The City

The City

by Max Weber

TRANSLATED AND EDITED

By DON MARTINDALE AND GERTRUD NEUWIRTH

THE FREE PRESS, *New York*
COLLIER-MACMILLAN LIMITED, *London*

Contents

Prefatory Remarks:
The Theory of the City

by Don Martindale

The closest approximations to a systematic theory of
urbanism that we have are to be found in a penetrating
essay, "Die Stadt," by Max Weber, and a memorable
paper by Robert E. Park, on "The City: Suggestions
for the Investigation of Human Behavior in the Urban
Environment."

Louis Wirth (A.J.S. Vol. XLIV,
July, 1938, no. 1, p. 8)

NO SUBTLETY of perception is required to determine
that the contemporary American theory of the city is in crisis. Each
season brings forth a new crop of books on the city. They are
mere produce not much as food for thought—dull fare as any
teacher will testify when his students turn up for examinations with
his city-texts unread. The student finds himself trapped behind a
boredom so great that he would sooner face the prospect of failing
the course. To change the imagery, too often in the presence of the
materials of the ordinary city book one feels as if he is in the
necropolis, the city of the dead from which all life has vanished.
And the writers of the books seem to feel it too, for as if in the
belated effort to breathe life into their materials they argue that in
response to the environment of the city the urbanite develops a
"segmental" culture and "schizoid" mentality. There seems to be
no stopping point in the interpretation of the city between visualiz-
ing it as a task exceeding the facilities of the department of sanitation or an insane asylum. Surely in this valley of dry bones one
may ask with Ezekiel, "can these bones live?"

The theory of the city somehow cannot account for what every journalist, poet, and novelist knows—the city is a living thing. As a system of life, the city penetrates the structure of biological evolution itself, creating new urban-insect and urban-animal forms. There are urban-insects like the silver fish, carpet beetle, bedbug, and the cockroach—as special to the city as the proletariat, as urban as the bureaucrat. The rat and the alley cat are animal denisens of the city with an outlook as urban as detachment and sophisticated cynicism. The city has its representatives from the feathered world in the sparrow, the starling, and the pigeon—dodging traffic with the same *sang froid* as the rest of the urbanites, disputing in the squares and holding council in the eaves—winning a livelihood from the by-products of commerce. There are moments in every city dawn when the circles, rectangles, polygons, and triangles—the geometry of the city—seem to float in the mist, like the essence of the human spirit emancipated from the earth. There are times, on starlit nights, when its towers and spires ram upward as if to tear the darkness loose from its riveting stars and the city seems to be a strident assertion of mankind against time itself.

When one examines the urban books it is not immediately apparent where they are deficient. It is certainly not in their statistical tables—since every city is a somewhat untidy statement in applied mathematics. It is an argument in millions of kilowatt hours, millions of short tons of coal, iron, steel, concrete, and brick. It is a metric assertion in linear miles of steel rails. It is a rebuttal in cubic feet of air space. It is a human petition in rates of infant morality, and tuberculosis. It is a protest expressed in percentages of criminality, juvenile delinquency, prostitution, recidivism, mental illness, and senility. It is a suave assurance pronounced in volumes of transactions, in gross sales, in amounts of credit, in retail and wholesale values, in the size of payrolls, in cash reserves and balances.

Nor can one say the urban books are deficient in the kind of items they include. What is a city without political parties, bosses, machines, chambers of commerce, credit associations, labor unions, factories, newspapers, churches, schools, welfare agencies, philanthropic societies, humane societies, museums, art galleries, lodges, zoos, auditoriums, parks, playgrounds, slums, red-light districts, riversides or park avenues, main streets, jungles, sanitation plants and taxi-cab companies?

One may find anything or everything in the city texts except the informing principle that creates the city itself. One is reminded of Pirandello's piece *Six Characters in Search of An Author*. Everything is present except the one precise essential that gives life to the whole. When all is said and done the question remains, What is the city?

The persistence in American sociology after all this time of the question can only be explained in terms of the peculiar developmental conditions of American sociological theory. Only recently has the question itself emerged in full clarity. This lends especial interest to the beginnings of a theory of the city in Europe among which the study by Max Weber stands out as of unusual importance. Weber's relevance to the question may be ascertained by way of a review of the stages of theoretical development of the concept of the city in America.

The First Form of American City Theory

The modern European city is centuries old; comparatively few American cities extend back of the nineteenth century. The American cities are cut off from the peculiarities of long-standing local traditions in a way that was true in Europe only in the newly-founded cities of the Germanic East. A newly founded city possesses a relatively simplified structure as against its parent model, for its starting point is inevitably a simplified version of the terminal stage of a developed city. American cities were such simplified versions of civic forms current in England at the time of their founding. And while in Europe, generally, national power partly grew coextensively with the evolution of the city, in America the establishment of national power preceded the formation of most of our cities. The few cities incorporated before the American Revolution were chartered on English pattern with limited powers granted to them by colonial legislatures. These powers were lodged in a council elected by limited suffrage. At the beginning of the 19th century only 4% of the population lived in cities of more than 8,000 population. As cities began to appear in the nineteenth century they were largely modeled on an imitation of the state governments with a council of two chambers one of which was elected by the city wards. The political activity promoted by this system was enormous for it facilitated avoidance of clear-cut responsibility. In the 1880's James Bryce insisted that city government in the United States represented the most conspicuous of all its political failures.[1] The events leading to this judgment were important for America's first urban theory.

As the effects of the industrial revolution were felt the growth in size of the cities of the western world was enormous. In the 1880's, for example, Prussia's cities grew by two million; those of France by a million; the cities of England and Wales increased by three quarters of a million and by 1890 London and Paris had more than doubled their populations as of the mid-century while the population of Berlin had increased fourfold.[2] In America the same phenomenon was apparent. By 1890 one third of the American population lived in towns of four thousand or more inhabitants.[3] Between 1880 and 1890 the number of cities with from 12 to 20 thousand population had increased from 76 to 107; cities of from 20 to 40 thousand population had increased in number from 45 to 91; cities of from 45 to 75 thousand population had increased from 23 to 39. In this decade Chicago increased from one half million to over a million. The Twin Cities had trebled in size. Detroit, Milwaukee, Columbus, and Cleveland had increased by eighty per cent. By 1890 there were already states and even whole sections where more than half of the entire population lived in cities of over four thousand inhabitants. (For example, more than 3/5 of the people of the North Atlantic section filled this category).

In the cities of both America and Europe the tremendous increase of population was correlated with a comparative decline of rural populations. In America the cities grew in considerable measure also by an increase in foreign-born populations. One fifth of all the denisens of American cities in 1890 were foreign born. There were as many foreign born persons in the cities as the entire population of the city in 1880. In 1890 there were only two German cities (Berlin and Hamburg) with greater German populations than Chicago; only Stockholm and Göteborg had more Swedes; only Christiania and Bergen had more Norwegians. One fourth of the

1. James Bryce, *American Commonwealth* (1888).
2. A. F. Weber, *The Growth of Cities in the Nineteenth Century* (New York: Macmillan, 1899).
3. *U. S. Eleventh Census*, I, 698-701.

Philadelphians and one third of the Bostonians were of alien birth. New York—Brooklyn was the greatest center of immigrants in the world: with half as many Italians as Naples; as many Germans as Hamburg; twice as many Irish as Dublin; one half as many Jews as Warsaw.[4]

The crowding of people into small space bears with it a tremendous increase in specialized demands. People need streets, public water supplies, public sewage systems, garbage disposal, police protection, fire protection, parks, playgrounds, civic centers, schools, libraries, transportation systems. A more complicated system of administration is necessary to handle the complex problems of engineering, law, finance and social welfare. The unprecedented speed of civic growth accompanying the industrial revolutions carried unprecedented problems in all these respects. A few familiar illustrations from a much told story may suffice for us here.

In the 1890's in America not a single one of the major municipalities had adequate traffic facilities. The majority of streets were ill paved, turning into seas of mud during rains, or paved with cobblestones or granite blocks. In the 1870's Washington laid more than four hundred thousand yards of asphalt. Buffalo and Philadelphia followed. During the same period Charleston, West Virginia and Bloomington, Illinois started paving with bricks which soon became popular, Des Moines, Columbus, and Cleveland leading the civic trend.[5] By 1900 Washington and Buffalo were the best paved cities in the world. Boston and the Borough of Manhattan followed and Chicago was only beginning.[6] Meanwhile, since most cities were built on waterways, bridge building was becoming a problem. The Brooklyn Bridge completed in 1883 by the Roeblings ushered in an era in the building of super-bridges. Before it was completed the New York traffic problem had become worse than it was at the time construction was started. Other cities were going through the same experience. Pittsburgh built the Seventh Street Suspension bridge over the Allegheny; Philadelphia completed a cantilever bridge over the Schuylkill; Richmond built a suspension

4. Kate H. Claghorn, "The Foreign Immigrant in New York City," *U. S. Industrial Comm., Reports*, XV, 465-492 and J. A. Riis, *How The Other Half Lives* (New York: 1890). For a general summary of this movement see Arthur Meier Schlesinger, *The Rise of the City* (New York: Macmillan, 1933), pp. 53-57.
5. G. W. Tillson, *Street Pavements and Paving Materials* (New York: 1900).
6. J. A. Fairlie, *Municipal Administration* (New York: 1901).

bridge.[7] Simultaneously the old horse cars, omnibusses and cabs from stage coach days were proving to be inadequate to move the urban masses. In 1879 New York completed an overhead railway which scattered oil and hot ashes on the unwary. It was so successful that a wing was quickly added. Other elevateds quickly followed in Kansas City, Chicago and Boston.[8] In 1901 Boston had begun to burrow underground ushering in an epoch of city tunnel building that still continues. Cable cars were introduced in San Francisco in 1873 and followed in Chicago, Philadelphia, and New York and from there to other cities. A practical dynamo was finally achieved in the 1870's with the possibility of producing adequate supplies of cheap electric current. By the 1880's trial electric trolley lines were tried in Boston and Denver and after the success in Richmond, Virginia, they spread almost universally until 51 cities had established trolley systems by 1890.[9] The tension on communications was no less and by 1878 the telephone had already ceased to be a toy. And once the legal battles between Western Union Telegraph and the Bell Company had been solved the full effects of Francis Blake's carbon transmitter, J. J. Carty's metallic circuit system and Charles E. Scribner's switchboard could be felt. By 1880 eighty-five towns already had telephone exchanges with fifty thousand subscribers and thirty-five thousand miles of wire.[10] Meanwhile, the telegraph, at first slowly, continued to expand. Tremendous urban pressures led to the eventual consolidation, speeding up, and streamlining of the postal system. The sale of postage stamps increased from around seven hundred million to over two billion during the 1880's. The same period saw the tremendous pressure for efficient methods of lighting with the change from kerosene lamps, to open-flame gas jets, to electric lighting made possible by the dynamo and Edison's invention of the electric light.[11] In the course of the competition of these utilities the process of making water gas was per-

7. H. G. Tyrrell, History. of Bridge Engineering (Chicago: 1911).

8. Allan Nevins, The Emergence of Modern America (New York Times, May 24, 1883), p. 90.

9. H. H. Vreeland, "The Street Railways of America" in C. M. Depaw, One Hundred Years of America (New York: 1895).

10. H. N. Casson, The History of the Telephone (Chicago: 1910).

11. J. B. McClure, ed. Edison and his Inventions (Chicago, 1879) and Henry Schroeder, History of the Electric Light (Smithsonian Miscel. Colls.) LXXVI, no. 2.

fected. Moreover, the same time period saw the construction of vaults and cesspools, to accommodate the waste of the city with the development of drainage systems that poured sewage into nearby bodies of water and poisoned the water supply. Systems of disposing of garbage developed from dumping into the oceans by barge in the coastal cities to the feeding of garbage to swine in inland cities. The poisoning of the water supplies became acute with epidemics of disease and initiated civic improvements in water systems and a beginning of more sanitary disposal of sewage and garbage. After a dramatic series of fires (the estimated total fire losses in 1878 were over sixty-four million, by 1882 they passed one hundred million dollars, by 1890 over one hundred fifty million),[12] more efficient fire fighting systems, the introduction of new fire fighting devices and equipment, the increased use of fire resistant materials for construction, and initiation of fire protection ordinances and inspections got underway. The problem of housing mass populations was met by a building of shanties, rooming houses, hotels of many kinds and inventions such as the tenement house which rapidly formed the slum sections of the cities.

Such details are not intended to be complete but illustrative of the opportunities and problems of the urban environment. The growing masses of consumers placed new values on standardizations and mass production. For if one only made a penny an item profit but captured the urban millions he became a millionaire. Meanwhile the masses of aliens came in response to the need of great quantities of cheap labor. As the results of handicraft vanished from the product, skill disappeared from the producer. It was as if the new urban environment had to tear down before it could build up; it had to simplify before it could complicate on a new principle. And the city itself was emerging as a most desirable consumer. Instrumented by the credit arrangements of modern industry it was possible for one generation to build what later generations paid for, the city was a monster with an endless appetite for anything that fertile imaginations could dream of supplying: brick, asphalt, concrete, steel, glass in endless arrangements and compounds. The city was also an economically important agent in other senses and able to grant monopolies in the form of franchises to an amazing series of "utilities" affecting access to and use of earth, water and sky.

12. World Almanac for 1929.

The first reactions to and interpretation of these phenomena hardly add up to a genuine theory of the city. They fall into two general categories: attempts to account for its location and its moral consequences.

Charles H. Cooley[13] tried to account for the location of cities. While in the past cities were located by proximity to a religious establishment or fort and while some cities have at all times been located by political considerations, the primary reasons for location of cities are found in transportation. A break in transportation, even if it involves no more than a transfer of goods from one carrier to another, involves much equipment and many facilities. Thus, it is at the mouths or key points of rivers, meeting points on hills and plains, and other such areas that city formations appear. When there is also a change of ownership with the possibility of temporary storage the center grows by leaps and bounds with stevedores, warehousemen, importers, exporters, merchants, money changers, accountants, secondary service personnel, and many other forms and types. The great majority of the larger cities of the United States are located on navigable rivers. The lake ports are among the American cities experiencing most rapid growth: Chicago, Buffalo, Cleveland, Detroit, and Milwaukee. New York depends for its importance on its location at the juncture of both land and water terminals.

Cooley's theory of transportation is evidence of the awakening theoretical concern with the city and the attempt, at very least to explain why cities locate where they do. A more general study of the same type is represented by Adna Weber's *Growth of Cities in the Nineteenth Century*.[14] This much quoted work performed a brilliant service in assembling a statistical picture of the recent quantitative growth of the city in the western world. Beyond this Adna Weber inquired into the causes of the concentration of people into cities concluding that this was primarily a product of economic

13. The literature on the origin and location of towns includes Roscher's *System der Volkwirtschaft*, Vol. III and *Die Nationalökonomie des Handels und Gewerbefleisses*. His theory of the location of cities is developed in "Ueber die geographische Lage der grossen Städte in *Ansichten der Volkswirtschaft*, Vol. I. Also see E. Sax, *Die Verkehrsmittel in der Volkswirtschaft* (Vienna, 1878) and A. de Foville, *De la Transformation des Moyens de Transport et ses Consequences economiques et sociales* (Paris, 1880). Cooley's *The Theory of Transportation* first appeared in Publications of the American Economic Association.

14. Adna Ferrin Weber, *The Growth of Cities in the Nineteenth Century* (New York: Macmillan, 1899).

forces and that these in turn were of the kind becoming significant with the industrial revolution: steam and machinery, trade and commerce, the solution of modern transportation problems, the industrialization and increased productivity of agriculture, the growth of commercial centers, transportation (with Cooley), industrialization and the factory system. In addition to such primary economic causes of city growth, Adna Weber thought there were a series of secondary causes of an economic, political and social type. In a secondary economic sense the city grows not only because of the revolution in transportation, finance, production, and commerce but also because of the lure of high wages and the inducements of more varied opportunities. Among the political causes of city growth Adna Weber listed the influence of: 1. legislation promoting freedom of trade; 2. legislation promoting freedom of migration; 3. centralized administration with its location of persons in civic centers and 4. free forms of land tenure politically defended in the city. Social causes of city growth were found in the advantages the city offered for 1. education; 2. amusements; 3. a higher standard of living; 4. the attractiveness of intellectual associations; 5. habituation to an urban environment; and 6. a diffusion of knowledge of the values of city life.

Adna Weber was not at all convinced that the city spelled the moral ruin of mankind and he devoted a chapter to the *Physical and Moral Condition* of the cities in which he reviewed one of the most systematic indictments of city life in favor of the country.[15] The basic arguments of this treatise made by many other thinkers in other forms were that: 1. The city-born reside in the poorest quarters of the city; 2. The city-born predominate in the lowest occupations of the lowest social classes; 3. the city-born contribute an unduly large proportion of degenerates, criminals, lunatics, and suicides; 4. the cities have a low rate of natural increase or even deficient births; 5. the city population consists of as many country-born as city-born; and 6. the typical city-class is incapable of self-perpetuation.[16] Adna Weber treated these propositions not simply as "moral" arguments but as testable hypotheses. After a review of the urban statistics he concluded that they are either mistaken or only partly justified. For example, Adna Weber denies that there

---

15. Georg Hansen's *Die Drei Bevölkerungsstufen* (Munich: 1889).
16. Weber, *op. cit.*, p. 370.

is a distinction in America between rural and urban illegitimacy rates. Moreover, in Europe while infanticide is more prevalent in the country, abortion is less prevelant there. Prostitution is a profession of the city, to be sure, but it is supplied in considerable measure by recruitment from corrupted country homes. Meanwhile "the amount of viciousness and criminality in cities is probably exaggerated in popular estimation" because of the facilities of the city press.[17] And against all these things, Adna Weber urges, one must not forget the manysided advantages of the city.

While an awakening theoretical consciousness is evident in the work of Cooley and Adna Weber, at least with respect to the growth, size and location of cities, another kind of theoretical interest is shown in Josiah Strong's concept of the moral effects of the city.[18] Strong thought that modern civilization shows a one-sided development of material in contrast to moral and spiritual properties. This material growth is manifest in the development of the "materialistic" city whose phenomenal growth was attributed to a redistribution of population because of the development of scientific agriculture, the substitution of mechanical for hand power, and the development of transportation. Society was seen as undergoing transformation from the farm to the city in an irreversible process. "We must face the inevitable. The new civilization is certain to be urban; and the problem of the twentieth century will be the city."[19]

A city, according to Strong, is materialistic when its intellectual and moral development are not commensurate with its physical growth. To illustrate: as a result of improper sanitation Strong believed there were at least 150,000 unnecessary deaths in the city in 1890. Among the basic problems the industrial revolution posed for the city was the adjustment of an aristocratic system of industry to a democratic system of government.[20] As civilization grows more complex the individual becomes segmental and dependent and performance failures on the part of the individual become more socially disastrous. As the city grows more prosperous and rich the administration of its interests affords increased opportunities for corruption. "If we have not sufficient moral sense or common sense to

17. *Ibid.*, p. 407.
18. Josiah Strong, *The Twentieth Century City* (New York: Baker and Taylor, 1898).
19. *Ibid.*, p. 53.
20. *Ibid.*, p. 61.

PREFATORY REMARKS: THE THEORY OF THE CITY   [19]

prevent saloon-keepers, thieves, gamblers, jail-birds, and prize fighters from dominating our municipal politics, we have as good officials as we deserve."[21] Homes are disappearing in the city at both social extremes. Among the rich, hotel and club life is being substituted for home life. At the other extreme appear homeless masses living in the lodging house, tenement houses and a migrant idle class. The church grows weaker in proportion to the size of the city. "Ignorance, vice, and wretchedness, combined, constitute social dynamite, of which the city slum is a magazine."[22] In Strong's opinion these evidences of civic moral decline were correlated with and further exaggerated by the increase in numbers of foreign born and Catholics.[23]

Between the extremes of an attempt to account for the growth and location of the city and concern for a presumed "moral decline" occurring in the city lay the vast area of interest in and concern with politico-economic corruption which elicited reactions of an outraged citizenry. This was documented by the muckrakers, as illustrated by Lincoln Steffens in the *Shame of Our Cities*, and the organization of municipal reform movements.

These various developments cast up fragments of explanations, and materials for a theory of the city but hardly a theory. Cooley and Adna Weber, for example, do not offer theoretical explanations of the city. They assume its existence only trying to account for its size, growth, and location. Their "theories" account only for the physical and external aspects of the city. On the other hand the moral reaction to the "materialism" of the city also constitutes only the most fragmentary of explanations of urban phenomena, quite apart from its domination of moral considerations. The city itself is treated as the "cause" of moral decline or—in Strong—at least the foreign born populations, the Catholics, and the slum are. Precisely those individuals and groups most victimized by the processes of the city are blamed for their fates. This, again, is hardly an explanation of the city. Finally the muckrakers and their outraged publics, alarmed at civic corruption, locate the problem in government and their solutions in civic reform. But here, too, only fragments of civic phenomena were being conceptualized.

21. *Ibid.*, p. 67.
22. *Ibid.*, p. 78.
23. For another expression of the moral reaction to the city see Jane Addams, *The Spirit of Youth* (New York: Macmillan, 1909).

Rise of the Ecological Theory of the City

At the time that increased attention was being paid by American thinkers to the nature and problems of their cities, sociology itself was assuming more definite shape. By 1900 the first academic departments of sociology were being established. The new field had as yet to found its first professional society and its first professional journal. The movement from a pre-professional to a professional stage was accomplished in the first decade of the 20th century. The first graduate school departments were set up. Moreover, if one were to find a point at which an autonomous science has appeared —not a mere area of special interest—it would be hard to find a more appropriate one than that time when assemblage by the discipline of its materials for study first hand occurs. Thereafter, the discipline does not rest on a mere re-hash of data gathered by some other discipline. Under the guidance of the brilliant staff assembled by Albion Small at the University of Chicago many of these steps toward the professionalization of sociology and establishment of it as an autonomous science were taken.

As a natural object of study for the new science of sociology, the city was subject to three kinds of requirements: 1. the search for a point of view permitting the approach to both aspects of urban phenomena, a. the objective aspects of location, size and growth (Charles Cooley, Adna Weber) and b. the social aspects (noted by moral critics, Strong; reformers, Jane Addams; and muckrakers, Steffens); 2. an "objective" point of view—that is a point of view permitting simple understanding without *a priori* value commitments either to defend or to destroy; and 3. a point of view providing for the first hand study of the "facts" of the urban environment. All of these objectives were present in a series of papers, theses, and special research projects that were being promoted at the University of Chicago between 1915 and 1925. Eventually they were collected in the very appealing little volume, *The City*[24] by Robert E. Park, Ernest W. Burgess and Roderick D. McKenzie, which marks the beginning of a systematic theory of the city by sociologists in the United States.

Park provided the general framework for the ecological theory

24. Robert E. Park, Ernest W. Burgess, Roderick D. McKenzie, *The City* (Chicago: The University of Chicago Press, 1925).

of the city, as this approach came to be known.[25] He took the position that the city is a "natural habitat of civilized man" in the sense that it represents a "cultural area" with peculiar cultural types. As a natural structure Park suggested that the city obeyed laws of its own and there "is a limit to the arbitrary modifications which it is possible to make: 1. in its physical structure and 2. in its moral order."[26] What holds for the entire city applies also to its sub-sections and every neighborhood takes on properties of the qualities of its inhabitants showing a historical continuity of its own. This, however, should not obscure the fact that the neighborhood tends to lose much of the significance it had in a tribal condition of mankind. Nevertheless, in the city, through isolation, the immigrant and racial colonies, or so-called ghettos, and areas of population segregation tend to maintain themselves.

Every device in the city facilitating trade and industry prepares the way for further division of labor and further specialization of tasks. As a result there is a continuous breakdown of older traditional, social and economic structures based on family ties, local associations, culture, caste, and status with the substitution of an order resting on occupation and vocational interests. Among other things this means that the growth of the city is accomplished by a substitution of indirect "secondary" relations for direct, face-to-face "primary" relations. The church, school and family are modified. The school takes over some of the functions of the family. The church loses influence being displaced by the printed page. This may have the effect of separating the vocational classes so completely that they live in an isolation almost as complete as a remote rural community.

The selection of city officials by popular vote becomes impracticable under these conditions. To meet the emergency of the election crisis created by city life two types of organizations appear for controlling the vote: the political boss and machine and the good-government organizations (independent voters' leagues, tax-payers' associations, and bureaus of municipal research). The political machine is based on local, personal and "primary" relations; good-

<hr>

25. Robert E. Park, *The City*, "Suggestions for the Investigation of Human Behavior in the Urban Environment." pp. 1-46.
26. *Ibid.*, p. 4.

government organizations rest on secondary relationships, depending upon organizing public opinion. The great cities not only create vocational—but temperamental types as well. Experience is of an increasingly fortuitous and casual character excluding the more intimate and permanent associations of the smaller community. The individual's status is determined by conventional signs such as fashion and "front" and "the art of life is largely reduced to skating on thin surfaces and the scrupulous study of style and manners."[27] This is correlated with a segregation of moral environments, a multiplication of competing milieus.

One may sum up Park's conception of the city in a sentence: the city represents an externally organized unit in space produced by laws of its own. The precise statement of this external organization of the city in space—the badge by which the ecological theory is most quickly identified—was made by Ernest W. Burgess. The systematic statement of its inner "laws" was the work of Roderick McKenzie.

The growth of the city was treated by Burgess in terms of its physical expansion and differentiation in space.[28] The expansion of the city, he thought, tends to take the form of the development of a series of concentric rings representing successive zones of urban

27. *Ibid.*, p. 40.

28. There were complex ties between these various students. Not a little of the original stimulus for the ecological point of view seems to have come from the study by C. J. Galpin, "The Social Anatomy of an Agricultural Community," Wisconsin Agricultural Experiment Station, Research Bulletin No. 3 (1915). Galpin collected data from families in a county showing where they banked, traded, sent their children to school. He prepared maps showing their spatial locations and the distribution of their activities. This was important for demonstrating that the actual units of living were often quite at variance with the political units. Also, it should be noted, however simple-minded this procedure, a sociologist was actually in the field gathering the data he needed himself. This fitted into the plans of R. E. Park who promoted urban research very actively between 1915 and 1921. In 1918 Park borrowed some concepts from the plant ecologist and turned them into a unified explanation. This was soon followed by the first hand study of various areas of the city—which were often thought of as "habitats" by analogy from plant ecology. R. D. McKenzie published a study of "The Neighborhood" *American Journal of Sociology*, Vol. XXVII (September 1921; November 1921; March 1922; May 1922). Columbus, Ohio was studied in terms of the distribution of dependency, delinquency, nationality and a number of other indices. The concept of "cultural areas" was utilized and maps were employed for delimiting urban areas. Other studies included Nels Anderson's *The Hobo* (Chicago: University of Chicago Press, 1923). The ideas of an overall spatial organization of the city was systematized by Burgess in "The Growth of the City" reprinted in *The City*, pp. 47-62.

extension. If nothing else interferes a town or city expands radially from its central business district like the Chicago "Loop," 1. This is the first area. Encircling the downtown area there is normally an area in transition, which is being invaded by business and light manufacture, 2., where property is being held for business use and while housing is poor, rent is low. A third area, 3. is inhabitated by the workers in industries who have escaped from the area of deterioration but who desire to live within easy access to their work. This area threatens to become the next slum. Beyond this zone is the "residential area," 4., of high-class apartment buildings or of exclusive "restricted" districts of single family dwellings. Still farther, out beyond the city limits, is the commuter's zone—suburban areas or satellite cities—within a thirty to sixty-minute ride of the central business district.[29]

In the argument supporting this physical description Burgess suggests that the phenomena of urban growth were a result of organization and disorganization in a kind of anabolic—katabolic process. Disorganization is preliminary to reorganization of attitudes and conduct and the newcomer of the city while discarding habitual points of view and traditional morality experiences mental conflict and personal loss. In the expansion of the city a process occurs which sifts and sorts and relocates individuals and groups by residence and occupation. Thus, within the "main stem" appears the "hobohemia" of homeless migratory men. In the zone of deterioration encircling the central business sections are always found the "slums" submerged regions of degradation, disease and the underworlds of crime and vice. And progressively as one moves outward the segregation and assemblage of other social adjustments are to be found.

The extent to which Park and Burgess had created an atmosphere actively promoting first-hand research into various aspects of the city is illustrated by the number of projects under their guidance at the time this essay was published. Some studies destined to be classics of American sociology were being conducted. Nels Anderson, *The Slum: An Area of Deterioration in the Growth of the City;* Ernest R. Mowrer, *Family Disorganization in Chicago;* Walter C. Reckless, *The Natural History of Vice Areas in Chicago;* E. H. Shideler, *The Retail Business Organization as an Index of Business Organization;* F. M. Thrasher, *One Thousand Boys' Gangs in Chicago;* H. W.

29. Park, *op. cit.*, p. 50.

Zorbaugh, *The Lower North Side; A Study in Community Organization.*[30]

Park and Burgess had assumed that the city presented a physical portrait characterized by typical areas and zones. They made numerous references to the laws which established them. The fullest statement of these so-called "laws" or "processes" was made by their colleague McKenzie.[31] Ecology was that phase of biology studying plant and animal forms as they exist in nature in relation to each other and to their environments. Human ecology was a parallel study of the spatial and temporal relations of humans as affected by the social environment. Society was thought to be made up of individuals territorially distributed by competition and selection. Human institutions are accommodated to spatial relations. As these spatial relations change social relations are altered, producing social and political problems.

The first use made of social ecology was to classify communities into four types: 1. Primary service communities are represented by agricultural towns, fishing, mining, or lumbering communities serving as a first step in the distributing process. 2. The second type fulfills a distributive function collecting basic materials from the surrounding area and distributing them in the markets of the world. These are commercial communities. 3. The third type of community is in the industrial town. 4. The fourth type lacks a specific economic base exemplified by recreational resorts, political or educational centers, communities of defense, penal or charitable colonies.

Communities are organized for defense and for mutual economic advantage. When a community reaches a point of culmination—the limits of the economic advantage that occasioned the population aggregation—it must either stabilize, re-cycle, or disintegrate. "A community which has reached a point of culmination and which has experienced no form of release is likely to settle into a condition of stagnation."[32] When it starts to decline disorganization and social unrest follow. Competition becomes keener, the weaker elements are forced lower in the community or even forced to with-

30. *Ibid.*, p. 62.

31. R. D. McKenzie, "The Ecological Approach to the Study of the Human Community," *American Journal of Sociology*, XXX 287-301 and "The Scope of Human Ecology," Pub. A. S. S., XX 141-54 and in E. W. Burgess, *Urban Community*, pp. 167-82. See also *The City*, *op. cit.*, pp. 63-79.

32. *The City*, p. 71.

draw. Thus, beyond a point the economic competition that organizes a city, becomes keen and acts a a depressing element in it. At this time innovating elements tend to be introduced into the adjustment of the community, forming the first stage of an invasion that may lead to a complete change in the structure and organization of the community. As a community increases in size it becomes better able to accommodate itself to invasions and sudden changes in the number of inhabitants.

In the course of this process there is a development from simple to complex, from general to specialized. Increased centralization is followed by decentralization. The axial or skeletal structure is determined by the routes of traffic and travel. As the community grows there is a multiplication of houses and roads and a process of differentiation and segregation. As competition for advantageous sites becomes keener with the growth of population economically weaker types of utilities are forced to lower-priced less accessible areas. Residential sections also segregate into types depending on economic and racial composition of the population. Some specialized utilities do not appear until a certain point of development is reached "just as the beach or pine forest is preceded by successional dominance of other plant species. And just as in plant communities successions are the products of invasion, so also in the human community the formations, segregations, and associations that appear constitute the outcome of a series of invasions."[33] The two main types of invasions are due to a changed use of land and a new type of occupants. Invasions are initiated by: 1. changes in transportation routes; 2. obsolescence and physical deterioration; 3. creation of structures, buildings, bridges; 4. introduction of new types of industries; 5. changes in the economic base for the redistribution of incomes and 6. real estate promotions. Invasions lead to a regular process of events with a distinct, initial stage, secondary stage, and climax. The climactic stage is reached when the invasion forces establish a dominant type of ecological organization able to withstand intrusions from others. Once a dominant use becomes established within an area, competition becomes less ruthless among the associating units, rules of control emerge, and the invasion of a different use is for a time obstructed. There are established, thus, units of communal life that may be called natural areas.

---

33. *Ibid.*, p. 74.

Thus, the major processes that form the city are in order of importance, competition, concentration, centralization, segregation, invasion, and succession. Their operation creates the "natural areas" that form the physical structure of the city.

When one reviews the literature on the city from the days of this interesting assemblage of essays to the 1950's, it is evident that the second quarter of the twentieth century in American sociology has been dominated by the ecological theory of the city. The primary architects of this theory were Park, Burgess, and McKenzie. As early as 1928 it was clear that the sociological study of the city was assuming a standard form based on these ideas. Nels Anderson and Eduard C. Lindeman brought out their Urban Sociology in 1928.[34] The first eighty-nine pages of their book are devoted to an extended ecological description of the city and its environs. Another division of the book is concerned with the so-called "functions" of the city. This includes such topics as the supplying of the city, its waste and sewerage, transportation, recreation, and the mechanization of the urban environment. Another section is devoted to urban personality and groups and breaks down into a review of some of the psychological effects of the speeded-up, mechanized urban environment on personality and the formation of urban social types with some review of the effects of professionalization on individuals and groups. The study is concluded with a review of problems of an urban environment: poverty, mental health, old age, the disorganization of the home, political disorganization and so forth.

There is little value here in reviewing all the studies of the city, but a volume or two chosen over time may illustrate the fundamental fact that if the city in America had changed as little as the interpretations of it, its problems could have been solved long ago. In 1932 two very responsible volumes appeared by Davie and Carpenter.[35] Davie's volume even shows a reluctance theoretically to exploit the Chicago concepts. The book opens with the proposition that the development of urbanism is just about the most important thing that has happened to society lately. However, it is concerned so little with the theory of urbanism that the question, "What is

34. Nels Anderson and Eduard C. Lindeman, Urban Sociology (New York: Alfred A. Knopf, 1928).

35. Maurice R. Davie, Problems of City Life (New York: John Wiley, 1932) and Niles Carpenter, The Sociology of City Life (New York: Longmans, Green, 1932).

the city?" is disposed of by a quotation from Munroe,[36] and after a rather quick review of the growth of the city based upon the study of Adna Weber, Davie took a quick look at city planning and the traffic problem and, dispensing with further nonsense, launched into a discussion of city problems. He devoted 119 pages to housing; 182 pages to health; 170 pages to education; and 149 pages to recreation. What did Davie contribute to the theory of the City? Nothing.

Carpenter's study is somewhat more rich theoretically, chiefly because of its continuities with the Chicago tradition. The first 188 pages were primarily devoted to the geology and ecology of the city. This was followed by a chapter on city growth and planning. The composition of the urban population was reviewed and some attention devoted to the effects of the city on personality. Once again the work trails off into a long review of the problems of the city—its effects on marriage and the family, the home, religion, and finally vice, crime, immorality, mental deficiency, mental disease and suicide.

In both of these books much larger quantities of research were made available. They are, in this sense, more complete and up to date. But Davie reduces this to a mere review of problems without a particular integrating theoretical framework. Carpenter's study takes the ecological theory as unquestioned and only amplifies it in rather minor ways by somewhat greater attention to institutions.

How remarkably little fundamental change there has been since then is shown by two volumes appearing in 1955.[37] In the study by Rose Hum Lee the old topic of the growth of cities is amplified a bit by materials from Western Europe, Asia, Africa, and the United States. But the fundamental explanatory framework is provided by a demographic and ecological picture. The tendency is manifest to pay more attention to institutions—in fact almost ninety pages are devoted to urban institutions, somewhat less than 1/5th of the study. The discussion of urban ways of life, leisure, personality, problems, and city planning are traditional.

In Bergel's study the same traditional formula is largely pre-

36. Davie, *op. cit.*, pp. 4-5. The reference is to William Bennett Munroe, *The Government of American Cities* (New York: Macmillan, 1926) pp. 13-16. It should be noted however, that Munroe's statement is theoretically superior to that of the Chicago school.

37. Rose Hum Lee, *The City* (New York: Lippincott, 1955) and Egon Ernest Bergel, *Urban Sociology* (New York: McGraw-Hill, 1955).

served. How little concerned he is with the basic theoretical meaning of the city may be indicated by the cryptic definition he is satisfied with. "We shall call a city any settlement where the majority of occupants are engaged in other than agricultural activities."[38] A military base would seem to constitute an almost perfect case. Rose Hum Lee's definition is as cursory: "Cities are basically population aggregates which are large, heterogeneous, and densely settled within a limited land area."[39] However, more important than the lack of interest in theoretic issues is the maintenance of the traditional composition. Roughly the first 168 pages of Bergel's study is devoted to physical and ecological descriptions of the city past and present. A long chapter is devoted to urban demography. The examination of urban institutions is reduced to about eighty pages—a smaller proportion than is found in Lee's study. Almost twice as much space is devoted to urban problems and planning.

In 1958 Louis Wirth's estimate of the state of city theory is almost as relevant as it was in 1938. Moreover, Wirth was a charter member of urbanism incorporated—the Chicago school of ecological theory. In his brilliant study of *The Ghetto* he had carried out one of the most able studies of urban sub-communities to be made. He had contributed the annotated index to the Park, Burgess, McKenzie volume on *The City*. He was familiar first hand with the great majority of studies carried out under Park's auspices. Yet, writing in 1938 he argues:

In the rich literature on the city we look in vain for a theory of urbanism presenting in a systematic fashion the available knowledge concerning the city as a social entity. We do indeed have excellent formulations of theories on such special problems as the growth of the city viewed as a historical trend and as a recurrent process, and we have a wealth of literature presenting insights of sociological relevance and empirical studies offering detailed information on a variety of particular aspects of urban life. But despite the multiplication of research and textbooks on the city, we do not as yet have a comprehensive body of compendent hypotheses which may be derived from a set of postulates implicitly contained in a sociological definition of the city, and from our general sociological knowledge which may be substantiated through empirical research.[40]

It goes without saying that minor modifications of the original proposals of Park, Burgess, and McKenzie are hardly the answer for

38. Bergel, *op. cit.*, p. 8.
39. Lee, *op. cit.*, p. 7.
40. Louis Wirth, "Urbanism as a Way of Life," *American Journal of Sociology*, XLIV (1938), p. 8.

an urban theory. The concentric zone theory has been toyed with and minor alternatives to it have been offered. And a "separate nucleus" theory and a "sector theory" have been proposed. But they imply acceptance of the original postulates. More up-to-date studies of tuberculosis, recidivism, juvenile delinquency, housing values, prostitution have been offered from time to time. New and more recent demographic descriptions of the population by area and zone have been carried out. None of these proposals and studies touch the basic structure of the original "theory" and one may retain Wirth's critique unmodified.

Basically there are three major theoretical difficulties with the ecological theory of the city. First it started analysis off on the wrong track by orienting it to the geo-physical aspects of the city rather than to its social life. Social life is a structure of interaction, not a structure of stone, steel, cement, asphalt, etc. It is, to be sure, not altogether inappropriate to suggest that one can understand much about the activities of a household by a careful analysis of what passes through its sewerage system and what ends up in the garbage can—but this is true only if these are taken as by-products of activity and as evidence on which to establish inferences. Too much of the ecological study of the city was devoted to the establishment of the properties of various zones—natural areas, habitats, and what not—too little attention was paid to the life that produced these properties. An extraordinarily patient study was made of the scene of the crime, the criminal was largely ignored. The ecological theory of the city was in part betrayed by the demand to make the science autonomous, independent, exact. Too many of the charts, maps, overlay maps, diagrams, and statistical rates and ratios were present for their own sake.

A second fundamental difficulty with the ecological theory of the city was the unnecessary "primitivism" of its crucial concepts. These were summarized most compactly by McKenzie as including competition, concentration, centralization, segregation, invasions, and succession. Civic social life can indeed be accounted for in such terms—that is not the issue. The difficulty was that it could not be sufficiently differentiated in those terms. They could account as easily for rural life as for city life. They could apply to social life in the past or the present. They could apply to non-human animal life as well as to man's life; or to plant life as well as to animal life. One does not account for monogamous marriage by the presence of a sex drive. Such a sex drive will as easily account for sex outside monogamous marriage. One may account for the fact that he eats because he is hungry; this will not account for the fact that on some particular occasions he eats canapes and drinks cocktails. The basic conceptualizations of the ecological theory were insufficiently precise to differentiate the theory of the city from any other branch of sociological theory. In fact they were not sufficient to distinguish sociological theory from political or economic theory or even to distinguish sociology from some branches of botanical theory.

Thirdly, and in part growing out of the first two difficulties, the ecological theory of the city omitted precisely those concepts most traditionally sociological—groups, institutions, social structure. Nels Anderson's and Lindesmith's study of the city had no need for institutions—they were mentioned only incidentally with reference to social problems. In Davie's study as well no formal admission of institutions is to be found. And after thirty years of development of the ecological theory institutions managed to find a place in the city texts but they are found to occupy less than a fifth of the space.

Positively the ecological theory of the city represented important advances. It facilitated the examination both of the external physical and internal social aspects of urban phenomena. Even more importantly the ecological theory demanded first hand research and the construction of an autonomous science. Finally, its very primitivism was a kind of advantage—it was so completely uncommitted theoretically that almost any kind of study could occur in its name. It was a sort of injunction: Go ye forth and gather facts. This favored the accumulation of a wide variety of data. Of course, this was an advantage won only at a great price, for ever and again the study of the city reduces to a mechanical framework for inventory, the social problems of an urban environment. The framework is so loose that normative judgments are able to obscure the requirements of empirical social theory.

Notes on a Social-Psychological Theory of the City

The observation that man thinks, feels, responds differently in the city than outside it is as old as the city itself. There is no more idle error than the supposition that the men of some previous age were any more unperceptive and unintelligent than we. Traditional evidence testifies to the fact that ancient men perceived and valued the special properties of their cities. A familiar concern of fathers for their children in ancient Egypt was that they learn to write and take up the "white collar" tasks of scribes in the imperial bureaucracy rather than suffer the privations of humbler occupations. Pressure and social ascent by way of an urban occupation are ancient. In nearby Babylonia the high value placed on specifically urban types of socio-political opportunities is shown in the care with which the attempt was made to restrict access to such opportunities to privileged groups of citizens. When the Jews were carried off into Babylonian captivity they were permitted much freedom but carefully excluded from access to the priestly schools and the political positions correlated therewith. In Ancient China the desirability of the urban roles is indicated by the devotion, patience, and hard work the individual was willing to devote in preparation for the civil service exams and the extent to which his family and clan might finance his activities in training for the mandarinate. In classical Greece, the citizen was proud of his membership in the city and he took this quality as a distinguishing difference between himself and the barbarian. Similar attitudes and evidences of civic pride differentiated the denisen of Rome.

However, it is one thing to recognize the development of a peculiar urban outlook, related to urban occupations and the city environment—this is as old as the city itself—it is another thing to isolate this as the peculiar core of urban phenomena making all explanations from it. The conditions that could lead to this rather curious result were present in the sociology of Georg Simmel.

Sociology was organized in the nineteenth century by non-academic thinkers like August Comte in France, Herbert Spencer in England and Lester Ward in the United States. The founders of the discipline were rather breezy, imaginative, and not a little imperialistic. They were empire builders establishing a new field out of territories carved from the older disciplines. They did their work very well—so well that sociology was in process of establishment as an academic discipline during the lifetime of some of the founders.

Simmel belonged to the second generation as an academic sociologist. He and his colleagues faced quite a different task from that of the founders—the need to define the field with precision and in limited terms, not in ways that brought it into conflict with every other field. Philosophically Simmel was a careful student of Immanuel Kant; sociologically he was a leader in the school often described as Neo-Kantianism. Ignoring the details, Neo-Kantian social science attempted to arrive at a precise and limited definition of the social sciences by analogy with a procedure in Kant's philosophy. This consisted in drawing a sharp distinction between the form and the content of experience, and finding everything of a general value for science in the study of forms.

The task of the social sciences, according to Simmel, is to study the whole range of man's interactive life. The special task of sociology is to study the forms of social interaction apart from their content. Simmel assumed that the same social forms could encompass quite different content and the same social content could be embodied in different forms. It should be noted, moreover, that interhuman behavior does not by any means reduce to physical action, but includes ideas, sentiments, and attitudes.

If one grants Simmel's approach to sociology and brings the city under analysis nothing could be more idle than to occupy one's self with demographic details and spend endless hours examining the physical characteristics of zones, neighborhoods, environs and all the rest. A sociological analysis of the city finds its proper field in the psychic forms of interhuman life in an urban environment. Precisely the mentality of the urbanite is its primary object. Sociologically, thus, for Simmel there is nothing whimsical, marginal, or incidental about a topic like "Metropolis and Mental Life"[41]— quite the contrary in it sociology finds its proper field.

Simmel agrees with many modern observers that the city is peculiarly central to the destiny of modern man. He argues that the deepest problems of modern life arise out of the attempt by the individual to preserve his autonomy and individuality in the face of the overwhelming social forces of a historical heritage, external culture and technique of life. To the sociologist who wishes to understand this problem, it is important to comprehend the psychological basis of the metropolitan forms of individuality. This is found by Simmel in the intensification of nervous stimulation result-

41. Translated by Kurt Wolff, *The Sociology of Georg Simmel* (Glencoe: The Free Press, 1950) pp. 409-424.

ing in the swift uninterrupted transition from outer to inner stimulation.

The metropolitan man is subject to an unusual volume of stimulation and he develops a mentality protecting himself against elements in the external environment which would uproot him. This means that he must react with his head rather than his heart—to yield to deep emotional reactions is to be crushed. His environment intensifies his awareness, not his feeling, leading to a dominance of intelligence. Intellectuality, which extends in many directions with the specialization of the urban environment, is characteristic of the city.

The institutions of the city confirm its mentality, for money economy and dominance of the intellect are intrinsically connected. Both involve a matter-of-fact attitude in dealing with men and things. Money is concerned only with what is common to all items of which it asks only exchange value, reducing all quality and individuality to the question: How much? It is, moreover, the natural institution of the market so central to the metropolis. City production is for the market, for completely unknown consumers who will never enter the producer's actual field of vision. The modern mind becomes ever more calculating. This calculation and the exactness which the money economy brings about also corresponds to the ideal of natural science which would transform the world into an arithmetic problem and fit its parts into mathematical formulae.

In city social life, punctuality, calculability and exactness are required by the very complexity of life, intimately connected with money economy and intellectualism. Simmel believed, this also explains why original natures like Ruskin and Nietzsche who found the value of life in unschematized existence not only hated the punctuality and exactness of the metropolis but extended the same hatred to the money economy and the intellectualism of modern existence and science.

The same factors which enhance exactness and minute precision and form them into a structure of highest impersonality tend also to promote a highly personal subjectivity. A blasé attitude develops in the city as a product of the rapidly changing context of contrasting experiences. Over-stimulation results in loss of the capacity to respond. The essence of the blasé attitude is found in a blunting of discrimination. And here, again, the role of the urban money economy is evident and appropriate to the urban attitude. It is colorless and indifferent as a common denominator of all value. It hollows out the core of things—their individuality, special value or incomparability. The larger the city the more central the role of seats of money exchange and the more completely the purchasability of things is brought to the fore. Meanwhile the self-preservation of personality is bought at the price of devaluing the world and can in the end only lead to the devaluing of the self.

The attitude of the metropolitan toward others tends to be one of formality and reserve. Simmel believed that the inner aspect of this reserve is not only indifference but a slight aversion or at least mutual strangeness and repulsion. Reserve with this overtone of aversion secures to the individual a kind of personal freedom impossible under any other conditions. In this connection Simmel thought that the great creativity of ancient Athens was due to its retention of some of the aspects of a small town in combustible tension with the stimulating intellectuality of the metropolis. While the number of persons makes the metropolis the locale of freedom, at a certain point in the economic, personal, and intellectual relations of the citizenry cosmopolitanism appears as well—this is manifest in the predominance of the city over the hinterland in a way growing in geometrical progression with the size of the city. Within the city, meanwhile, life has been transformed from a struggle for a livelihood with nature into an interhuman struggle for gain. And life is increasingly composed of impersonal components that displace personal colorations leading the individual to summon the utmost in uniqueness and particularization to preserve the personal core of the self.

Simmel's essay *Die Grosstädte und das Geistesleben*[42] did not seem to have nearly as much direct influence upon the founders of the ecological theory of the city as the treatment of the city by Oswald Spengler—which from its very phrasing appears in large measure to have been drawn from Simmel. Park's famous essay opened with reference to Spengler not Simmel. "The city . . . is something more than a congeries of individual men and of social conveniences—streets, buildings, electric lights, tramways, and telephones, etc.; something more than a mere constellation of institutions and administrative devices—courts, hospitals, schools, police,

42. Published in Dresden, 1903.

and civil functionaries of various sorts. The city is, rather a state of mind, a body of customs and traditions, and of organized attitudes and sentiments. . . . The city has, as Oswald Spengler has recently pointed out, its own culture: 'What his house is to the peasant, the city is to civilized man. As the house has its household gods, so has the city its protecting Deity, its local saint. The city also, like the peasant's hut, has its roots in the soil.' "43 While the description of urban mentality by Spengler is essentially Simmel's—as evident already in the ideas and quotation drawn from Spengler by Park—the framework for the interpretation of urban mentality is different.

Spengler developed his interpretation of the city in the *Decline of the West*44 which was written during World War I and published in July, 1918. It became so popular that 90,000 copies were printed. Translated it became a best-seller in the English-speaking world. It contained powerful ideological themes from Western development. It is interesting to locate Spengler's study in relation to the German city.

The career of the city in Germany has been checkered. The Romans had established a system of fortress cities in German lands along the natural transportation routes represented by the Rhine and Danube rivers. These vanished with the fall of Rome. With the revival of trade in the late Middle Ages these old Roman settlements revived for they were astride the routes for inner-continental trade. Later civic development in German lands occurred with the formation of cities into protective leagues like the Hanse on the North Sea and the Baltic, and the league of southern cities. Moreover, the pioneering movement of Germans into the frontier lands to the East was accompanied by the founding of many cities. These thriving cities underwent rapid internal evolution and formed the social basis for impressive developments in art, science, and literature. The religious wars, however, resulted in unbelievable devastation and impoverishment of the cities throughout German lands—the Thirty Years War left some cities with only a quarter of their former personnel and precisely the most civic types liquidated. Meanwhile, the opening of the new hemisphere reoriented trade away from continental Europe cutting the very economic base out from under such

43. *The City*, p. 1.
44. Oswald Spengler, *The Decline of the West* (New York: Alfred A. Knopf, 1928), 2 vols. Translated by Charles Francis Atkinson.

civic leagues as the Hansa. City life was annihilated. City life began
to revive again in Germany in the 18th century but at the same time
it was rural Prussia of the German north-east which led the way in
consolidating the German Empire. By and large Prussia's policies
were determined by the attempt to keep the city and its typical
strata under political control while political dominance—in the state,
the administration, and higher ranks of the Army—was in the hands
of rural aristocrats (the Junkers). Thus while in other Western
lands and the United States urban types had the major voice in the
affairs of the nation, in Germany the city man was peculiarly deprived of political responsibility.

As a result of these events in German lands, the urbanite tended
to display an unusually intense concentration on urban talents and
skills correlated with antipathy to and ineptness in politics. The
strata that ran the government were shrewd, able chess players in
the game of power while they were remarkably crude and uncul-
tured. The urban strata were over-cultured and politically inept.
This supplied the basis for the savage tides of agrarian mysticism
and the passionate rejection of the city which the Nazis could exploit. Spengler took over Simmel's description of the city and reset
it in a frame of agrarian mysticism. The vast popularity of Spengler's
work in post-war Germany is accounted for in terms of the fitness
of this combination of agrarian mysticism and rejection of the city
to the bewildered disillusionment of a defeated nation. The popularity of Spengler's work in America is to be accounted for somewhat differently—it provided a systematic rationale for the outraged sentiments generated in contexts of urban corruption and
focussed to a point by the Pre-World War I muckrakers but drama-
tized by the heightened patriotism of War and the post-war let
down.

The fundamental contrast in the order of human life for
Spengler[45] is found between country and city. The roots of human
life are always in the soil. Only in civilization with its giant cities
do we disengage ourselves from such roots. The civilized man is an
intellectual nomad, quite homeless, a microcosm, as intellectually
free as the hunter and herdsmen were sensually free. World history
is the history of civic men. The soul of a town is a mass-soul of a

45. The fullest treatment of *The City* by Spengler is contained in Volume II
of the *Decline of the West*, Chapters 4-6, pp. 85-186.

fundamentally new kind. The city quickly reduces the countryside to something experienced only as "environs."

Human civilization is cyclical. Every springtime of culture sees the birth of a new city-man and type of civism. It involves the creation of a situation in which man becomes more languid, while sensation and reason become ever more powerful. Man becomes "intellect," "*Geist*," "*esprit*." In the specifically urban form of understanding, all religion and science becomes intellectualized and more alien to the land, incomprehensible to the peasant.

We cannot, Spengler continues, comprehend political and economic history unless we realize that the city with its gradual detachment from the land eventually bankrupts the country. World history is city history and every culture is oriented in the type of the capital city. In all countries in the periods of late culture great parties, revolutions, Caesarisms, democracies and parliaments appear as the form in which the capital tells the country what is expected of it and what to die for. The classical forum and the Western press are the intellectual instruments of the ruling city. Moreover all style-history is played out in cities where the life experience of man speaks to the eye in the logic of visual form. Gothic art was a growth of the soil but Renaissance style flourished only in the city. The village peasant remained Gothic; the Hellenic countryside preserved the geometrical style. The Epic belongs to *Platz* and *Burg*; the drama in which an awakened life tests itself is city poetry.

The city is intellect, the "megapolis" is free intellect. Intelligence originates in resistance to the feudal powers of blood and tradition against which the bourgeoisie as an intellectual class becomes conscious of its own existence. As it develops the urban intellect reforms the religion of the springtime and sets aside the old religion of noble and priest for the new religion of the *Tiers Etat*, liberal science. The city assumes control of the land replacing the primitive values in land—which are everywhere inseparable from the life and thought of the rustic—with the absolute idea of money as distinct from goods. Thus, the city not only implies intellect but money. And like money itself genuine "megalopolitans" are at home wherever their postulates are satisfied. Money not only serves for understanding economic intercourse but subjects the exchange of goods to its own evolution. As the city expands the money market itself emerges for money is power. Money becomes for man a form of activity of waking consciousness no longer having any roots in being. Civilization always represents an unconditional dictatorship of money.

Finally, the city itself, the stone colossus, the "Cosmopolis" stands at the end of the life course of every great culture. The mass of stone is the absolute city. The final city is pure intellect. Civilization is nothing but pure tension; and intelligence is the capacity for understanding at high tension. In every culture the intellectuals are the final types of men. When tension becomes intellectual no other form of recreation is open to it but that of the world city itself—*detente*, relaxation, distraction. Civilized man tends toward sterility with a metaphysical turn toward death. And the last man of the world city no longer wants to live—at least as a type. This is the conclusion of the city as it grows from the primitive barter center to the city of culture, in the course of its majestic evolution flowering as civilization and wilting in a final destruction.

Louis Wirth[46] was far too much an urban type himself to find any comfort in the anti-urbanism and agrarian mysticism of Spengler. At the same time he was too theoretically perceptive to be satisfied with the substitution of a shallow external formula for serious study. Moreover, he agreed that the distinctiveness of all that is specifically modern is tied in with the growth of the great cities in the Western world. In reaction to the ecological point of view he urged that "as long as we identify urbanism with the physical entity of the city . . . we are not apt to arrive at an adequate concept of urbanism."[47] Rather a sociologically significant definition of the city seeks to select the elements which mark it as a distinctive mode of human group life.

It is noteworthy that Park's famous essay began with almost the same idea and nearly the same phrasing. However, Park had Spengler in mind, Wirth took the point of departure from Simmel.[48] Urbanization, he urged, refers to the cumulative accentuation of

46. Louis Wirth, "Urbanism as a Way of Life." *American Journal of Sociology*, XLIV (July, 1938), 1-24.

47. *Ibid.*, p. 4.

48. Wirth got up the annotated bibliography on the city for the Park, Burgess, McKenzie volume. It is noteworthy that he included Simmel's *Die Grosstädte und das Geistesleben*. He observed that it was "The most important single article on the city from the sociological standpoint." *The City*, p. 219.

the mode of life typical of the city. This is not to be confused with industrialism or modern capitalism. The central problem of the sociologist of the city is to discover the forms of social action and organization that typically emerge in relatively permanent compact settlements of large numbers of heterogeneous individuals.

The multiplication of the number of persons in interaction, Wirth argues, makes full contact of personalities impossible. The result is a "schizoid" property of urban personality. Urbanites meet in highly segmental roles. Their relations are secondary rather than primary. Contacts are impersonal, superficial, transitory, and segmental, leading to reserve, indifference, a blasé outlook and the immunization of one's self against the claims of others. The superficiality, anonymity, and transitory character of urban social relations makes intelligible the sophistication and rationality of city dwellers. Freedom from personal emotional control of intimate groups leaves them in a state of *anomie* (a kind of normlessness) as Durkheim put it. The segmental character and unitary criteria of interpersonal relations emphasized the need for professional codes and the operation of a pecuniary nexus. A premium is placed on utility and efficiency and leads automatically to the employment of corporative devices for the organization of enterprises.

The simultaneous interdependence and instability is increased by the tendency in the city for the individual to specialize in those functions from which he receives greatest advantage. This further separates individuals. It becomes necessary to communicate through indirect media and individual interests are articulated through delegation. Density re-enforces the effect of numbers further by diversifying men and their activities and increasing the complexity of social structure. Hence, a premium is placed in the urban world on visual recognition. We see the uniform as denoting the role of the functionary and are oblivious to personal eccentricities hidden behind it.

Groups and interests separate out under such conditions. Density, land values, rentals, accessibility, healthfulness, prestige, aesthetic considerations, absence of nuisances, such as noise, smoke, and dirt determine the desirability of various areas of the city as places of settlement for different segments of the population. Place and nature of work, income, racial and ethnic characteristics, social status, custom, habit, taste, preference and prejudice are among the significant factors in accord with which the urban population is selected and distributed into more or less distinct settlements.

Nervous tensions deriving from personal problems and accentuated by a rapid tempo of life and complicated technology are always at work. The urban milieu tends to break down the rigidity of class lines and to complicate class structure.

Urbanism as a way of life, Wirth believes, may be empirically approached from three interrelated perspectives: as a physical structure with a population base, technology and ecological order; as a system of social organization with a structure and series of institutions; as a set of attitudes, ideas and constellation of personalities. With respect to the first, urban population shows selection and differentiation on a number of factors. There are more persons in the prime of life, more foreign born males, more women, more negroes, there are fewer births, a failure to reproduce, and a higher death rate. As a social order urbanism is characterized by the substitution of secondary for primary contacts. Related to this is the weakening of kinship ties, the declining significance of neighborhood, the undermining of the traditional bases of social solidarity, the transfer of industrial, educational and recreational activities to specialized institutions. Along with this since the individual actor is ineffectual alone and efficiency is only achieved in groups there is a multiplication of voluntary organizations. Finally urban personality and collective behavior show all the properties noted above along with increased personal disorganization, mental breakdown, suicide, delinquency, crime, corruption and disorder.

The property that holds the conceptions of urbanism by Simmel, Spengler, and Wirth together is the location of the focal point of study in the "urban mentality." It can hardly be said that all the theoretical problems this poses have been resolved. Spengler's treatment is at once most complete and most questionable. Spengler's theory represents a reification of collective psychology. It is one thing to think of people as possessing a point of view, or system of attitudes; it is quite another thing to conceive of a point of view as possessing people. Nor does Spengler merely rest content with this. He not only assumes that collective psychology reified and visualized as a mass-soul has an independent reality but that it is an organic phenomenon with a birth, growth, or death—in his rural imagery, with a springtime, summer, fall and winter. And all spiritual entities when they die, it seems, return their spiritual potential to the all encompassing world-spirituality or proto-spirituality of the soil and peasantry. This is not responsible theory formation but the pyramiding of figures of speech. Such, it seems, is the technique for setting up metaphysical holding companies.

Simmel's analysis is at least theoretically consistent with his definition of the task of sociology as the discovery of the contentless inter-psychic forms of inter-human life. Consistently Simmel set about to epitomize the urban mind. On this topic he wrote an intuitive essay of great imagination, delicacy and charm. However, neither his conception of sociology nor his treatment of the city is wholly satisfactory to the overwhelming majority of sociologists. It may be seriously doubted—at least it has been doubted—that the study of contentless inter-psychic forms is the task of sociology. In practice, it may be noted, Simmel never adheres to his own rules, but is at his best in the incisive comparisons of wide varieties of evidence. Moreover, the suggestion that form and content are intrinsically separable—that they may even have different origins—tends also to point toward the reification of forms. There is almost a Platonic note in this concept of a world of blue prints looking for a draftsman. Simmel has by no means completely avoided the reification appearing in Spengler's work. Finally, while Simmel does not make the mistake of presenting urbanism in a framework of agrarian mysticism, he tends to define his materials in a way that places them outside empirical study.

When one takes into account the fact that Wirth was a relatively hardheaded urbanite it can easily appear strange that he was attracted by either Spengler or Simmel. To be sure, that he passed over Spengler in silence is understandable—Wirth was under no delusions as to the intrinsic superior spirituality of the country over the city. At the same time he was not inclined to trade the parlor game of spinning out imaginative insights for the scientific process. Wirth's judgments become fully understandable only in terms of his obvious attempt to correct the simple-minded physics of ecological theory. His judgments, thus, have the properties of a corrective overstatement. To be sure, the social-psychological theory of the city exists only as a program possibility not as an accomplished fact and one is in position only to criticize tendencies with all the risks this involves. Nevertheless, it seems to point toward a simple-minded psychological approach just as ecology led to an over-simplification on a physical level. There is a strong tendency for the relevant world of action to be reduced to mere matters of increase, density, and heterogeneity of population which have psychological effects. All indications point to the possibility that institutions tend to receive as cursory and incidental a treatment as they did from ecology.

Perhaps it is of some significance that though Wirth's brilliant statement is some twenty years old the reconstruction in urban theory it demanded has not been forthcoming.

European Developments in Urban Theory

In the last quarter of the nineteenth and first two decades of the twentieth century the theory of the city was undergoing a remarkable internal evolution. Some peculiarities of American urban theory account for the fact that American theorists to a remarkable degree have cut themselves off from these European beginnings—except in the case of two, as when Spengler's ideas because of their sheer popularity forced themselves on attention and when because of their sheer "urbanity" Simmel's views are belatedly taken into account. It will be recalled, however, that in the early days of the twentieth century when sociology became an academic discipline with limited rather than unlimited claims, it rejected its founders and their distinguishing peculiarities—which, incidentally, included the use of historical writings for sociological evidence. Sociology, in general, and urban sociology in particular were striving to become autonomous sciences—gathering their own evidence first hand by their own methods. Moreover, the popular attitude toward the city in America was marked by the serious concern with current problems of urban corruption and the disasters to various areas of social life possible in urban environments. While European students of the city were oriented toward historical materials, American students were oriented toward the present. While European students had materials available from cities that had been going-concerns for a thousand years; American cities were often not more than a few decades old. When an American student did happen to dip into the work of a European theorist he tended to react to it as mere "ancient history." Once in a great while he was even willing to admit that it was interesting. He rarely saw in it any relevance to his own problems except as a curious contrast. Under these circumstances American students of the city largely cut themselves adrift from the urban theory of Europe.

Among the consequences for American urban theorists of cutting themselves off from research into the historical past of the city was the toleration of a degree of naivete that had been banned from other areas of their science. Human social forms, once they have been stabilized, and their difficulties have been worked out sometimes amount to something like solutions of a maximum efficiency to a given set of social problems. People are remarkably unwilling or unable to give up successful solutions. When they came to the new hemisphere, for example, they neither lost their language nor invented a new one. Sociologists who would not make the mistake for a moment of assuming that each new family represents a new family institution seem to have assumed something of the sort with regard to their cities.

A single illustration may suffice to illustrate the value of historical knowledge in interpreting some of the happenings in American cities. The patterns of city government in European cities evolved gradually and only stabilized after some centuries of development. As this stabilization occurred the administrative focus of city government came to center in the structure of the mayor and council. American cities were set up by people of European culture, but the large majority of cities established in the nineteenth century followed the pattern of government of the state rather than the more normal European civic form. Sociologists might well have taken this as a kind of unconscious "experiment" in city government in America. Approached in this way the American experiment —heralded as a device of securing greater democracy in the city— made possible the influence of every interest in city affairs except the public interest. Bryce has been quoted by everyone on the state of American civic affairs in the 1880's. City government, he thought, was the most conspicuous political failure in America. Under these circumstances a series of events began to occur which should have excited every sociologist in America—*American cities began to set up traditional mayor and council types of government along the European plan.* The more limited administrative structure and more clear location of responsibility were critical to the adequate functioning of city government in the system of institutions of the city. A certain degree of "visibility" as to its operations was necessary for the control of power.

This was a tremendous concession to the fact that the cities in America were "new" only in a physical sense—not in a sociological sense. The city was a peculiar system of institutions that had gradually arrived at an economical functioning in time. Within limits it could not be varied arbitrarily without paying an exceptionally heavy price. The price paid in nineteenth century America for its "experiments" was the tolerance of almost unbelievable quantities of graft. Not only did most sociologists completely miss this point but when the return to the more traditional relations of mayor and council occurred in American cities the implications of this fact were radically misinterpreted.

The struggle for liberty has been a struggle to wrest power from one, or the few, and to lodge it with the many; that is, to decentralize government. When popular government fails, society is saved from anarchy by the strong man; that is, power is again centralized. The movement, therefore, to centralize government by transferring power from the council to the mayor was a confession that popular government in our great cities had failed.[49]

Thus, instead of seeing this as the partial return to a more stable community form it was interpreted by Strong as a failure of democracy itself. Strong completely overlooked the fact that sometimes the decentralization of government permits the centralization of graft.

There are other examples of theoretical naivete. What are sometimes viewed as rather uniquely American contributions to civilization are enactments of a traditional civic drama. In 1901 in Galveston, Texas the city stricken by wind and flood set up a commission which worked so well in meeting the disaster that it was continued as the governing organ of the city. Its success was copied and it worked very well in small cities and was present in 327 out of 2,033 small cities of 5,000 or less population in 1945. In larger cities the city manager plan represents the equivalent of commission government. A city manager is appointed by the city council which retains full authority to enact ordinances, make plans, plan developments and select and discharge the manager. The city charter usually

49. Josiah Strong, *Twentieth Century City*, p. 86.

directs that the choice of a manager be made independent of party. He usually has power to choose all his own assistants and technicians. The plan was instituted at Staunton, Virginia in 1908 and became nationally important following adoption by Dayton, Ohio after 1914. In 1945 it was in effect in 350 cities of the United States of more than 5,000 population; the largest was Cincinnati with a population of one-half a million. Under the city manager plan a body of professional city administrators has developed who are fairly free of political considerations.

In America under the old system of diffused civic authority such complex structures of party patronage developed that even the return to the traditional form of city government with a council and mayor was often unsuccessful. Such powerful party machines had developed that they immediately distorted city government to their pattern and continued to operate with hardly a pause. Commission government and the city manager are the exact parallel of the *podesta* system of the Middle Ages, arising for similar reasons and having somewhat the same results. There, too, party conflicts had become so destructive to the general interests of the citizens that an uncommitted outsider was brought in for administrative purposes and was free to choose his own subordinates. There, too, the *podesta* system led to the development of a body of professionals trained in city administration. Such examples illustrate the value of acquaintance with European urban theory to which we now turn.

The ancients, as André Piganiol observed, generally had little understanding of the city. Plato and Aristotle held the middle classes —typical urban strata—in contempt and wished to subordinate them to warriors and philosophers. Private property (that is, urban alienable property) was suspect and money thought to be dangerous. The location of the city on the sea was thought to be a mistake. Their own choice for a city was Sparta, hardly a true city but a permanent open military camp.

As "the city" increasingly presented itself as a problem to modern social scientists one characteristic explanation was that the origin of the modern urban community was a survival of Roman cities. While there is little doubt that a considerable number of medieval cities took form at the same location points as old Roman garrisons and trade centers—such as Cologne, Mayence, Strasbourg, Rheims, and Paris—becoming feudal garrisons and episcopal sees, later evolving into modern cities, this does not explain the city but thrusts the problem it presents back into history.

There are two general properties of the theories of the city emerging in the late nineteenth and early twentieth centuries in Europe despite many differences between them—they all assume that the characteristics of any unit of social life are determined by institutions. Secondly, they all generally assume that human society is an evolutionary or historical product, hence explanation of social events consists in a discovery of origins. Thus, in contrast both to the ecological theory of the city and the rather fragmentary social-psychological theory of the city, European urban theory at the turn of the century held an *institutional theory of the city*. The explanation of the city was found in the peculiar order and historical primacy of its institutions. The various special theories differed in terms of the particular institution they took to be central or original.

Fustel de Coulanges who pioneered city theory took the critical institution of the city to be a religion. The original nucleus of pre-urban society was thought to be the family finding its point of integration in the hearth, its religious symbol, and worship of the father as its priest. The union of several families could establish the hearth of the phratry.

The tribe, like the family and the phratry, was established as an independent body, since it had a special worship from which the stranger was excluded. Once formed, no new family could be admitted to it.
Just as several phratries were united in a tribe, several tribes might associate together, on condition that the religion of each should be respected. The day on which this alliance took place the city existed.[50]

The critical point in the founding of the city was religious synoecism and establishment of the hearth of the city. The city assumed the form of a new sanctuary for common worship. The ancient city was a religious community.

Glotz considerably advanced beyond Fustel de Coulanges in his conception of the range of possible city types in terms of different relations of family and city to each other. Like Coulanges he treated the family as the core structure from which both state power and

---

50. Fustel de Coulanges, *The Ancient City* (New York: Doubleday Anchor Books, 1956), pp. 126-7.

individualism could emerge. Thus three stages in Greek city life were assumed—each with its peculiar institutional order.

The Greek city, while retaining the institution of the family, grew at its expense. It was compelled to appeal to individual forces which the original group repressed. For a long time the city had to fight against the *genos* and each of its victories was gained by the suppression of some form of patriarchal servitude.

We shall not see two opposing forces—the family and the city—but three—the family, the city and the individual each in its turn predominant. The history of Greek institutions thus falls into three periods: in the first, the city is composed of families which jealously guard their ancient right and subordinate all their members to the common good; in the second, the city subordinates the families to itself by calling to its aid emancipated individuals; in the third, individualism runs riot, destroys the city and necessitates the formation of larger states.[51]

This represents genuine advance over Fustel de Coulanges in that it conceives of the possibility of a more complex inter-institutional development making the city possible and of more varied city types. The family dominated or patrician city is clearly visualized.

A third institutional factor was brought into central focus as determinative for the rise of the city by the students of comparative jurisprudence. Henry Sumner Maine, for example, in one of the great pioneering works[52] of social science argued that comparative jurisprudence proves that the original condition of the human race was one of dominance by the patriarchal family. From England to India in ancient times, he believed, society was organized in patriarchal families under dominance of the eldest parent with dominion extending even to life and death over his children. Law was the parent's word. Guilt was a community affair for which the kin had joint responsibility. At this stage kinship was the only ground for political functions. For all more complex social forms, Maine felt that the critical problem lay in the substitution of a principle of territoriality for kinship and a transformation of the legal order isolating the individual from his status in the family, freeing him for the plastic entry into multiple "contractual" relations. One social role after the other was freed according to Maine. The son was

---

51. G. Glotz, *The Greek City* (New York: Alfred A. Knopf, 1930). Translated by N. Mallinson, pp. 4-5.

52. Henry Sumner Maine, *Ancient Law* (London: John Murray, 1894).

delivered from the *Patria Potestas* first, probably because it had always been necessary for him to become a patriarchal house-head himself. The status of the slave disappeared, being superseded by a contractual relation between servant and master. In time even women won contractual freedom. As Maine put it "The movement of the progressive societies has hitherto been a movement from Status to Contract."[53] The city in Maine's analysis is a legal structure resting on contract and territory rather than kinship and family. The effect of his analysis was to bring the relations of kinship and territory into central focus institutionally, shifting the attention of urban theory to the evolution of the law. This was the starting point for rich additional developments and the consideration of the importance of a whole series of legal or semi-legal phenomena for the development of the city. These include such things as: 1. the importance of charters for the possibility of the city and the basis of its law; 2. the role in the appearance of the city of the development of special civic courts and law; 3. the importance for the city of the (Roman) legal notion of a civic corporation with a legal personality of its own.

Maitland, who did brilliant work on the evolution of the city in England, partly agreed with Maine. At least he urges that "the borough community is corporate; the village community is not."[54] However, its existence as a legal entity and as a fictitious personality resting its identity on incorporation as the result of the grant of a royal charter is a later stage of city development. Its origins trace back to the castle or burg or borough and to a special burgess obligated for the upkeep of the fortress. "It seems to me possible that the great men of the shire were bound to keep house and retainers, burgmen, *burgenses*, knights in this stronghold and place of refuge."[55] Maitland himself designated this as the garrison theory. Closely parallel with Maitland's garrison theory was the "military" theory of the city advanced by Keutgen in Germany. Towns were regarded as strongholds for emergency purposes, where the inhabitants surrounding the place could retreat for protection. In times of

53. *Ibid.*, p. 170.

54. Frederick William Maitland, *Township and Borough* (Cambridge: Cambridge University Press, 1898), p. 18.

55. *Ibid.*, p. 24.

peace the lords kept a skeleton staff of retainers on duty; these were the first civic personnel. Some towns like Chichester and Canterbury in England at the time of Doomesday had between 100 and 200 houses attached to 44 and 11 manors respectively.

The attempt to explain the city in terms of economic institutions was made by Marx and others and much more completely by Pirenne.[56] He maintained the two attributes necessary to constitute a city are a middle class population and a communal organization. From this standpoint the *town* or *gorod*, originally enclosures where people might seek refuge in time of danger, were not yet cities. People might resort to them on religious occasions so that they became the sites of temples as well as the seats of officials. However, although they grew in complexity they were still not cities. Historically the municipal system of Rome was identified by its constitutional system. In time Roman municipal centers declined until in the eighth century they were in extensive decay. Meanwhile the Church based its diocesan boundaries on the boundaries of Roman cities. This, in turn, meant that the cities where the bishops resided fell under episcopal domination as Roman cities decayed. Areas that had been centers of municipal administration under Rome lost their civic functions. In the ninth century *"civitas"* had come to be synonymous with the bishopric and the so-called episcopal "city." The episcopal "city" for Pirenne is a city in name only. The influence of the bishops became unrivaled precisely because the last vestiges of civic life were being annihilated. These centers often had a weekly market where peasants brought their produce. Sometimes there was an annual fair. The bishop enjoyed both religious and secular power over them for he even had loosely-defined police powers under which he supervised the markets, regulated tolls, took care of bridges and ramparts. These towns were fortresses as well as episcopal establishments. However, for Pirenne they were not cities, though many cities took them as points for development. They played a role in the history of cities as "stepping stones." Round about their walls cities were to take shape after the "economic renaissance."[57] The cities took form as a byproduct of

56. Henri Pirenne, *Medieval Cities* (Princeton: University Press, 1946). Trans. by Frank D. Halsey.

57. *Ibid.*, p. 76.

the activities of merchant caravans which settled outside the walls and in crisis could use them for defence.

Under the influence of trade the old Roman cities took on new life and were repopulated, or mercantile groups formed round about the military burgs and established themselves along the sea coasts, on river banks, at confluences, at the junction points of the natural routes of communication. Each of them constituted a market which exercised an attraction proportionate to its importance, on the surrounding country or made itself felt afar.[58]

The critical point for Pirenne was the development of a new class of merchants who found themselves at odds with the countryside and its institutions. They fought for a new code of laws, a private jurisdiction, free property, and eventually distinct communal organization—for Pirenne the city is the community of the merchants.

Max Weber and European Urban Theory

The abbreviated review of the highlights of European urban theory illustrates the variety of points of view and the accumulating mass of historical research at special points and for particular areas. Thoughtful sociologists recognized the need for a more special or more comprehensive theory of urbanism. Simmel and Weber were responding to the same problem. Simmel sought to solve the problem of the city by way of a specialization in terms of neo-Kantian formalism. Weber was familiar with Simmel's formulation and he opened his study with the observation that the city is often thought of as a densely settled area of crowded dwellings forming a colony so extensive that personal reciprocal acquaintance of the inhabitants is lacking. But while recognizing the importance of this, Weber immediately pointed out that this could not serve as more than a fragment in the full theory of the city for not only would it restrict the concept of the city to densely settled areas of large size but it would even then be inconclusive for cultural factors play a role in the point where impersonality makes its appearance in human affairs. It would be difficult to touch its limitations more quickly. Besides Weber's theoretical starting point was different and in principle he could not have found Simmel's concept of the city completely adequate.

Max Weber's theoretical point of view may best be described as

58. *Ibid.*, p. 102.

a form of social behaviorism. He was unwilling, like Simmel, to confine sociological analysis to the delineation of inter-psychic forms. On the other hand he was strongly nominalistic and suspicious of any sociological procedure that had to invent artificial entities such as "over-souls" like Spengler's reified social psychology. Finally, Weber thought that the task of sociology was to explain human conduct in its meaningful dimensions and not merely externally. One can determine a person's loss of weight objectively by weighing him repeatedly but it makes a lot of difference if he is losing weight because he is dying of an illness or because he is engaging in ascetic practices in connection with his religion. The task of sociology is to explain inter-human actions in terms of the meanings they have to the parties involved as well as in terms of specific physical changes they entail.

The idea of "social relation" for Weber was a kind of conceptual shorthand by which one speaks of the maintenance of a pattern in inter-human actions. If when two people interact one gives orders and the other carries them out, one may speak of a relation of dominance-subordination between the two. Weber was suspicious of the German tendency toward reification and he was careful to insist that a relation exists only so far as inter-human actions actually occur.

Granting this meaning of "social relations" it is possible to take an additional step and conceive of the possibility of a complex "system" of relations. An institution such as a state, a family, a religion, or a system of law is a "system of relations." It has no different status from that of a single isolated relation—it has no further reality. The institution actually exists only so far as people act in certain ways. Just as the concept of "social relation" is a useful economy for expressing the comparative identity in a number of specific social actions so "institution" is an economy for speaking about the occurrence of complex sets of social interactions.

In Max Weber's terms all forms of European urban theory reviewed above are "institutional" theories of the city. They are different from each other only with respect to the particular institution taken to be central or original to the city. Weber's own position was not advanced by way of a review and critique of current urban theories—but as an independent inquiry into the nature of the city. But he automatically took these theories into account.

One of the values of Weber's approach to the problems of the city from the standpoint of the sociology of social action may be seen by further comparisons with Simmel. For both men society eventually reduces to social interaction or meaningful inter-human behavior. Simmel, however, would analyze this into form and content and confine sociology to the study of form. This reduces the science to an inventory of inter-psychic forms and leaves aside large blocks of the materials generally included by sociology. Max Weber, by contrast, set aside the distinction between form and content conceiving the task of sociology to be causal interpretation of social action. One of the most immediate consequences of this was the fact that Weber's theory of the city could encompass Simmel's while the reverse was not true. There was room in Weber's theory for attention to mentality in the city. He was able, also, to recognize and account for the appearance in the city of most varied social types. As he put it. "The city . . . has always contained elements from the most varied social situations. Office candidates qualified by examinations and mandarins rub shoulders with illiterates despised as rabble and practitioners of the (few) unclean occupations in East Asia. Many kinds of castes carry on their activities beside one another in India. Blood relatives organized in clans appear together with landless artisans in the Near East. In Antiquity free men, bondsmen, and slaves emerged alongside noble landlords, their court officials and servants. And in the early medieval city ministerial officials and mercenaries, priests and monks encounter one another in the city." Weber thus had provided for the fact that in the city all sorts of people meet and mingle, often without understanding one another. Slums may be separated from fine residences by a few hundred yards but while they are geographically close they may be miles apart in points of view. He recognized the absence of psychological homogeneity such that the intelligentsia, middle class, political reformers, stand-patters, and go-getters, in Monroe's phrases, all pull apart to such an extent that city dwellers can only think effectively in groups. Weber's point of view permitted him to move in either direction—toward the mentalities, conceptual traditions, and segmented *milieus* of the city or toward the stabilized patterns persistent through time, the institutions of the city. In fact, his theory required that he consider both.

With Simmel, Weber was able to recognize that in the city every occupation—including mendicancy and prostitution—tends to become a profession. The city dweller's mind is crowded with impressions with little time for reflection, developing a craving for novelty, an impatience with repetition, a yearning for the bizarre. Simmel's theory of the city was reduced to a sub-part of his own. However, this does not indicate how he dealt with the many conflicting institutional theories of the city. His procedure is a model of sound theory construction. He successively reviewed one type of concept of the city after another—the economic, the relation of the city to agriculture, the political-administrative concept of the city, the fortress and garrison concepts of the city, the concept of the city as fusion of fortress and market, the social and status concept of the city (legal concept of the city), the city as a sworn confederacy, the city as a body of militarily competent citizens— he attempted thereby to isolate and retain whatever was correct in each special concept of the city.

This may suggest that Weber's procedure was eclectic. But theory construction is not a mere matter of carpentry—sawing out little bits from existing theories and gluing them into a new inlay work of one's own. Theory construction is neither carpentry nor the solving of jigsaw puzzles with pre-cut pieces. Weber's procedure was no mechanical assembling of theoretically unrelated fragments but one of testing the various concepts of the city against the evidence noting what they do explain and what they do not. For example, in reviewing the economic concept of the city Weber isolated the distinguishing property of the city in the conduct of life on the basis of non-agricultural activities. In terms of the dominant economic features of their life a typology of cities is possible and one may distinguish producers' cities from consumers' cities, commercial from industrial cities, main and satellite cities with many sub-types. However, when all is said and done the economy of a city is a necessary *but not sufficient* condition of the city. Similar judgments apply to other concepts of the city and the evidences upon which they rest.

The concept formation in terms of which Weber brought together and surpassed the various forms of the *institutional theory of the city* current in his day was in the *theory of the urban com-*

munity. The relation of the concept "community" to other of Weber's ideas may be seen easily if his key concepts are outlined in terms of their comparative abstractness and complexity.

1. *Social actions,* the ultimate units of analysis for the sociologist. These are inter-human behaviors having a meaning to the parties involved.

2. *Social Relations.* One may use this term to speak of the stable arrangement of elements appearing in social action. They do not exist outside social actions, they merely represent the abstractly conceived arrangements or patterns an action displays.

3. *Social Institutions,* a similar way to abstractly conceptualize the social relations in a whole network of social actions. Social institutions bear the same relation to patterns of action that social relations do to single actions. In practice social institutions are always manifest as more or less stable patterns of behaviors. However, important institutions are they are not, by themselves, sufficient to account for all of social life, for individuals live out their experience in more than single institutions. They act as members of families, agents of economic institutions, as citizens of states, etc. How an individual acts in accordance with one institutional pattern like the family is modified by how he acts in accord with others. The state condones special kinds of marriage arrangements, not others; economic success or failure modifies activity in family contexts. One is led, thus step by step to the total systematic units of inter-human life of which the institutions are separate aspects.

4. *Community.* In the concept of the urban community as a total systematic unit of inter-human life distinguished not by a single institution but by an order of institutions Weber found a theoretical formulation which was able to take account of the many partial concepts of the city current in his time. As he phrased the problem neither the "city" in the economic sense nor the garrison of inhabitants accoutred with a special politico-administrative structure necessarily constitutes an urban community. "An urban 'community' in the full meaning of the word appears only in the Occident. Exceptions occasionally were to be found in the Near East (in Syria, Phoenicia, and Mesopotamia) but only occasionally and in rudiments. To constitute a full urban community the settlement had to represent a relative predominance of trade-commercial relations with the settlement as a whole displaying the following features:

1. a fortification, 2. a market, 3. a court of its own and at least partially autonomous law, 4. a related form of association, and 5. at least partial autonomy and autocephaly, thus, also, an administration by authorities in the election of whom the burghers participated."

Weber's general procedure was to review the concept of the city in terms of the evidence from world history. On this basis he established the concept of the urban community. Any community, including an urban community, is not an unstructured congeries of activities but a distinct and limited pattern of human life. It represents a total system of life forces brought into some kind of equilibrium. It is self-maintaining, restoring its order in the face of disturbances. One need only recall the illustrations given previously of the unexpected consequences in corruption emerging in American cities facilitated by their awkward political structures. As noted, American cities were forced back into an older more tested form of political organization. The city, as a limited pattern, obeys its own laws.

As a peculiar system of forces the urban community could not have emerged everywhere. Weber argues rather convincingly that it did not. It did not appear in Asia and only fragmentarily in the Near East in part for the very reason that the city was a center of state administration. Weber's arguments on this point are also relevant today for some capital cities such as Washington, London, and Paris, precisely because they are centers of national government, lack some of the political autonomy of the normal city. They are prevented from becoming full urban communities.

The city as a peculiar system of forces could appear only under special conditions and in time. A good part of Weber's study is devoted to the gradual emergence and structuring of the force-composition of the city in various areas under different conditions and its gradual stabilization into a distinct form. As the changing composition of forces is traced from the ancient kingships through the patrician city to the demos of the ancient world, from the episcopal structures and fortresses through the city of notables, to the guild dominated cities on the continent, from the buroughs with their assigned garrison personnel through a peculiar evolution due to ties with kinship in England, many penetrating observations are made. And ever and again the complex processes accompanying the emergence of the urban community are laid bare. It is not difficult to accept Wirth's proposition that Weber's study is one of the closest approximations to a systematic theory of urbanism we have.

Max Weber's Relevance for American Urban Theory

If one grants that the analysis of the city as a peculiar community formation with a special arrangement of institutions is sociologically legitimate, a rather novel fact emerges: this kind of urban theory has been more frequent among American political scientists than among sociologists. Though this may seem startling at first it is not difficult to explain. By the very definition of his activity the political scientist has to approach his problems from the point of view of one institution, the state. When he deals with the city his point of departure is found in city government. The moment he generalizes his problems and follows out their implications his study becomes a more or less systematic review of the forces and institutions of the civic community by way of their bearing upon government, the charter, city law, city courts, the political party, the boss, the pressure groups, the good-government league, etc.

Two illustrations may suffice to show this tendency of the discussion of the urban community by political scientists to assume a form approximating Weber's:

In 1904 Wilcox carried out a study of the American city.[59] In a series of felicitous phrases he formulated the problem of the American city in quite sociological terms. He observed that in the city the sheer volume of stimulation to which the individual was subject inevitably places some pressure on democracy. "In the cities the gossip of the world comes buzzing in our ears twice a day at least, and perhaps through a score of channels."[60] All the forces affecting life in ways unfavorable to democracy tend to concentrate in cities. "The city is, indeed, the visible symbol of the annihilation of distance and the multiplication of interests."[61] Here all institutions tend to undergo change. "The neighborhood, the natural primary unit of local organization is weakened, and in many cases nearly destroyed. Home life is little more than a name whereas a hundred

59. Delos F. Wilcox, *The American City: A Problem in Democracy* (New York: Macmillan, 1904).

60. *Ibid.*, p. 8.

61. *Ibid.*, p. 9.

people, often of different nationalities, live in a single tenement house.... Among the business and professional classes, a man's most intimate associates may be scattered over the whole city, while he scarcely knows his next door neighbor's name...there is an... organization of industry on so large a scale that, in cities, only an insignificant proportion of the people work for themselves."[62] Nor does the problem stop here for "the city is the distributing center of intelligence as well as of goods."[63] It tends to become dominant in the same way as a great employer of labor who deals with his men individually. The city transforms men as if by magic and newcomers are absorbed and changed into city men. "There is little difficulty making city men out of countrymen, it seems well-nigh impossible to reverse the process."[64] And for many reasons the city assumes national importance. "Democracy...has been badly damaged by its contact with city conditions...Secondly, the city, as the center of civilization and the distributing center of the nation's intelligence, tends to impose its ethical and social ideals upon the whole people irrespective of residence. Thirdly, as the accumulation of enormous wealth in the hands of one man without a corresponding responsibility for its use with reference to the social welfare, it is a positive menace to the general well-being."[65] Thus in a striking sense the approach to the city by way of one of its institutions, and in terms of the bearing of various social processes upon it, leads toward the kind of theoretical formation one finds in Max Weber's study.

With an exciting and distinctly "sociological" imagination Wilcox goes on to present "the street" as the symbolic model of the problems of the city. The street, represents first and last the greatest material problems of the city for here by the cooperation of the whole community, a free way is provided, an "open road," a challenge for traffic and transportation for all alike. "The street is the symbol of the free city wherein all cooperate to secure opportunity for all."[66] Similarly, one may locate dangers to the city here. "It is no wonder that the curtailment of the people's rights in the street

---

62. *Ibid.*, p. 10.
63. *Ibid.*, p. 14.
64. *Ibid.*, p. 15.
65. *Ibid.*, p. 21.
66. *Ibid.*, p. 28.

through the grant of special privileges to individuals and corporations is widely regarded as a menace to popular institutions and a step toward the overthrow of the principles of free government. The control of the streets means the control of the city."[67]

It is difficult to imagine a more appropriate symbol of the city as a community. Every community is an organization of individual and general interest. Institutions determine at what points the line is drawn between these explosive forces. One may use the "street" as a symbolic meeting ground for the conflicts of private and public interest and hence for all the problems of regulation and control, of government, as well as for the penetration of private interests, by way of franchises and other monopolies to advantageous position over public life. The value of the street as a symbol does not stop here and one could as well use it as a point of departure to all urban life.

That Wilcox's strongly sociological tendencies were no accident, but the product of an analysis of the city when made by way of one of its institutions can be illustrated by Munroe's study.[68] After summing up the major aspects of urban growth and considering its basic causes as lying in an improved productivity of agriculture, the development of modern industry and commerce and after reviewing various typologies of the city (for example, the primary service city, industrialized city, industrial-commercial city, and metropolitan city) Munroe raised the question as to just what the city is. His discussion bears comparison with Weber's:

Off hand one might say that it is a large body of people living in a relatively small area. That, however, would be a very inadequate definition, for it would convey no intimation of the fact that the city has a peculiar legal status, a distinct governmental organization, a highly complicated economic structure, and a host of special problems which do not arise when an equal number of people live less compactly together. A comprehensive definition of the modern city must indicate that it is a legal, political, economic, and social unit all rolled into one.[69]

Munroe goes on to urge that the city is a corporation at law endowed with an artificial personality such that it may sue and be sued, hold property, make contracts, employ officials and agents,

67. *Ibid.*, p. 29.
68. William Bennett Munroe, *The Government of American Cities* (New York: Macmillan, 1926).
69. *Ibid.*, p. 13.

levy taxes, borrow money, exercise the right of eminent domain. It is a unit of government with a charter proving its warrant for existence granted by the state. It has a form of government, a mayor and council or elective commission, or council and city manager all with complex powers and functions. Economically the city is an agency of economic enterprise and purveyor of water and often gas, electricity and transportation, it is an employer of labor, a purchaser of supplies and materials, a seller of services. The city is also an agency for promotion of social welfare with officials providing free education, health protection, poor relief, public recreation, and social welfare activities of many kinds. It was Munroe's opinion that the many problems faced by the city could hardly, in good theory or conscience, be blamed on the newcomers or foreign born in the city. If they have a general cause it is probably the clumsiness of much governmental machinery.

American municipal development was interpreted by Munroe against a background of social-historical conditions. At a time when most sociologists either missed the fact altogether or misinterpreted it, Munroe saw that the corruption of the American city was made possible in considerable measure by the overly-clumsy governmental machinery of the early nineteenth century civic structure. He correctly interpreted the civic return to a more traditional structure not as a failure of city democracy but as a product of the normal operation of its laws.

Furthermore, the development of municipal government was seen against a background of the social structure of the city. Munroe observed that even as a body of population the city has a peculiar social structure. In the city there is a reversal of many of the ratios of the countryside with greater numbers of women, greater numbers of people in the middle age groups. The city has rural influence which in part drains off many of the most intelligent persons of the country. Foreign born persons collect in the city where they are subject to special concentrations and special political manipulations. In the city birth rates fall, marriage and death rates go up. While there is no evidence of a change in physical virility as between country and city, in the city there is relatively higher intellectual achievement. Moral standards may possibly go down in the city and certainly many crimes are peculiarly associated with city life: forgery, perjury, embezzlement, business frauds are peculiarly urban crimes. And beyond these phenomena there are psychological differences which emerge in the city. Here, again, analysis moves step by step through the charter, city law, city court, political party, etc.

It should not for a moment be supposed that political scientists like Wilcox and Munroe fully carry out a sociological analysis of the urban community with its peculiar institutional order. They were political scientists and as such ninety percent of their analyses remained concerned with government and its problems. For the reasons already noted, in the remaining ten percent of their argument they sometimes expressed a clearer sense of the urban community than many of their sociological colleagues. The task of carrying out theory construction on a full scale and the kind of sociological analysis of the city suggested by Weber remains.

A final point should be noted concerning the possible application of Weber's theory of the city. Weber found that one essential component of the fully developed urban community was the presence of a city fortification and a city army. This is the one element completely absent for the modern city. When one considers the multiple evidences from the historic past of the city which Weber brought to bear upon this point, the disappearance of the city fortification and city army cannot be without importance. In the ancient world outside the West the presence in the locale of military-political powers different from the local residents often prevented the full emergence of an urban community. In ancient India at the time of the appearance of the great heterodox religions, Buddhism and Jainism, a considerable development toward urbanism was present. However, the cities of India were pacifistic and the "city" religions were very much so—this had as one consequence that at any time they chose the Indian princes could crush the cities. They did so choose. On the other hand, in all areas of the world the presence of a fortress and a local militia were powerful factors in establishing a nucleus around which the city could appear. Again and again the city took shape around the castle. In Europe in contrast to India when crisis deepened the burghers manned the walls and fought to maintain the integrity of the city.

It is of decisive importance, which units of social life are able to maintain themselves by armed force. In many parts of the pre-literate world the ultimate military unit was the tribe. Feudal systems of the human society were determined by the decisive military importance of castle-based aristocratic landlords. For a time, in the Ancient Near East, more completely in the Ancient Occident and in the Middle Ages, the ultimate military units were cities—maintaining themselves in the surrounding world by means of their fortifications, their armies, and their navies. The ultimate armed units of modern society are not tribes, or castle-dwelling nobles, nor cities, but states. The modern city is militarily negligible even as politically it has become a subordinate unit. With atomic weapons the city may have become the great death trap of modern man.

The modern city is no longer a community with a firm military shell. The individual is no longer required to take up arms and man its walls—and with this the city no longer figures in his hopes and dreams as a unit of survival, as a structure that must marshal his supreme loyalties since it may ask his very life. The destruction of the city no longer represents the extinction of the institutions of social life. Modern government, business, and religion are more interlocal with every passing year. At any time they choose the decisively militarily competent social formations of the modern world, the national states, can crush the city. This is not merely a possibility. In Russia, cities are governed by a city soviet elected by the workers in various industries and other units of the system. The city soviet is large, often with as many as a thousand members. It elects on nomination of the Communist party a president and praesidium or executive committee of eleven to seventeen members. Democratic civic autonomy in the Soviet Union is, thus, approximately what it was in classical Greece at the time of Homer where the public assembly represented the occasions on which the decisions of the king could be announced and the people were permitted to respond by acclamation. Modern dictators have not been interested in permitting the independent urban community—for they know practically, if not theoretically, that independent communities support the formation of independent thought. In Italy Mussolini replaced elected syndicos and councils of a French model by a *podesta* appointed by the government in whom all authority was vested. In Prussia prior to World War I the government of the cities rested on a three-class system of voting in which membership in the city council was secured to a limited group of taxpayers: one third representation going to the relatively small group paying most taxes;

a third to a larger second group; a final third to the rest. This tax-payers' council chose an executive board or magistrate of salaried professional officers, chairman, or a Burgomaster. The Weimar Republic introduced universal suffrage in German cities permitting them to become more free and democratic. But the Nazis changed all this. The city was coordinated into the party structure and the Mayorality and other principle salaried offices were staffed by party officials.

Max Weber's theory of the city, thus, leads to a rather interesting conclusion. We can grant the phenomenal increase and aggregation of modern populations as a concomitant of the industrial revolution. We should not, however, confuse physical aggregation with the growth of the city in a sociological sense. The urban community has everywhere lost its military integrity—its right to defend itself by military means. In many areas of the world it has, temporarily at least, lost its very legal and political autonomy—the same fate is possible everywhere. Meanwhile, within the city itself greater masses of residents pursue interlocal interests—as representatives of the national government, as agents in business and industries of the national government, as agents in business and industries of national and international rather than of civic scope.

The modern city is losing its external and formal structure. Internally it is in a state of decay while the new community represented by the nation everywhere grows at its expense. The age of the city seems to be at an end.

The City

Chapter 1

The Nature of the City[1]

Economic Character of the City: Market Settlement

THE MANY definitions of the city have only one element in common: namely that the city consists simply of a collection of one or more separate dwellings but is a relatively closed settlement. Customarily, though not exclusively, in cities the houses are built closely to each other, often, today, wall to wall. This massing of elements interpenetrates the everyday concept of the "city" which is thought of quantitatively as a large locality. In itself this is not imprecise for the city often represents a locality and dense settlement of dwellings forming a colony so extensive that personal reciprocal acquaintance of the inhabitants is lacking. However, if interpreted in this way only very large localities could qualify as cities; moreover it would be ambiguous, for various cultural factors determine the size at which "impersonality" tends to appear. Precisely this impersonality was absent in many historical localities possessing the legal character of cities. Even in contemporary Russia there are villages comprising many thousands of inhabitants which are, thus, larger than many old "cities" (for example, in the Polish colonial area of the German East) which had only a

1. First published in *Archiv für Sozialwissenschaft und Sozialpolitik*, Vol. 47, p. 621 ff. (1921). Last edition: *Wirtschaft und Gesellschaft* (Tübingen: J. C. B. Mohr, 1956) Vol. 2, p. 735 ff.—All the notes in this translation are those of the editors.

few hundred inhabitants. Both in terms of what it would include and what it would exclude size alone can hardly be sufficient to define the city.

Economically defined, the city is a settlement the inhabitants of which live primarily off trade and commerce rather than agriculture. However, it is not altogether proper to call all localities "cities" which are dominated by trade and commerce. This would include in the concept "city" colonies made up of family members and maintaining a single, practically hereditary trade establishment such as the "trade villages" of Asia and Russia. It is necessary to add a certain "versatility" of practiced trades to the characteristics of the city. However, this in itself does not appear suitable as the single distinguishing characteristic of the city either.

Economic versatility can be established in at least two ways: by the presence of a feudal estate or a market. The economic and political needs of a feudal or princely estate can encourage specialization in trade products in providing a demand for which work is performed and goods are bartered. However, even though the *oikos* of a lord or prince is as large as a city, a colony of artisans and small merchants bound to villein services is not customarily called a "city" even though historically a large proportion of important "cities" originated in such settlements.[2] In cities of such origin the products for a prince's court often remained a highly important, even chief, source of income for the settlers.

The other method of establishing economic versatility is more generally important for the "city"; this is the existence in the place of settlement of a regular rather than an occasional exchange of goods. The market becomes an essential component in the livelihood of the settlers. To be sure, not every "market" converted the locality in which it was found into a city. The periodic fairs and yearly foreign-trade markets at which traveling merchants met at fixed times to sell their goods in wholesale or retail lots to each other or to consumers often occurred in places which we would call "villages."

Thus, we wish to speak of a "city" only in cases where the local inhabitants satisfy an economically substantial part of their daily

2. For the place of the household or oikos-economy cf. Max Weber, *General Economic History*, trans. Frank H. Knight (Glencoe: The Free Press, 1950) pp. 48, 58, 124 ff., 131, 146, 162 and Johannes Hase Broek, *Griechische Wirtschafts-geschichte* (Tübingen: J. C. B. Mohr, 1931) pp. 15, 24, 27, 29, 38, 46, 69, 284.

wants in the local market, and to an essential extent by products which the local population and that of the immediate hinterland produced for sale in the market or acquired in other ways. In the meaning employed here the "city" is a market place. The local market forms the economic center of the colony in which, due to the specialization in economic products, both the non-urban population and urbanites satisfy their wants for articles of trade and commerce. Wherever it appeared as a configuration different from the country it was normal for the city to be both a lordly or princely residence as well as a market place. It simultaneously possessed centers of both kinds, *oikos* and market and frequently in addition to the regular market it also served as periodic foreign markets of traveling merchants. In the meaning of the word here, the city is a "market settlement."

Often the existence of a market rests upon the concessions and guarantees of protection by a lord or prince. They were often interested in such things as a regular supply of foreign commercial articles and trade products, in tolls, in moneys for escorts and other protection fees, in market tariffs and taxes from law suits. However, the lord or prince might also hope to profit from the local settlement of tradesmen and merchants capable of paying taxes and, as soon as the market settlement arose around the market, from land rents arising therefrom. Such opportunities were of especial importance to the lord or prince since they represented chances for monetary revenues and the increase in his treasure of precious metal.

However, the city could lack any attachment, physical or otherwise, to a lordly or princely residence. This was the case when it originated as a pure market settlement at a suitable intersection point *(Umschlageplatz)*[3] where the means of transportation were changed by virtue of concession to non-resident lords or princes or usurpation by the interested parties themselves. This could assume the form of concessions to entrepreneurs—permitting them to lay out a market and recruit settlers for it. Such capitalistic establishment of cities was especially frequent in medieval frontier areas, particularly in East, North, and Central Europe. Historically, though not as a rule, the practice has appeared throughout the world.

---

3. Charles H. Cooley's theory of transportation took the break in communication either physical or economic as the most critical of all factors for the formation of the city.

Without any attachment to the court of a prince or without princely concessions, the city could arise through the association of foreign invaders, naval warriors, or commercial settlers or, finally, native parties interested in the carrying trade. This occurred frequently in the early Middle Ages. The resultant city could be a pure market place. However, it is more usual to find large princely or patrimonial households and a market conjoined. In this case the eminent household as one contact point of the city could satisfy its want either primarily by means of a natural economy (that is by villein service or natural service or taxes placed upon the artisans and merchants dependent on it) or it could supply itself more or less secondarily by barter in the local market as that market's most important buyer. The more pronounced the latter relation the more distinct the market foundation of the city looms and the city ceases by degrees to be a mere appendaged market settlement alongside the *oikos*. Despite attachment to the large household it then became a market city. As a rule the quantitative expansion of the original princely city and its economic importance go hand in hand with an increase in the satisfaction of wants in the market by the princely household and other large urban households attached to that of the prince as courts of vassals or major officials.

Types of Consumer and Producer City

Similar to the city of the prince, the inhabitants of which are economically dependent upon the purchasing power of noble households are cities in which the purchasing power of other larger consumers, such as rentiers, determines the economic opportunities of resident tradesmen and merchants. In terms of the kind and source of their incomes such larger consumers may be of quite varied types. They may be officials who spend their legal and illegal income in the city or lords or other political power holders who spend their non-urban land rents or politically determined incomes there. In either of these cases the city closely approximates the princely city for it depends upon patrimonial and political incomes which supply the purchasing power of large consumers. Peking was a city of officials; Moscow, before suspension of serfdom, was a land-rent city.

Different in principle are the superficially similar cities in which urban land-rents are determined by traffic monopolies of landed property. Such cities originate in the trade and commerce consolidated in the hands of an urban aristocracy. This type of development has always been widespread: it appeared in Antiquity; in the Near East until the Byzantine Empire; and in the Middle Ages. The city that emerges is not economically of a rentier type but is, rather, a merchant or trade city the rents of which represent a tribute of acquisitors to the owners of houses. The conceptual differentiation of this case from the one in which rents are not determined by tributary obligations to monopolists but by non-urban sources, should not obscure the interrelation in the past of both forms. The large consumers can be rentiers spending their business incomes (today mainly interest on bonds, dividends or shares) in the city. Whereupon purchasing power rests on capitalistically conditioned monetary rentier sources as in the city of Arnheim. Or purchasing power can depend upon state pensions or other state rents as appears in a "pensionopolis" like Wiesbaden. In all similar cases one may describe the urban form as a consumer city, for the presence in residence of large consumers of special economic character is of decisive economic importance for the local tradesmen and merchants.

A contrasting form is presented by the producer city. The increase in population and purchasing power in the city may be due, as for example in Essen or Bochum, to the location there of factories, manufactures, or home-work industries supplying outside territories—thus representing the modern type. Or, again, the crafts and trades of the locality may ship their goods away as in cities of Asiatic, Ancient, and Medieval types. In either case the consumers for the local market are made up of large consumers if they are residents and/or entrepreneurs, workers and craftsmen who form the great mass, and merchants and benefactors of land-rent supported indirectly by the workers and craftsmen.

The trade city and merchant city are confronted by the consumer city in which the purchasing power of its larger consumers rests on the retail for profit of foreign products on the local market (for example, the woolen drapers in the Middle Ages), the foreign sale for profit of local products or goods obtained by native producers (for example, the herring of the Hansa) or the purchase of foreign products and their sale with or without storage at the place to the outside (intermediate commercial cities). Very frequently a combination of all these economic activities occurred: the *com-*

menda and *societas maris* implied that a *tractator* (travelling merchant) journied to Levantine markets with products purchased with capital entrusted to him by resident capitalists.[4] Often the *tractator* traveled entirely in ballast. He sold these products in the East and with the proceeds he purchased oriental articles brought back for sale in the local market. The profits of the undertaking were then divided between *tractator* and capitalist according to pre-arranged formulas.

The purchasing power and tax ability of the commercial city rested on the local economic establishment as was also the case for the producers' city in contrast to the consumers' city. The economic opportunities of the shipping and transport trade and of numerous secondary wholesale and retail activities were at the disposal of the merchants. However the economic activity of these establishments was not entirely executed for the local retail trade but in substantial measure for external trade. In principle, this state of affairs was similar to that of the modern city, which is the location of national and international financiers or large banks (London, Paris, Berlin) or of joint stock companies or cartels (Duesseldorf). It follows that today more than ever before a predominant part of the earnings of firms flow to localities other than the place of earning. Moreover, a growing part of business proceeds are not consumed by their rightful receivers at the metropolitan location of the business but in suburban villas, rural resorts or international hotels. Parallel with these developments "city-towns" or city-districts consisting almost exclusively of business establishments are arising.

There is no intention here of advancing the further casuistic distinctions required by a purely economic theory of the city. Moreover, it hardly needs to be mentioned that actual cities nearly always represent mixed types. Thus, if cities are to be economically classified at all, it must be in terms of their prevailing economic component.

Relation of the City to Agriculture

The relation of the city to agriculture has not been clear cut. There were and are "semi-rural cities" *(Ackerburgerstaedte)* locali-

---

4. Weber, *General Economic History*, pp. 205, 206 and W. Silberschmidt, *Die Commenda in ihrer Frühesten Entwicklung* (1884).

ties which while serving as places of market traffic and centers of typically urban trade, are sharply separated from the average city by the presence of a broad stratum of resident burghers satisfying a large part of their food needs through cultivation and even producing food for sale. Normally the larger the city the less the opportunity for urban residents to dispose of acreage in relation to their food needs at the same time without controlling a self-sufficient pasture and wood lot in the manner of the village. Cologne, the largest German city in the Middle Ages, almost completely lacked the *Allmende* (commons) from the beginning though the commons was not absent from any normal village of the time. Other German and foreign medieval cities at least placed considerable pastures and woods at the disposal of their burghers.

The presence of large acreages accessible to the urbanite is found more frequently as one turns attention to the south or back toward antiquity. While today we justly regard the typical "urbanite" as a man who does not supply his own food need on his own land, originally the contrary was the case for the majority of typical ancient cities. In contrast to the medieval situation, the ancient urbanite was quite legitimately characterized by the fact that a *kleros, fundus* (In Israel: *chelek*) which he called his own, was a parcel of land which fed him.[5] The full urbanite of antiquity was a semi-peasant.

In the Medieval period, as in Antiquity, agricultural property was retained in the hands of merchant strata. This was more frequently the case in the south than in the north of Europe. In both medieval and ancient city states agricultural properties, occasionally of quite exorbitant size, were found widely scattered, either being politically dominated by municipal authorities of powerful cities or in the possession of eminent individual citizen landlords. Examples are supplied by the Cheronesic domination of the Miltiades or the political or lordly estates of medieval aristocratic families, such as the Genoese Grimaldi, in the provinces or overseas.

As a general rule inter-local estates and the sovereign rights of invididual citizens were not the objects of an urban economic policy. However, mixed conditions at times arose such that according to the circumstances estates were guaranteed to individuals by the city.

---

5. Pöhlmann, *Aus Altertum und Gegenwart,* p. 124 ff.; Weber, *General Economic History,* p. 328; Weber, *Ancient Judaism* (Glencoe: The Free Press, 1952), p. 465.

In the nature of the case this only occurred when the individuals whose estates were guaranteed by the city belonged to the most powerful patricians. In such cases the estate was acquired and maintained through indirect help of civic power which in turn might share in its economic and political usufruct. This was frequently the case in the past.

The relation of the city as agent of trade and commerce to the land as producer of food comprises one aspect of the "urban economy" and forms a special "economic stage" between the "household economy" on the one hand and the "national economy" on the other.[6] When the city is visualized in this manner, however, politico-economic aspects are conceptually fused with pure economic aspects and conceived as forming one whole. The mere fact that merchants and tradesmen live crowded together carrying on a regular satisfaction of daily needs in the market does not exhaust the concept of the "city." Where only the satisfaction of agricultural needs occurs within closed settlements and where—what is not identical with it—agricultural production appears in relation to non-agricultural acquisition, and when the presence or absence of markets constitutes the difference, we speak of trade and commercial localities and of small market-towns, but not of cities. There were, thus, hidden non-economic dimensions in the phenomena brought under review in the previous sections. It is time to expand the concept of the "city" to include extra-economic factors.

The Politico-Administrative Concept of the City

Beside possessing an accumulation of abodes the city also has an economic association with its own landed property and a budget of receipts and expenditure. Such an economic association may also appear in the village no matter how great the quantitative differences. Moreover, it was not peculiar to the city alone, at least in the past, that it was both an economic and a regulatory association. Trespass restrictions, pasture regulations, the prohibition of the export of wood and straw, and similar regulations are known to the village, constituting an economic policy of the association as such.

6. Weber has in mind distinctions introduced by Gustave Schmoller.

The cities of the past were differentiated only by the kinds of regulations which appeared. Only the objects of political economic regulation on behalf of the association and the range of characteristic measures embraced by them were peculiar. It goes without saying that measures of the "urban economic policy" took substantial account of the fact that under the transportation conditions of the time the majority of all inland cities were dependent upon the agricultural resources of the immediate hinterland. As shown by the grain policies of Athens and Rome this was true for maritime cities. In a majority, not all, of urban trades areas, opportunity was provided for the natural "play of the market." The urban market supplied the normal, not the sole, place for the exchange of products, especially food.

Account also must be taken of the fact that production for trade was predominantly in the form of artisan technology organized in specialized small establishments. Such production operated without or with little capital and with strictly limited numbers of journeymen who were trained in long apprenticeship. Such production was economically in the form of wage worker as price work for customers. Sale to the local retailers was largely a sale to customers.

The market conditions of the time were the kind that would naturally emerge, given the above facts. The so-called "urban economic policy" was basically characterized by its attempt to stabilize the conditions of the local urban economy by means of economic regulations in the interest of permanently and cheaply feeding the masses and standardizing the economic opportunities. of tradesmen and merchants. However, as we shall see, economic regulation was not the sole object of the urban economic policy nor, when it historically appears, was it fully developed. It emerges only under the political regime of the guild. Finally it can not be proved to be simply a transitional stage in the development of all cities. In any case, the urban economic policy does not represent a universal stage in economic evolution.

On the basis of customer relations and specialized small establishments operating without capital, the local urban market with its exchange between agricultural and non-agricultural producers and resident merchants, represents a kind of economic counterpart to barter as against systematically divided performances in terms of work and taxes of a specialized dependent economy in connection with the *oikos*, having its basis in the accumulation and integration of work in the manner, without exchange occurring inside. Following out the parallel: the *regulation* (urban economic policy) of the exchange and production conditions in the city represent the counterpart to the *organization* (traditional and feudal-contractual) of activities united in the economy of the *oikos*.

The very fact that in drawing these distinctions we are led to use the concepts of an "urban economic area" and "urban area," and "urban authority," already indicates that the concept of the "city" can and must be examined in terms of a series of concepts other than the purely economic categories so far employed.

The additional concepts required for analysis of the city are political. This already appears in the fact that the urban economic policy itself may be the work of a prince to whom political dominion of the city with its inhabitants belongs. In this case when there is an urban economic policy it is determined *for* the inhabitants of the city not *by* them. However even when this is the case the city must still be considered to be a partially autonomous association, a "community" with special political and administrative arrangements.

The economic concept previously discussed must be entirely separated from the political-administrative concept of the city. Only in the latter sense may a special *area* belong to the city. A locale can be held to be a city in a political-administrative sense though it would not qualify as a city economically. In the Middle Ages there were areas legally defined as "cities" in which the inhabitants derived ninety percent or more of their livelihood from agriculture, representing a far larger fraction of their income than that of the inhabitants of many localities legally defined as "villages."

Naturally, the transition from such semi-rural cities to consumers', producers' or commercial cities is quite fluid. In those settlements which differ administratively from the village and are thus dealt with as cities only one thing, namely, the kind of regulations of land-owning, is customarily different from rural land-owning forms. Economically such cities are differentiated by a special kind of rent situation presented in urban real estate which consists in house ownership to which land ownership is accessory. The position of urban real estate is connected administratively with special taxation principles. It is bound even more closely to a further element decisive for the political-administrative concept of the city and standing entirely outside the purely economic analysis, namely, the fortress.

Fortress and Garrison

It is very significant that the city in the past, in Antiquity and the Middle Ages, outside as well as within Europe, was also a special fortress or garrison. At present this property of the city has been entirely lost, but it was not universal even in the past. In Japan, for example, it was not the rule. Administratively one may, with Rathgen,[7] doubt the existence of cities at all. In contrast to Japan, in China every city was surrounded with a gigantic ring of walls. However, it is also true that many economically rural localities which were not cities in the administrative sense, possessed walls at all times. In China such places were not the seat of state authorities.

In many Mediterranean areas such as Sicily a man living outside the urban walls as a rural worker and country resident is almost unknown. This is a product of century-long insecurity. By contrast in old Hellas the Spartan polis sparkled by the absence of walls, yet the property of being a "garrison-town" was met. Sparta despised walls for the very reason that it was a permanent open military camp.

Though there is still dispute as to how long Athens was without walls, like all Hellenic cities except Sparta it contained in the Acropolis a castle built on rock in the same manner as Ekbantama and Persepolis which were royal castles with surrounding settlements. The castle or wall belonged normally to Oriental as well as to ancient Mediterranean and ordinary medieval cities.

The city was neither the sole nor oldest fortress. In disputed frontier territory and during chronic states of war, every village fortified itself. Under the constant danger of attack in the area of the Elbe and Oder Rivers Slavic settlements were fortified, the national form of the rural village seems early to have been standardized in the form of the "hedge-enclosed" circular area with a single entrance which could be locked and through which at night cattle were driven to the central protection of the village area. Similarly,

---

7. Karl Rathgen, "Gemeindefinanzen" in *Verein für Sozialpolitik* (Leipzig: Duncker & Humblot, 1908-10) and *Allgemeine Verfassungs und Verwaltungsgeschichte* (Leipzig: Huebner, 1911).

walled hill retreats were diffused throughout the world from Israelite East Jordan to Germanic territories. Unarmed persons and cattle
took refuge within in times of danger. The so-called "cities" of
Henry I in the German East were merely systematically established
fortresses of this sort.

In England during the Anglo-Saxon period a "burgh" (borough)
belonged to each shire whose name it took. Guard and garrison
duty as the oldest specifically "civic" obligations were attached to
certain persons or pieces of land. When in normal times such fortresses were occupied, guards or vassals were maintained as a permanent garrison and paid in salaries or in land. There were fluid
transitions from the permanently garrisoned fortress to the Anglo-
Saxon burgh, the "garrison-city," in the sense of Maitland's theory,
with a "burgess" as inhabitants. The burgess received its name from
its political position which like the legal nature of its civic land and
house property was determined by the duty of maintaining and
guarding the fortress.

However, historically neither the palisaded village nor the emergency fortification are the primary fore-runners of the city fortress,
which was, rather, the manorial castle. The manorial castle was a
fortress occupied by the lord and warriors subordinated to him as
officials or as a personal following, together with their families and
servants.

Military castle construction is very old, doubtlessly older than
the chariot and military use of the horse. Like the war chariot the
importance of the castle was determined by the development of
knightly and royal warfare. In old China of the classic songs, in
India of the Vedas, in Egypt and Mesopotamia, in Canaan, in Israel
at the time of the Song of Deborah, in Greece during the period
of the Homeric epics, and among the Etruscans, Celts, and Irish,
the building of castles and the castle-principality were diffused universally. Old Egyptian sources speak of castles and their commanders
and it may be assumed that they originally accommodated just as
many small princes. From old documents it can be inferred that in
Mesopotamia the development of the provincial kingships was preceded by a castle-dwelling princedom such as existed in Western
India at the time of the Vedas and such as was probable in Iran at
the time of the oldest *Gathas*. The castle was certainly universally
dominant in Northern India on the Ganges during the time of politi-

cal disintegration. In this last instance, the old Kshatriyas whom the sources show to be peculiarly sandwiched between the king and nobility, were obviously princes.

In the period of Christianization, castle construction was pressed in Russia. It appears also during the dynasty of Thutmose in Syria at the time of the Israelite confederation (Abmilech). Old Chinese literature also provides irrefutable evidence of its original occurrence. The Hellenic and Asia Minor sea-castle was as universally diffused as piracy. There must have been an interim period of especially deep pacification to allow the Cretan unfortified palaces to arise in the place of the castle. In this area later castles like the Decelia,[8] so important in the Peloponnesian Wars, were originally fortresses of noble families.

The medieval development of a politically independent gentry opened with the *castelli* in Italy. In Northern Europe the independence of the vassals was also bound up with enormous castle construction as established by Below.[9] Even in modern times individual deputyship in Germany has been dependent upon possession by the family of a castle, even if only the meager ruins of one. Disposal of a castle originally signified military dominion over the country. The only question was: In whose hands? It could be in the hands of the individual lords, or confederations of knights, or of a ruler who could depend on the trustworthiness of his vassals, ministers, or officers.

The City as the Fusion of Fortress and Market

In the first stage of its development into a special political form the fortified city was incorporated in or dependent upon a castle, the fortress of a king, noblemen, or association of knights. Such nobles either resided in the fortress themselves or maintained a garrison of mercenaries, vassals, or servants therein. In Anglo-Saxon England the right to possess a "haw," a fortified house in a "burgh," was bestowed as a privilege on certain land owners of the surrounding countryside. In Antiquity and Medieval Italy the cityhouse of

8. Hill commanding the pass between Pentelicus and Poenes, occupied by the Spartans in 413.

9. Georg Below, *Der deutsche Staat des Mittelalters* (Leipzig: Zuelle & Meyer, 1914); *Territorium und Stadt* (München: R. Oldenberg, 1900).

the nobleman was held in addition to his rural castle. The inhabitants or residents adjoining the castle, sometimes all, sometimes special strata, were bound as citizens (burgess) to the performance of certain military duties such as building and repair of the walls, guard duty, defense service and, at times, other military services such as communication and supply for the urban military noble. In this instance the burger is a member of his estate because, and insofar as, he participates in the military association of the city.

Maitland[10] has worked this out with especial clarity for England. The houses of the "burgh" were in the possession of people having the duty of maintaining the fortification. This contrasts with the village. Alongside royal or aristocratically guaranteed market peace appears military jurisdiction. The politically oriented castle and economically oriented market with the market area of the towns at times simultaneously serving both functions, again drill field and assembly area of the army and the place of pacific economic exchange on the other, often stand in plastic dualism beside one another.

The military drill field and economic market are not everywhere spatially separated. The Attic *pnyx* was a much later development than the *agora* which originally served the economic traffic as well as political and religious activities. On the other hand in Rome from ancient times the *comitium* and *campus martius* were separated from the economic *fora* as in the Middle Ages the *piazza del campo* at Siena (a tournament place still used today as a place for holding races between the wards of the city), as the front of the municipal place, is distinct from the *mercato* at the rear. Analogously in Islamic cities the *kasbeh*, the fortified camp of the warriors, was spatially separate from the *bazaar*. In Southern India the political city of notable men appears separately alongside the economic city.

The relation between the garrison of the political fortress and the civil economic population is complicated but always decisively important for the composition of the city. Wherever a castle existed artisans came or were settled for the satisfaction of manorial wants and the needs of the warriors. The consumption power of a prince's

10. Frederic William Maitland, *The Charters of the Borough of Cambridge* (Cambridge: University Press, 1901) and *The Court Law* (London: Quaritsch, 1891).

military household and the protection it guaranteed attracted the merchants. Moreover the lord was interested in attracting these classes since he was in position to procure money revenues through them either by taxing commerce or trade or participating in it through capital advances. At times the lord engaged in commerce on his own, even monopolizing it. In maritime castles as ship owner or ruler of the port the lord was in a position to procure a share in piratical or peacefully won sea-borne profits. His followers and vassals resident in the place were also in position to profit whether he voluntarily gave them permission or, being dependent on their good will, was forced to do so.

The evidences of the participation of the ancient city lords in commercial activities are many. Vases from old Hellenic cities like Cyrene picture the king weighing goods *(silphion)*. In Egypt at the beginning of historical time a commercial fleet of the Lower-Egyptian Pharaoh is reported. Widely diffused over the world, but especially in maritime "cities" where the carrying trade was easily controlled, the economic interest of resident military families flourished beside the monopoly of the castle chieftain, as a result of their own participation in commercial profits. Their capacity to participate in the civic economy often shattered the monopoly (if it existed) of the prince. When this occurred the prince was considered only to be *primus inter pares* in the ruling circle or even simply as equal. The ruling circle comprised the urban sibs domiciled through landed property and deriving capital from some form of peaceful commerce, especially the *commenda* capital in the Middle Ages, or from personal participation in piracy or sea war. Often the prince was elected for short times and in any case he was decisively limited in power. In ancient maritime cities since Homer's time yearly municipal councils gradually appeared. Quite similar formations often occur in the early Middle Ages. In Venice they formed a counter balance to the doges though with very different leadership positions depending on whether a royal count or vicomte or bishop or someone else was lord of the city. Equivalent developments also appear in other typical commercial cities.

Thus in early Antiquity and in the Middle Ages the urban commercial capitalists, the financiers of commerce, the specific notable persons of the city, have to be separated in principle from the domiciled holders of commercial "establishments," the merchants proper. To be sure the strata often blended into each other. However, with this we already anticipate later explanations.

In the hinterland, shipping points, terminals, crossings of rivers and caravan routes (for example, Babylon) could become locations of similar developments. At times competition arose between the priest of the temple, and priestly lord of the city, for temple districts of famous gods offered sacred protection to inter-ethnic elements. Such areas could provide locations for politically unprotected commerce. Thus a city-like settlement, economically supplied by temple revenues, could attach itself to the temple district in a manner similar to the princely city with its tributes to the prince.

Individual cases varied depending on the extent to which the prince's interest in monetary revenues predominated in the granting of privileges for merchandising and manufacturing independent of the lordly household and taxed by the lord. On the other hand, the lord could be interested in satisfying his own needs hence in acting in ways strengthening his own powers and monopolizing trade in his own hands. When attracting foreigners by offering special privileges the lord also had to take into consideration the interests and "established" ability (which was also important for himself) of those already resident, who were dependent on his political protection or manorial supplies.

To this variety of possible development must be added the effects of the political-militaristic structure of the dominating group within which the founding of the city or its development occurred. We must consider the main antitheses in city development arising therefrom.

Associational and Status Peculiarities of the Occidental City

Neither the "city," in the economic sense, nor the garrison, the inhabitants of which are accoutred with special political-administrative structures, necessarily constitute a "community." An urban "community," in the full meaning of the word, appears as a general phenomenon only in the Occident. Exceptions occasionally were to be found in the Near East (in Syria, Phoenicia, and Mesopotamia) but only occasionally and in rudiments. To constitute a full urban community a settlement must display a relative predominance of trade-commercial relations with the settlement as a whole displaying the following features: 1. a fortification; 2. a market; 3. a court of its own and at least partially autonomous law; 4. a related form of association; and 5. at least partial autonomy and autocephaly, thus also an administration by authorities in the election of whom the burghers participated.

In the past, rights such as those which define the urban community were normally privileges of the estates. The peculiar political properties of the urban community appeared only with the presence of a special stratum, a distinct new estate. Measured by this rule the "cities" of the Occidental Middle Ages only qualify in part as true cities; even the cities of the eighteenth century were genuine urban communities only in minor degree. Finally measured by this rule, with possible isolated exceptions, the cities of Asia were not urban communities at all even though they all had markets and were fortresses.

All large seats of trade and commerce in China and most of the small ones were fortified. This was true also for Egyptian, Near Eastern, and Indian centers of commerce and trade. Not infrequently the large centers of trade and commerce of those countries were also separate jurisdictional districts. In China, Egypt, the Near East, and India the large commercial centers have also been seats of large political associations—a phenomenon not characteristic of Medieval Occidental cities, especially those of the North. Thus, many, but not all of the essential elements of the true urban community were at hand. However, the possession by the urbanites of a special substantive or trial law or of courts autonomously nominated by them were unknown to Asiatic cities. Only to the extent that guilds or castes (in India) were located in cities did they develop courts and a special law. Urban location of these associations was legally incidental. Autonomous administration was unknown or only vestigial.

If anything, even more important than the relative absence of autonomous administration, the appearance in the city of an association of urbanites in contradiction to the countryman was also found only in rudiments. The Chinese urban dweller legally belonged to his family and native village in which the temple of his ancestors stood and to which he conscientiously maintained affiliation. This is similar to the Russian village-comrade, earning his livelihood in the city but legally remaining a peasant. The Indian urban dweller remained a member of the caste. As a rule urban dwellers were also members of local professional associations, such as crafts and guilds of specific urban location. Finally they belonged to administrative districts such as the city wards and street districts into which the city was divided by the magisterial police.

Within the administrative units of the city, wards and street districts, urban dwellers had definite duties and even, at times, rights as well. In the attempt to secure peace, city or street districts could be made liturgically responsible collectively for the security of persons or other police purposes. It was possible thus for them to be formed into communities with elected officials or hereditary elders. This occurred in Japan where one or more civil-administrative body (*Machi-Bugyo*) was established as superior to self-administered street communities. However, a city law similar to that of Antiquity or the Middle Ages was absent. The city as corporate *per se* was unknown. Of course, eventually the city as a whole formed a separate administrative district as in the Merovingian and Carolingian Empires, but as was still the case in the Medieval and Ancient Occident, the autonomy and participation of the inhabitants in local administration were out of the question. As a matter of fact, local individual participation in self-administration was often more strongly developed in the country than in the relatively large commercially organized city.

In the village, for example, in China, in many affairs the confederation of elders was practically all-powerful and the Pao-Chia[11] was dependent on them, even though this was not legally expressed. Also in India the village community had nearly complete autonomy in most significant circumstances. In Russia the mir enjoyed nearly complete autonomy until bureaucratization under Alexander III. In the whole of the Near Eastern world the "elders" (in Israel, *sekenim)*[12] originally of the family and later chiefs of noble clans were representatives and administrators of localities and the local court. This could not occur in the Asiatic city because it was usually the seat of a high official or prince and thus under the direct super-

11. Even until recent times every ten families constituted a "pao" formally under a headman. A hundred families constituted a "Chia" under a "Pao Chia" also called "Ti Pao." We read Pao-Chia for Taotai.
12. Weber, *Ancient Judaism*, p. 16.

vision of their bodyguards. However, the city was a princely fortress and administered by royal officials (in Israel, *sarim*)[13] who retained judicial power.

In Israel the dualism of officials and elders can be traced in the royal period. Royal officials everywhere triumphed in bureaucratic kingdoms. Such royal bureaucrats were not all-powerful but subject to public opinion often to an astonishing degree. As a rule the Chinese official was quite powerless against local associations such as the clans and professional associations when they united in a particular case. At every serious united opposition of the clans and local associations the Chinese Official lost his position. Obstruction, boycott, closing of shops, and strikes of artisans and merchants in response to oppression were a daily occurrence, setting limits on the power of officials. However, such limits on official power were of a completely indeterminate kind.

In China and India the guilds and other professional associations had competencies with which the officials had to reckon. The chairman of the local associations often exercised extensive coercive powers even against third parties. However all their powers involved only special competencies of particular association in particular questions of concrete group interest. Moreover, there was ordinarily no joint association representing a community of city burghers *per se*, even the concept of such a possibility is completely lacking. Citizenship as a specific status quality of the urbanite is missing. In China, Japan, and India neither urban community nor citizenry can be found and only traces of them appear in the Near East.

In Japan the organization of estates was purely feudal. The *samurai* (mounted) and *kasi* (unmounted) ministerial officials confronted the peasant *(no)* and the merchants and tradesmen who were partly united in professional associations. However, here too, the concepts of a "citizenry" and an "urban community" are absent. This was also true in China during the feudal period. After the feudal period in China a bureaucratic administration of literati qualified for office in terms of examinations leading to academic degrees confronted the illiterate strata among whom appeared economically privileged guilds of merchants and professional associations. But in this period in China, too, the ideas of an "urban citizenry" and "urban community" are missing. This was true even though in

13. *Ibid.*, p. 18.

China as well as in Japan the professional associations were self-administered. Moreover while the villages were self-administered the cities were not. In China the city was a fortress and official seat of imperial authorities in a sense completely unknown in Japan.

The cities of India were royal seats or official centers of royal administration as well as fortresses and market places. Guilds of merchants and castes largely coinciding with professional associations were present, enjoying considerable autonomy especially with respect to their own legal competence and justice. Nevertheless, the hereditary caste system of Indian society with its ritualistic segregation of the professions, excluded the emergence of a citizenry and urban community. And though there were numerous castes and sub-castes of traders and artisans they cannot be taken together and equated with the Occidental burgher strata. Nor was it possible for the commercial and artisan castes of India to unite in a form corresponding to the medieval urban corporations for caste estrangement hindered all inter-caste fraternization.

To be sure in India during the period of the great salvation religions, guilds appeared with hereditary elders *(schreschths)* uniting in many cities into an association. As residues from this period there are, at present, some cities (Allahabad) with a mutual urban *schreschth* (elder) corresponding to the occidental mayor. Moreover, in the period before the great bureaucratic kingdoms there were some politically autonomous cities in India ruled by a patriciate recruited from families supplying elephants to the army. Later this phenomenon almost completely disappeared. The triumph of ritualistic caste estrangement shattered the guild associations and royal bureaucracies in alliance with the Brahmans swept away, except for vestiges, such trends toward a citizenry and urban community in Northwestern India.

In Near Eastern Egyptian antiquity the cities were fortresses and official administrative centers with royal market privileges. However, in the period of the dominion of the great kingdom they lacked autonomy, community organizations, and a privileged citizen estate. In Egypt during the Middle Empire office feudalism existed; in the New Empire a bureaucratic administration of clerks appeared. "Civic privileges" were bestowed on feudal or prebendal office holders in localities comparable to the privileges of bishops in old Germany. However, civic rights were not bestowed on an autonomous citizenry and even the beginnings of a "city patriciate" have not been found.

In contrast to the complete absence of a citizenry in ancient Egypt were the phenomena in Mesopotamia, Syria and especially Phoenicia, where at an early period typical city-kingdoms emerged at intersection points of sea and caravan traffic. Such civic kingdoms were of intensified sacred-secular character. They were also typified by the rising power of patrician families in the "city-house" (*bitu* in the Tel-el-Amarna tablets) in the period of charioteering.[14] In the Canaanite city an association of chariot-fighting knights possessing urban residences appeared. This knighthood kept the peasant farmers in a state of debt servitude and clientship as in the case of the early Hellenic polis. It was obviously similar in Mesopotamia where the "patrician" as a land-owning full burgher economically qualified for war service is separated from the peasant. Immunities and privileges of this stratum were chartered by the king. However, with the mounting military power of the government this also disappeared. Politically autonomous cities and a burgher stratum of Occidental type are as little to be found in Mesopotamia as is a special urban law alongside royal law.

Only in Phoenicia did the landed patriciate engaging in commerce with its capital manage to maintain its dominion over the city state. However, the coins of the time *am Sôr* and *am Karthadast* in Tyre and Carthage hardly indicate the presence of a ruling "demos" and if such was ever the case it was only at a later time. Thus a true citizenry only partly developed. In Israel, Juda became a city-state but the elders (*sekenim*) who in the early period governed the administration as chieftains of patrician sibs were thrust into the background by the royal administration. The *gibborim* (knights) became royal attendants and soldiers. In contrast to the countryside, the royal *sarim* (officials) ruled in the large cities. Only after the exile did the community (*kahal*) or fellowship (*cheber*) appear as an institution on a confessional basis under the rule of priestly families.[15]

Nevertheless, all these phenomena indicate that here on the coasts of the Mediterranean Sea and on the Euphrates appeared the first real analogies of a civic development equivalent to that of Rome

14. Weber, *Ancient Judaism*, p. 14 f.
15. *Ibid.*, p. 385 f.

at the time of the reception of the Gens Claudia. The city is ruled by a patriciate resident in the city with powers resting on monetary wealth primarily won in commerce and secondarily invested in landed property, debt slaves and war slaves.[16] The military power of the urban patriciate was a product of its training for knightly warfare, a training often spent in feuds against one another. The patricians were inter-locally diffused and united with the king or *schofeten* or *sekenim* as *primus inter pares*. Such a patriciate like the Roman nobility with consuls was threatened by the tyranny of the charismatic war king relying upon recruited bodyguards (Abimelech, Jepthah, David). Prior to the Hellenic period this stage of urban development was nowhere permanently surpassed.

Obviously such a patriciate also dominated in cities of the Arabian coast during the period of Mohammed, remaining in existence in those Islamic cities where the autonomy of the city and its patriciate was not completely destroyed as in the larger state. Under Islamic rule ancient oriental conditions were often preserved, whereupon a labile ratio of autonomy between urban families and princely officials appears. Resident city families enjoyed a position of power resting on wealth from urban economic opportunities and invested in land and slaves. Without formal legal recognition the princes and their officials had to take account of the power of the patriciate in the same manner that the Chinese Pao Chia had to take account of the obstruction of clan elders of the villages and merchant and professional associations. However, the city was not thereby necessarily formed into an independent association. Often the contrary occurred, as may be exemplified.

Arabian cities like Mecca were settlements of clans such as remained typical in the Middle Ages to the threshold of the present. Snouck Hurgronje[17] has proven that the city of Mecca was surrounded by the *bilad* representing lordly property of an individual *dewis* of sibs descending from Ali—such were the *hasnaidic* and other noble sibs. The *bilad* was occupied by peasants, clients, and protected Bedouins. *Bilads* were often intermixed. A *dewis* was any

---

16. In all these areas in the early period enslavement for debt appears and debt slaves are found alongside slaves captured in battles—battles at times being actually slave raids.

17. Snouck Hurgronje, *Mekka in the Latter Part of the 19th Century* (London: Luzac, 1931).

sib one ancestor of which was once a sherif. Since 1200 the
sherif himself belonged without exception to the Alidic family
Katadahs. Legally the sherif should have been installed by the governor of the caliph (who was often unfree and once, under Harun
al Rashid, was a Berber slave). However in reality the sherif was
chosen from the qualified family by election of the chieftains of
the *dewis* who were resident in Mecca. For this reason as well as
the fact that residence in Mecca offered opportunities to exploit
pilgrims, the heads of the class *(emirs)* lived in the city. Between
them at times alliances obtained with agreements for preserving
the peace and establishing quotas for dividing chances for gain.
Such alliances were terminable at any time, dissolution signaling
the start of a feud inside and outside the city. Slave troops were
employed in such feuds and the defeated group was exiled from
the city. However, despite defeat the community of interest between hostile families as against outsiders led to observance of the
courtesy of sparing the goods and lives of members of the families
and clientele of the exiles. Such courtesies were observed under the
threat of general mutiny of one's own partisans.

In modern times the city of Mecca recognizes the following official authorities: 1. On paper the collegiate administrative council
(Medschlis) installed by the Turks appears as the authority; 2. In
fact the Turkish governor is the effective authority, occupying the
position of protector (in former times usually the ruler of Egypt);
3. authority is shared by the four *cadis* of the orthodox rights
who are always noble men of Mecca, the most eminent (schafitic)
for centuries being nominated from one family by the sherif or
proposed by the protector; 4. The sherif simultaneously is head
of the urban corporation of nobles; 5. The guilds, especially the
cicerones, followed by the butchers, corn merchants and others.
6. The city ward with its elders is partly autonomous. These authorities competed with each other in many ways without fixed com-
petences. A party to a legal suit selected the authority appearing
most favorable or whose power against the accused seemed to be
most strong. The governor was unable to prevent an appeal to the
cadi who competed with him in all matters of ecclesiastical law.
The sherif was held to be the proper authority of the natives especially in all matters concerning the Bedouins and caravans of pilgrims. The governor was dependent on the willingness of the sherif

to cooperate. Finally, here as in other Arabic areas, particularly in the cities, the cooperation of the nobility was decisive for the effectiveness of authority.

In the ninth century a development reminiscent of Occidental circumstances occurred when with the flight of the Tuluniden and Deschafariden, in Mecca the position of the richest guilds, that of the butchers and corn merchants, held the balance of power. However, it was still unconditionally true at the time of Mohammed that only the noble *koreischitic* families were militarily and politically important, thus, a government by guilds never arose. Slave troups sustained by profit-shares of resident urban families continually sustained their power. In a similar manner, in medieval Italian cities power continually tended to glide into the hands of the knightly families as wielders of military power.

The idea of an association which could unite the city into a corporate unit was missing in Mecca. This furnished its characteristic difference from the ancient polis and the early medieval Italian commune. However, when all is said and done, this Arabic condition—of course omitting specific Islamic traits or replacing them by Christian counterparts—may be taken to typify the period before the emergence of the urban community association. It is also typical for Occidental commercial sea cities.

So far as sound information extends, in Asiatic and Oriental settlements of an urban economic character, normally only extended families and professional associations were vehicles of communal actions. Communal action was not the product of an urban burgher stratum as such. Transitions, of course, are fluid but precisely the largest settlements at times embracing hundreds of thousands even millions of inhabitants display this very phenomenon. In medieval Byzantine Constantinople the representatives of urban districts were leaders of party divisions who financed circus races (as is still the case for the horse race of Siena.) The Nika revolt under Justinian was a product of such local cleavages of the city. Also in Constantinople, from the time of the Islamic Middle Ages until the sixteenth century, only merchants, corporations, and guilds appear as representatives of the interests of the burghers beside purely military associations such as the *Janitscharen* and *Sipahis* and the religious organizations of the *Ulemas* and *Dervishes*. However, in sixteenth century Constantinople there is still no city representation. Similarly in late Byzantine Alexandria, beside the power of the patricians, relying upon the support of very sturdy monks, and the competitive power of the governor relying on a small garrison there was no militia of particular city districts. Within the districts of the city only the circus parties of rival "greens" and "blues" represented the leading organizations.

Chapter 2

The Occidental City

Property Rights
and Personal Legal Situation

THE MEDIEVAL occidental city presents striking con-
trasts to its Asiatic counterparts. This was particularly true for urban
formations north of the Alps where the Western city developed in
its purest form. Like the Asiatic and oriental city it was a market
place, a center of trade and commerce, and a fortress. Merchant and
artisan guilds can be found in both areas. Even the creation of autonomous constitutions for the urbanites is common, differing only in
degree. Moreover, the ancient as well as the medieval occidental
city—though with qualifications for the latter—contained farms held
in socage and the domiciles of families possessing manorial land
outside the city in addition to often large urban properties enlarged
by profits from participation in the economic activities of the city.

There are other similarities between the cities of East and West.
The medieval occidental city also had as its paramount protector
or official a political lord, exercising varying degrees of authority
within the walls. As in most of the world, the law applying to urban
landed property differed from that applying to agricultural land.
Apart from transitional phenomena, the difference between the land-
law of the medieval occidental city and that of the city elsewhere
was hardly essential. In principle civic landed property is always
alienable without restriction or it is hereditary in an unencumbered
form or obligated only with a fixed land rent while outside the city

in multiple ways manorial and peasant land is restricted in the favor
of the village, the market community or both. In Asia and in the
ancient world this did not occur with the same frequency as for
the city of the Medieval Occident. However, to this merely relative contrast in the land law corresponded an absolute contrast in
personal legal condition.

Everywhere that it made its appearance—in the Middle Ages, in
Antiquity, in the Near and Far East—the city arose as a joint settlement by immigration from the outside. Because of the sanitary conditions of the lower classes the city was able to maintain itself only
through continuous new immigrations.[1] The city, thus, has always
contained elements from most varied social situations. Office candidates qualified by examinations and mandarins rub shoulders with
illiterates despised as rabble and practitioners of the (few) unclean
occupations in East Asia. Many kinds of castes carry on their activities beside one another in India. Blood relatives organized in clans
appear together with landless artisans in the Near East. In Antiquity
free men, bondsmen and slaves emerge alongside noble landlords,
their court officials and servants. And in the early medieval city
ministerial officials and mercenaries, priests and monks encounter
one another in the city.

The mixture of social types in the city arises not only from the
fact that manors of all kinds could be located in the city, but the
city itself could belong as a whole to the manor of a lord. Thus, in
the city even such activities as repair work and guarding of the walls
could be entrusted to vassals of the castle or by tenure of the castle
to other legally privileged persons.

All these facts issue in an inevitable status differentiation of
urbanites such as was particularly sharp in Mediterranean Antiquity
and to a lesser degree was true for the cities of the early Middle
Ages and of Russia to the threshold of the present, even after the

1. Weber, of course, was trying to account for the fact that the city in the
past was not a self-sustaining community, for more people died than were born
in the city. However, it is rare in Weber for an unconscious bit of class snobbery to slip into the account. To be sure, the sanitary condition of the lower
classes of the ancient and medieval city was abominable—but so too was the
sanitary condition of the upper classes. After all the germ theory of disease was
only a nineteenth century phenomenon. A complex play-back of social as well
as economic factors in the city are important for its differential birth-death rates.
Moreover, it should not be forgotten that the birth rate of the upper classes also
tends to be lowered while the death rate of urban lower classes tends to be raised.

freedom from bondage of the serfs. To be sure there were varia-
tions everywhere in the social stratification of individuals flowing
into the city from the outside. In India, for example, the emergence
of special urban activities necessarily resulted in the formation of
castes which in fact though not in law were specific to the city. In
the Near East, in Antiquity, in the Early Middle Ages and in Russia,
particularly before release of the serfs from bondage, the emergence
of distinctly urban strata occurred by stages.

In the city as a matter of fact, though at first not legally, the
broad strata of city residents, unfree or bondsmen, only paid a tribute to their lord. They formed a class of economically independent
petty burghers together with others who were legally free. The fact
that the city was a market with relatively permanent opportunities
to earn money through trade and commerce induced many lords to
exploit their serfs and bondsmen not as workers in their own houses
and enterprises but as income investments by training them to be
artisans or small merchants and eventually (as in Antiquity) equip-
ping them with working capital and permitting them to pursue their
livelihood in the city in return for their freedom. For this reason
it was possible to find in public construction in Athens both slaves
and freemen employed for wages in the same piece-work category.
During the Roman period free and unfree men either as *instmen*[2]
of the lord or as small burghers working for the *merx peculiaris*
stand independently alongside one another in trade and commerce,
belonging to the same mystery communities. The opportunity to
purchase one's freedom intensified the economic activity of unfree
petty burghers.

It is no accident that in Antiquity and in Russia a large part of
the first wealth acquired by rational management of trade or commerce accumulated in the hands of the freed. In Antiquity as in
Russia, the Occidental city was already a place where the ascent
from bondage to freedom by means of monetary acquisition was
possible. This phenomenon became even more important in the
medieval city, chiefly the continental city where the older the community the more this was true. Here the burghers of the city as a
conscious policy of their estate, aspired to the achievement of freedom in contrast to nearly all other known civic developments.

---

2. Workers on the land, married and living at home. *General Economic
History*, p. 90 f.

In the early period the ample economic opportunities of the cities established for their inhabitants a common interest in their exploitation. In order to increase the chances for sale and acquisition, immigration was facilitated. A solidarity of interests emerged among urbanites in avoiding the possibility that as soon as each bondsman became prosperous in the city he be ordered to boots and saddle service by his lord if for no other reason to extort a ransom from him. This was repeatedly practiced by Silesian noblemen in the eighteenth century and by Russians still in the nineteenth century. The urbanites therefore usurped the right to violate lordly law. This was the major revolutionary innovation of medieval occidental cities in contrast to all others.

In Central and North European cities the principle appeared: "City air makes man free." The time period varied, but always after a relatively short time, the lord of a slave or bondsman lost the right to subordinate him to his power. The principle was carried out in varying degrees. Very often, in fact, cities were forced to promise not to admit unfree men and when there was a restriction of economic opportunities such barriers were also often welcomed by the cities. However, despite such exceptions, as a rule the principle of freedom prevailed. Thus estate-based differences vanished in the city at least so far as they rested on a differentiation between freedom and bondage. On the other hand in North Europe in numerous civic settlements, originally resting on an internal political equality of the settlers and free elections of municipal officials, a patrician stratum developed.

As differentiation in terms of the medieval estates declines, thus, a new status differentiation appears with the emergence of patrician families monopolizing office by virtue of their economic independence and power over and against the other burghers. Moreover, from the beginning, in numerous rich cities of the North as well as South (including German cities) even as in Antiquity there appear knights who maintain a stable (today we would speak of a "racing stable" because it is assumed to be for the purpose of tournaments). Such knights or "constables" constituted a city nobility alongside the common burghers. Stratification in terms of status has appeared.

However, this is confronted by another development enhancing the status identity of the citizens as such irrespective of whether

they are differentiated as nobles or otherwise—this was the mounting tension with the nobility outside the city. Toward the end of
the Middle Ages, at least in Northern Europe, the urban patriciate
participated in economic acquisition and—this was particularly insisted upon—sat together with the guilds in municipal government.
However the "nobility" of this civic patriciate was not acknowl-
edged by the knightly nobility of the countryside. Moreover, the
urban patriciate was denied qualification for the tournament and
for the canonate. It was also denied connubium and escheatment
(the latter in Germany with only temporary exceptions of the
privileged burghers of Imperial Cities). In the wider society, thus,
there were powerful forces tending the bring about a relative level-
ling of the city as a whole. In face of the strong internal differentiation within the city, generally, the latter retained preponderance.

At the close of the Middle Ages and at the beginning of modern
times and so far as they did not become, as in Italy, monarchical
city states, nearly all cities, Italian, English, French and German,
were dominated by an urban patrician council or a corporation of
burghers. This was exclusive as against outsiders but for insiders it
implied a domination by notable persons. This was true even in
cases where, as hold-over from the period of guild power, such
honorable persons were formally obligated to belong to a guild.

The cutting of status connections with the rural nobility was
carried out in relatively pure form only in the civic corporations
of Northern Europe. In the South, chiefly Italy, the reverse occurs
when, with mounting power of the cities, rural nobles took up
urban residence. This latter phenomenon also appears in augmented
form in Antiquity where the city originated precisely as the seat
of nobility. Thus the ancient and to a lesser extent, the southern
medieval European city form a transitional stage between the
Asiatic and North-European cities.

In addition to these differences the decisive quality of the ancient
and typical Mediterranean city was found in the institutional association of burghers endowed with special, characteristic organs.
In this, the burgess was subordinated to a common law which
formed it into a guild of "legal associates." As far as is known this
legally autonomous "polis" or "commune" was only rudimentary
in other areas, except those of Mediterranean and occidental cities.
Nevertheless, it was most likely characteristic in Mesopotamia,

Phoenicia, and in Palestine at the time of the battles of the Israelite
sworn confederacy with the Canaanite city nobility. Perhaps it
was also to be found in some maritime cities of other areas and
times. In the cities of the Fanti Negroes of the Gold Coast described
by Cruickshank[3] and later by Post,[4] a "council" appeared under
the chairmanship of a city king as *primus inter pares*. The members
of the council comprised: 1. the *kabossirs* who were heads of families distinguished by wealth and a socially appropriate style of life
(hospitality and display); 2. the elected foreman of city quarters,
which as military associates were organized by the election of chairmen with elders quite independent of each other and often feuding
with each other; 3. the hereditary police officers *(pyrine)* of the
city wards in whose hands were the court and administration.
Similar preliminary stages of the constitution of a polis or commune
may have appeared repeatedly in Asia and Africa. However, nothing
is known of a legal status of "citizenship."

Fraternization and the Formation of the Polis

More than anything else the fully developed ancient and medieval
city was formed and interpreted as a fraternal association.[5] Therefore, as a rule these cities had a corresponding religious symbol
standing for the associational cult of the burghers as such. There
was usually a city-god or city-saint specifically available to the
burghers. Such was not even lacking in China (often an apotheosized
mandarin), though in China they retained the character of functional deities in the pantheon.

In the Occident the city association owned and controlled property. This contrasts with practice elsewhere such as is illustrated by
the dispute of the Alides (Descendants of Ali, the fourth caliph)
with the community over the "Gardens of Fadak"—a dispute which
provided the first occasion for the economic separation of the
Schîâh. This was a dispute over family or communal property. The

3. Earl F. Cruikshank, *Morocco* (Philadelphia: 1935).
4. Albert Herman Post, *Grundriss der ethnologischen Jurisprudence* (Leipzig: Schwartz, 1894-5) and *Afrikanische Jurisprudence* (Leipzig: Oldenburg,
1887).
5. The classical study of the religious and civil institutions of the cities of
Greece and Rome is Fustel de Coulanges, *The Ancient City* (Garden City:
Doubleday, 1956).

community in whose name the caliph claimed the land was a religious community of Islam and not a political community of Mecca—indeed, the latter did not exist. But in the Occident the political association itself appears as a property owner. Typical of such property was the commons of urban settlements which may have existed elsewhere and even for village communities. Similarly though the princes sometimes had urban tax sources, there is a unique finance structure for the urban community in the ancient and medieval city. At best only the barest rudiments appear elsewhere. Foremost among the reasons for the peculiar freedom of urbanites in the Mediterranean city in contrast to the Asiatic is the absence of magical and animistic caste and sib constraints. The social formations preventing fusion of urban dwellers into a homogeneous status group vary. In China it was the exogamous and endophratric sib; in India—since the victory of the patrimonial kings and the Brahmans—it has been the endogamous caste with its exclusive taboos which has prevented the fusion of city dwellers into a status group enjoying social and legal equality, into a connubium sharing table community and displaying solidarity toward the outgroup. Because of the intensity of exclusive caste taboos this possibility was even more remote in India than in China. Moreover, India possessed a population which was 90% rural in contrast to China where the city was of greater importance. While the inhabitants of India had no possibility for communal cult meals, the Chinese, due to their sib organization, had no occasion for them, particularly since the ancestor cult was more important to the Chinese than anything else. Of course, only a taboo-bound people like the Indians and (to a much lesser degree) the Jews went so far as to exclude even the private communal meal. In India, however, this was the case to such a degree that even the glance of one outside the caste was sufficient to defile the kitchen.

It was still true in Antiquity that the social ceremonies of the family were as inaccessible to non-members as was the Chinese ancestor cult. The historical evidence suggests that one component (real or fictitious) in the establishment of the community was the substitution of the city cult meal or prytaneium for that of the family.[6] The *prytaneium* of the polis was originally indispensable

6. This is the central thesis of Fustel de Coulanges. the Feast of Synoikia was still celebrated in Athens in historical times.

for the city, for it symbolized the community of urban families as a consequence of their fraternization.

Originally the ancient polis was officially based on an organization of families. Some were super-ordinate over others for purely local reasons which often (at least according to fiction) rested on communities of descent. Such communities of descent formed externally-strict, exclusive, cult associations. It is a significant fact that in the minds of their members the ancient cities were freely-willed associations. They were confederations of groups partly of consanguineous and partly—in the case of the phratries—of military character. The groups that composed them were later systematically reorganized into civic divisions of a technical administrative nature. Thus the cities of Antiquity were not only sacred structures closed to the outside but inwardly closed to anyone not belonging to the confederated families: closed to the plebeian. For this very reason, at first, they constituted exclusive cult associations.

The confederations of noble families in Southern European cities in the early Middle Ages, especially but not only in the maritime cities, closely resemble those of the ancient city. Within the walls of the city each noble family had its own fortress or, if not, it shared a fortress with others, in which case its use (as in Siena) was regulated in detail. Feuds between families raged as violently within as outside the city and many of the oldest civic districts (for example the *alberghi*) were presumably such areas of feudal power. However, there were no residues—such as were still present in Antiquity—of sacred exclusiveness of families against each other and toward the outside. This was a consequence of the historically memorable precedent in Antioch justly thrust into the foreground by Paul in his letter to the Galatians. There Peter administered the (ritualistic) communal meal to uncircumcised brethren. Already in the ancient city ritualistic exclusiveness had begun to disappear. The clanless plebs accomplished ritualistic equalization in principle. In the medieval period, chiefly in Central and North European cities, the clans were weak from the beginning and they soon lost all importance as constituencies of the city. Thus the cities became confederations of individual burghers (house owners). In fact even in extra-civic affairs the exclusiveness of the burghers also lost all practical importance for the urban community.

It has been noted that the ancient polis increasingly tended to

become an "institutionalized community"[7] in the mind of its inhabitants. Even in Antiquity the concept of the "community" began
to differentiate from that of the "state." To be sure this only
occurred with incorporation into the large Hellenistic and Roman
states which robbed the city communities of their political independence. By contrast, the medieval city was a "commune" from
the beginning of its existence irrespective of the degree to which
the legal concept of " corporation" as such was brought to clear
consciousness.

Magical Barriers to Oriental Civic Development

In the Occident taboo barriers like those of the Indian equatorial
area were absent. So too were the totemic, ancestor cult and caste-
like magical supports of clan organization which prevented fraternization from leading to civic corporation in Asia. The effects of
totemism and the casuistic execution of clan endogamy long remained established and in effect precisely in those areas where large
scale political militaristic and urban associations never developed.
Totemism left only residues in the ancient religions. So far as they
are not specifically religious the reasons for this can only be vaguely
determined. The enlistment in foreign legions, participation in
piratical activities in the early period, military adventures, and
numerous continental and over-seas colonial establishments must
unavoidably have led the persons involved to permanent intimate
associations with tribal or at least clan strangers. Such experiences
must have unavoidably shattered the magical rigidity of clan exclusiveness. And if, as tradition suggests, clan distinctions were everywhere re-instituted artificially by the division of the newly-founded
communities into new "clans," associations, and phratries, it was
actually no longer clan associations but the military organizations
of the polis that now supplied the basis for unity.

Similar factors can be presumed at work in the north. The
century-long wanderings of conquering war bands of Teutons
before and during the migrations of peoples, their enlistments in
foreign legions and their adventurous expeditions under self-elected
heads, must have formed multiple barriers against the intensification

---

7. Weber is here using the term in the sense of consciously established or
"freely-willed" or "intentional."

of taboos and totemic ties. According to what we know of the Teutonic tribes settlements may have been most expediently made in terms of real or fictitious clans. In any case logistic and military association by "hundreds," the hide-constitution as an administrative basis for the imposition of taxes, and, later, the relation of followership and vassaldom to the princes remained the decisive elements in the structure of the city in this area rather than the magical bonds of the extended family which never achieved full development perhaps precisely due to those very circumstances.

Christianity became the religion of these people who had been profoundly shaken in all their traditions. Indeed, it was possible for Christianity to become so important precisely because of the weakness or absence of this kind of magical barriers and taboos. Christianity itself was the final element in the destruction of the religious significance of the clans. The role, often quite significant, played by the ecclesiastical community in the political-administrative organization of the medieval city is only one of the many symptoms of the characteristic influence of Christianity in dissolving clan associations and thus becoming fundamentally important for the very founding of the medieval city. In contrast to this, the whole history of the internal conflicts of the caliphate indicates that Islam never overcame the rural ties of Arabic tribal and clan associations, but remained the religion of a conquering arm structured in terms of tribes and clans.

Disruption of the Clans as a Prerequisite of Fraternization

Wherever it appeared the city was basically a resettlement of people previously alien to the place. Chinese, Mesopotamian, Egyptian and occasionally even Hellenistic war princes founded cities and transferred to them not only voluntary settlers but other kidnapped according to demand and possibility. This occurred most frequently in Mesopotamia where forced settlers had first to dig the irrigation canals which made possible the emergence of the city in the desert. The prince with his official apparatus and administrative officials remained absolute master of the city. This tended to prevent the appearance of any communal association whatsoever or, at best, permitted only the appearance of the rudiments of one. The people settled together in the area often remained as connubially segregated tribes.[8] Where this was not the case the newcomers remained members of their former locality and clan associations.

The urban resident in China normally belonged to his native rural community. So, too, did broad strata of the non-Hellenic population of the Hellenic Orient. Moreover, the legend of the New Testament locates the birth of the Nazarene at Bethlehem because the family of the father (using the German translation of Heliand) had its *Hantgemal* there; hence, according to the legend, it had to be counted there. Until recently the situation of the Russian peasants who had migrated to the city was similar; they retained their right to the land as well as, upon demand of the village community, their duty to share in the village work. Under such circumstances no civic rights arose but only a duty-encumbered and privileged association of city residents. The Hellenic *synoecism* was based on clan groups. According to tradition the reconstitution of the city of Jerusalem by Esra and Nehemiah was affected by clans, namely the settling together of delegations from each rural resident clan possessing full political rights.

In the ancient city only the clan-less, politically-illegitimate plebs were organized in terms of local residence.[9] The individual could be a citizen in the ancient city, but only as a member of his clan. In early Antiquity, at least according to fiction, each Hellenic and Roman *synoecism* as well as each colonial establishment occurred in a manner similar to the reconstitution of Jerusalem. Even democracy was initially unable to disrupt the organization of the burghers into families, clans, phratries, and phyles. Purely personal, cult associations were in fact dominated by the noble families and democracy was able to render them politically innocuous only through indirect means. In Athens everyone wishing to qualify for office had to prove the existence of a cult center of his clan *(Zeus epkaios)* in Athens.

Roman legend also reports the appearance of the city through the conjoint settlement of natives with people alien to the tribes. Through ritualistic fraternal acts they were formed into a religious community with a communal hearth and a god serving as communal

---

8. The Babylonian exile of the Jews was only a particularly famous case.

9. The substitution of locality for kin groups was particularly emphasized by H. S. Maine.

saint. However, they were simultaneously organized into gentes (clans), *curia* (phratries) and tribes (phyles). Such routine composition of the ancient city was initially imposed quite arbitrarily for tax purposes as is indicated by the round numbers of such associations (the cities were typically formed into 3, 30, or 12). But despite this in Rome participation in the *auspicia* remained the distinguishing mark of the burgher entitled to participation in the city cult and qualified for all offices requiring communication with the gods. This was indispensable precisely for ritual purposes. A legitimate association could only rest on traditional or ritualistic forms such as the clan, the defense associations (phratry) or the political or tribal association (phyle).

All this was changed in the medieval city, particularly in the North. Here, in new civic creations burghers joined the citizenry as single persons. The oath of citizenship was taken by the individual. Personal membership, not that of kin groups or tribe, in the local association of the city supplied the guarantee of the individual's personal legal position as a burgher.

The North European city often expanded to include not only persons originally foreign to the locality, but merchants foreign to the tribes as well. New civic foundations extended the civic privilege as an attraction to newcomers. To some degree this also occurred incidental to the transformation of older settlements into cities. At times, to be sure, merchants such as are mentioned in Cologne, recruited from the entire circuit of the Occident from Rome to Poland, did not join the local oath-bound urban community, which was founded by the native propertied strata. However, enfranchisement of complete strangers also occurred.

A special position corresponding to that of Asiatic guest people was characteristically occupied in medieval cities only by the Jews. Although in Upper Rhine documents the bishop insists that he called in the Jews "for the greater glory of the city," and though in Cologne shrine-documents the Jews appear as landowners mingling with Christians, ritualistic exclusion of connubialism by the Jews in a manner foreign to the Occident as well as the actual exclusion of table community between Jews and non-Jews and the absence of the Lord's Supper, blocked fraternization. The city church, city saint, participation of the burghers in the Lord's Supper and official church celebrations by the city were all typical of the Occidental

cities. Within them Christianity deprived the clan of its last ritualistic importance, for by its very nature the Christian community
was a confessional association of believing individuals rather than a
ritualistic association of clans. From the beginning, thus, the Jews
remained outside the burgher association.

While it is true that the medieval city retained cult ties and
often (perhaps always) religious parishes were part of its constitution it was nevertheless a secular foundation like the ancient city.
The parishes were not incorporated as church associations by their
church representatives but by secular civic aldermen. The decisive
legal formalities were undertaken by lay presidents of parochial
communities and, eventually, guilds of merchants. Moreover, the
qualification of an individual as a citizen was found in communal
religious equality rather than membership in the proper clans as in
antiquity.

Initially in the medieval city there was no fundamental religious
difference from Asiatic conditions. The God of the Asiatic city corresponds to the local saint of the Middle Ages; even determination
of citizenship in terms of the ritualistic community was characteristic of the cities of Near Eastern Antiquity. However, the pacification policies following conquests by the great Near Eastern kings
tended to destroy the ritualistic community. The great kings sought
to pacify conquered areas by transplanting whole populations, thus
destroying systems of local ties which could become nuclei of
resistance. The effect of this policy was to transpose the city into
a mere administrative district within which all inhabitants with
differences of ritual and family membership shared similar life
situations.

The effects of such Near Eastern policies of grafting populations
on civic structures may be seen in the fate of the Jews who were
carried into exile. In their exile location only those public offices
which demanded knowledge of writing and thus, also, ritualistic
qualification[10] were closed to them. While the Jews were permitted to enter without restriction almost every occupation the Babylonian city offered they did not become "officials" of the city.

10. Writing in considerable measure originated in the employment of magical
signs by magician priests and, in any case, remained a monopoly of priestly
strata for a long time in early civilization. Qualification for religious ministra-
tions, for public office, and possession of writing skills thus were early linked
phenomena still preserved in Babylonia at the time of the Jewish exile.

In this area of the ancient world just as was the case among the exiled Jews the individual members of foreign tribes had their own elders and priests. Thus they assumed the form of "guest tribes."[11] In Israel before the exile, the metics[12] (gerim) stood outside the ritualistic communities as indicated by the fact that they were not originally circumcised. The *gerim* comprised nearly all the craftsmen in Ancient Palestine. The counterpart to such craftsmen in India also were guest tribes, where ritualistic fraternization of city inhabitants was excluded by caste taboos.

Similar phenomena to these also appear in China where each city had its god, often a former mandarin of the city who had become transformed into a cultural hero and was the central object of a cult of worship. However, here, too, as in almost all Asiatic and Near Eastern cities the community is missing or, at best, rudimentary. When the urban community appears at all it is only in the form of a kin-association which also extends beyond the city. In the case of the Jews after the exile the confessional community was ruled in a purely theocratic manner.

Significance of the Clan for the Ancient and the Medieval City

The city of the Medieval Occident was economically a seat of trade and commerce, politically and economically a fortress and garrison, administratively a court district and socially an oath-bound confederation. In Ancient Greece the joint election of the *prytanis*[13]

---

11. This phenomenon of the transfiguration of the situation of an entire community into an often landless and certainly socio-politically under-privileged unit within the wider society so that it tends to form a closed community within the wider whole was of great interest to Weber. All the forces leading in this direction were seen by Weber as resulting in the emergence of the caste system of India. It is possible, of course, for a social unit to be transformed into a "guest people" even in the land of its origin. This occurred throughout the society in India and to the Jews in ancient Palestine. See Max Weber, *Ancient Judaism*. Translated by Hans Gerth and Don Martindale (Glencoe: The Free Press, 1952).

12. The metics were a class of resident aliens without full citizenship in Athens and in certain other city states of classical Greece. The *gerim* was the contemporary counterpart in the Hebraic world.

13. The *prytanis* in certain Greek states was a chief magistrate. In Athens a member of any of the ten sections of the council or senate during the presidency of that section, each section presiding for a period of five weeks.

was at times the proud symbol of the civilized city. In the Middle Ages the symbol of the city was eventually found in the sworn community which legally assumed the form of a corporation.

The emergence of the medieval urban community as a legal corporation occurred only by degrees. Still in 1313, according to Hatschek, English cities were not able to obtain the franchise because, speaking in modern terms, they had no "legal personality." It was only under Edward I that cities acquired the status of corporations.

Not simply in England but throughout Europe the citizenry of the emerging cities were initially dealt with politically through the sponsor of the city as a passive liturgical association the members of which were qualified through possession of urban landed property and enjoying specific tasks, duties, and privileges. The specific privileges accorded the citizenry included market monopolies, staple rights, trade privileges and the rights of eliminating competing trades, participation in the city court and special positions for military and tax purposes. The economically most important of all civic privileges did not appear in a formal legal sense as an acquisition of the citizen's association, but of the political or manorial city sponsor.

It was the city's protector rather than the burgher who formally acquired those important rights which in fact benefitted the burgher in direct economic ways. They actually benefit the sponsor only indirectly by way of the taxes imposed on the burghers. As in Germany such rights are, in the oldest instances, privileges of the king granted to the bishop who in turn was permitted to treat his urban subjects as privileged. At times, as in Ango-Saxon England, permission to establish a market was an exclusive privilege of neighboring manorial lords to be bestowed only upon their bondsmen whose profits were taxed.

The city court initially was either royal or manorial. Its aldermen and other functionaries were not representatives of the burghers even in cases where they were elected by the burghers rather than being appointed as officials of the lord. For such functionaries urban law was the statute of the lord. The "universitas civium" as it was soon everywhere called was initially heteronomous and heterocephalous and incorporated in other political and manorial associations. However, this state of affairs did not persist.

In varying degrees the city became an autonomous and autocephalous institutional association. As a societal[14] rather than a communal movement the city was tending to become an active "territorial corporation." Urban officials were completely or partly organs of this new institution. From the very beginning of this institutional development, the privileged position of the burgher was valued as a right of the individual with respect to third parties. In some measure this was a product of the conception of personal-legal subordination to a common "objective" law as a status quality of the persons involved. The idea was peculiar to Antiquity and the Middle Ages. The evaluation of citizenship as an individual right was also, as emphasized by Beyerle[15] a product of the concept still alive in German court constitution in which each legal colleague is a "contractual party": that is an objective participant in a con-tractual community under objective law to which the burgher is entitled and which he co-creates as a judge in the court itself.[16] Such a law was absent from the courts of the major number of the cities of the world. Only in Israel can traces of one be found due to rather special circumstances.

It was of central importance for the emergence of the medieval city that at the time when the economic interests of the burghers thrust them toward the formation of an institutional association they were neither prevented therefore by the presence of magical or religious barriers on the one hand nor by the rational adminis-tration of a super-ordinate political association on the other. Where

14. Since Toennies in German sociology the distinction has been drawn be-tween the *Gemeinschaft* and *Gesellschaft*. As societal types the first represents a close knit, kin based, strongly local and familistic type of social interaction, the second a relatively impersonal, territory-based, political and economic type of social interaction. Weber did not make use of these ideas so much as societal types but as interactive tendencies and *Vergemeinschaftung* and *Vergesell-schaftung* refer to "communal" and "societal" interactive tendencies respec-tively.

15. Franz Beyerle, *Gesetz der Burgunden* (Weimar: H. Böhlaus, 1936).

16. *Dinggennossenschaft:* The folk community in its legal aspect. The sepa-ration of law finding from enforcement has often been claimed to be a peculiar trait of German law. In fact, the German council of aldermen took the place of old charismatic prophets. The unique feature of German legal development is located by Weber in the way the separation of law finding and enforcement was maintained. Members of the legal community who were not judicial hon-oraries took part in the process of adjudication and their acclamation was indis-pensable for the ratification of the verdict arrived at by the lawfinders. Max Weber, *Law in Economy and Society*. Trans. by Edward Shils and Max Rhein-stein (Cambridge: Harvard University Press, 1954) p. 90.

even a single one of these circumstances occurred, as in Asia, even despite strong conjoint economic interests, urban residents were unable to arrive at more than transitory unification. In the Middle Ages the emergence of the autonomous and autocephalous city association with its administrative sponsor and its "Konsul" or "Majer" or "Burgermaster" at its head is an occurrence differentiating it from both Asiatic and ancient civic development. As will be seen later, where the polis first developed its characteristic features, the urban constitution represents a transformation of the power of the city king on the one hand and the clan elders on the other into a reign of notable persons from "families" fully qualified for military service. The "familistic" city that tended to emerge in Antiquity was quite distinct from the typical medieval city.

The Oath-Bound Confederation in the Occident

When analyzing the various early civic phenomena, formal legal and socio-political factors are best kept separate, although this precaution is not always observed in the battle of the various "city theories." In a formal legal sense the corporation of citizens and their authorities was "legitimized" in terms of (real or fictitious) privileges granted by political or manorial powers. In actuality legitimation of the city corporation only at times occurred in this manner. From a formal legal point of view a revolutionary usurpation of rights by the burghers had occurred.

To be sure, this origin of urban rights does not hold everywhere. It is possible to distinguish between an original and derived emergence of the medieval city association of burghers in which legitimation only confirmed an illegitimate act, for often formal legal certification of rights achieved by the citizenry by the legitimate authorities only occurred later. Thus, in the derived sense the citizens' association often emerged through contractual agreement with the chartering authority, the city founder or his successors, and with varying rights to autonomy and autocephaly.

This pattern was especially frequent for new foundations of cities as a product of the attempt to guarantee civic rights to the new settlers and their legal successors. The original usurpation in the course of community development and the establishment of an

oath-bound fraternity *(conjuratio)* of burghers was the primary
event in some large old cities such as Genoa and Cologne. As a
rule, however, the establishment of the medieval urban community
was a product of a combination of events of another kind. The
historical document of the city, naturally overemphasizes the legitimate continuities and rarely mentions such usurpatory fraternizations. Hence, it is often accidental when the occurrence of a
revolutionary fraternity is documented. As a result of such biased
reporting the "derived" emergence of the city—that is, its origin
in formal legitimation by a princely or lordly sponsor—is over-
represented as against the real facts of existing cities. For example,
only one single laconic note refers to the Cologne *conjuratio* of 1112.

In Cologne the bench of aldermen of the old city and the parish
representatives particularly of the Martins suburb which was the
new settlement of the *mercatores*, was recognized by the "legitimate" authorities or they may have sought documentary confirmation
of their acts. In Cologne in disputes over formal legitimacy with their
opponents, the city sponsors used the pretext that there were aldermen present who among other things were not under oath. Many
usurpatory innovations have received the same form of expression
and reluctant confirmation. The edicts of the petty princes directed
against civic autonomy speak quite a different language. They not
only prohibit single acts of legalization but the very *conjurationes*
as well.

It speaks sufficiently of the nature of such acts of usurpation that
in Cologne even at a much later time the Richerzeche (a guild
of prosperous persons) which was no more than a private club of
wealthy individuals not only successfully managed to appropriate
for itself as self-evident the right to grant membership in the club
but citizenship as well which was legally quite independent of the
club. Similarly in the majority of the larger French cities, constitutions were in principle obtained in a similar way by oath-bound
citizens' associations.

Sociological Significance of Civic Unity

Italy was the proper home of the *conjuratio*. In the overwhelming majority of cases, the Italian city constitution originated by
conjuratio. Thus it is here, despite a comparative poverty of sources,

that the significance of civic unification can be most easily ascertained. The most general presupposition of city unification is found in the semi-feudal semi-prebendal appropriation of sovereign powers in the Occident. Before the *conjuratio* civic conditions, though varying in individual cases, may be conceived as approximately as anarchic as those in the city of Mecca. As a matter of fact it was for this very reason that the civic conditions of Mecca were described above in some detail. Numerous conflicting claims to authority simultaneously criss-cross each other. Side by side one finds: 1. episcopal powers of manorial and political content; 2. the power of vicounts and other appropriated political office powers resting partly on granted privileges and partly on usurpation; 3. the power of large urban resident holders of fiefs or freed ministers of the king and bishop (capitani) of most varied origin; 4. the powers of countless lords of castles administered in their own name or that of someone else which as a privileged estate had strong clientele either bound or free; 5. the powers of professional unions of resident urban economic classes. And reflecting these social groupings as sources of diverse and competing powers, judicial powers based on court law, on feudal law, on provincial law and ecclesiastical law can be found side by side. Essentially similar to the "connections" of the Mecca families, temporary contracts interrupted the feuds of interest groups competent for military service within and outside the city walls. The legitimate official lord of the city was either an imperial vassal or, often, a bishop. By virtue of his combined secular and sacred powers the bishop had the best chance of establishing effective sovereign power.

The *conjuratio* which as *campagne communis* (or under similar name) prepared the way for the political association of the later city was concluded for concrete purposes and limited time periods or until further notice. Thus it was terminable. At times in the early period several *conjurationes* can be found within the same walls. However, only the oath-bound association of the whole community won permanent importance. This was the association of all those powers which in the relevant moment were able to sustain a monopoly of military and police power within the walls.

In Genoa at first the political association was renewed every four years. Moreover, the political association varied in terms of whom it opposed. At Milan in 980 the militarily competent urban residents concluded a *conjuratio* against the bishop. In Genoa, the bishop together with the vicount's families to whom secular seigniorial rights were assigned (at a later time reduced to mere claims to tribute) were parties to the *conjuratio*. Later here as elsewhere the *compagne communis* opposed the power claims of both the bishop and the visconti.

The initial aim of the oath-bound fraternity was the union of locally resident land-owners for offensive and defensive purposes, for the peaceable settlement of internal disputes, and for the safeguarding of the administration of justice corresponding to the interests of urban residents. Not to be forgotten was the further aim of monopolizing the economic opportunities of the city. Only confederates were allowed to participate in urban trade. In Genoa, for example, membership in the confederacy was prerequisite for participation in capital investments of commenda type in transoceanic commerce. Similarly, membership in the sworn brotherhood carried with it a fixation of duties toward the lord of the city. Thus a kind of collective bargaining established lump sums or fixed tribute instead of arbitrary taxation. Moreover, the political association undertook military organization for the purpose of enlarging the political and economic power sphere of the commune.

The *conjurationes* were only in process of formation at the time of the beginning of the wars of the communes against one another. By the early eleventh century these wars had already reduced the country to a state of chaos. The wars accelerated the internal structuring of the communes for within the city the mass of the burghers were forced to join the sworn communal brotherhood. Resident urban noble and patrician families often led the way in the institution of the fraternization, taking under the civic oath all inhabitants qualified by land ownership. Whoever did not enter voluntarily was forced to join. This was not correlated, initially, by any formal change in the existing organization of offices. The bishop or secular city lord often retained his position as formal head of the civic district which continued to be administered through his ministers. The great transformation was felt only in the presence of the burgher assembly.

In face of the changing composition of the city the old political organization could not indefinitely continue. Already in the last decades of the eleventh century "consuls" elected yearly (sometimes as many as a dozen per city) appear. Such consuls are either elected officially by the totality of the burghers directly or by a representation of noble men as a *collegium* of delegates for election. Such a premium of noblemen elected by the burghers and certified only by acclamation always in fact usurped the right to vote. The consuls, salaried and equipped with prerequisites, completed the revolutionary usurpation, engrossing the major part of jurisdiction and supreme command in time of war. They increasingly administered all the affairs of the commune. In the beginning the consuls were often recruited from noble judicial officials or seignorial curia. The only basic difference in the initial recruitment of consuls is their election by the sworn citizens' confederation rather than appointment by the sovereign of the city.

A *collegium* (association) of *sapientes* (sages) or *credenza* stood beside and rigidly controlled the consuls. This association was formed out of old aldermen and nobles—the chiefs of economically and politically powerful families—who distributed the positions among themselves.

The first oath-bound civic confederations guaranteed the separation of the estates into: main vassals *(capitani)*, lower vassals, ministers, lords of castles *(castellani)* and *cives miliores* (persons economically qualified for military service). These groups were granted proportionate representation in the officialdom and council. However, the social revolution soon gained momentum and resistance developed against the internal remnants of feudalism. The consuls were prohibited from accepting fiefs or prebends as vassals of the lord and in this manner locating their loyalties outside the sworn confederation. A major political acquisition achieved by force or purchase was the right to demolish imperial, episcopal or seignorial castles within the city walls (as in the case of privileges won from the Salic emperor). The further principle was secured prohibiting the construction of castles within a specified area around the city. Furthermore, the emperor or other city sovereign lost the right to take up quarters within the city.

Among the legal acquisitions secured in the course of the city revolutions was the establishment of a special urban law. The burgess was particularly anxious to exclude irrational means of proof, particularly the duel—as illustrated in numerous grants of privilege of the eleventh century. Parallel interests of the burghers led to similar concessions in the English and French kingdoms. Among other legal gains by the burghers was the prohibition of summons of burghers to non-urban courts. They also pressed for the codification of a special rational law for urbanites to be applied by the court of the consuls.

Among the products of such revolutionary urban movements was the development of a permanent political association the members of which were legal colleagues enjoying special legal status as urbanites. In this manner the purely personal oath-bound confederation concluded from case to case was permanently institutionalized. Formally the new urban law implied the extinction of the old principle of the personality of the law. Materially it involved the breaking up of the fief-system and patrimonial estates, but not yet in favor of an institutionalized territorial corporation.

Burgher law, thus, is a half-way house between the old feudal law and the law of territorial units. It is an estate law of the members of an oath-bound confederacy. One was subject to such a law by virtue of membership in the burgher stratum or to copyholders dependent on them. Even in sixteenth century cities where the dominion of noble families was maintained as in most Dutch communities, representation in the provincial and general estates was not a representation of the city as such but of the resident urban nobility. This is revealed by the fact that beside representatives of the noble families, representatives of the guilds and non-noble strata of the city also frequently appear. Such additional representatives often voted separately and were by no means necessarily united with the representatives of the noble families of the city.

In Italy this particular phenomenon did not appear, though in principle the situation was often similar. Though normally the resident urban nobility should have been detached from the fief system they possessed country castles and manorial land in addition to their city houses. Thus, besides their participation in the communal association they were also included as lords or colleagues in other political associations. In the early Italian commune the city regiment was actually monopolized by families living as knights who, regardless of whether social development formally supplied something different, had obtained a temporary share in the regiment. The knightly nobility was militarily predominant.

In Northern Europe, particularly in Germany, the old aldermanic families played a much more decisive role than in the South. At first they even formally retained administrative control and later consolidated effective influence in their hands as a closed clique. Moreover, depending on the local distribution of power the ministers of the bishop as previous bearers of city sovereignty retained a share in administration. This was particularly true in cases where the usurpation of civic sovereignty by the burghers was not completely successful; the bishop and his ministers participated in the council of city estates. In some large cities such as Cologne and Magdeburg the bishop had originally executed his administration in part through free aldermen who, after the civic revolution, were transformed from sworn officials of the bishop into sworn officials of the communes.[17]

However, when such members of old aldermanic families retained power along with former ministers of the bishop or lord, representatives of the *conjuratio* (oath-bound association) always joined them or shared the administration with them. For example, in the cities of Flanders, Brabant and the Netherlands beside aldermen nominated by the court, town counsellors or jurymen or "burghermasters" began to appear. These administrative representatives of the burgher strata were usually formed in separate boards though at times meeting together with the older administrative personnel. Their very name, jury-men—*juratio*—already indicates the usurpatory origin of the *conjuratio*.

The jurymen were representatives of the burghers who formed a union still persisting at a later time as the corporation of the "*vroedschap*." These early conditions were very labile, being quite unregulated precisely with regard to the actual distribution of power. Personal influence was at a premium as individuals consolidated manifold functions in their hands. Even a formally separate civic administrative plant such as our offices and town hall was missing. As in Italy the burghers ordinarily assembled in the cathedrals while administrative committees met, as in Rome, in private

17. Modern parallels to such continuities of personnel with a reversal of institutional anchorage appear in situations when American city officialdoms established by political party machines have been transformed in the course of periodic reform movements from party workers in patronage schemes into civil service workers through the expedient of administering civil service examinations to them and permitting them to retain their former patronage positions under civil service administration if they pass. For example, the clean-up of the Pendergast Machine in Kansas City.

residences or more usually in club rooms. During the revolutionary usurpation in Cologne the "house of the rich" *(domus divitum)* united with the "house of burghers" *(domus civium)* to carry on administration. Thus Beyerle's explanation is certainly correct, the leaders of the "Millionaires' Club" *(Richerzeche)* were in extensive personal fusion with the incumbents of aldermen's chairs and other important civic' offices.

From place to place the composition of the dominant political strata of the city varied. In Cologne, for example, there was no resident knighthood with the importance of the Italian. In England and France merchant corporations played the leading roles. In Paris the chairmen of the Water Guild were formally recognized as representatives of the burghers. However, it was also generally true in most old French cities that urban communities originated in revolutionary usurpations carried out by associations of burghers. Frequently merchants and resident urban rentiers united with resident knights as in the South or with fraternities and corporations of artisans as in the North to form the decisive combinations able to usurp political rights. France, thus, represents a transitional mixture of the patterns manifest in South and North respectively.

Fraternization in the Germanic North

The associations playing the decisive role in the origin of the urban community in the North were not identical with the southern *conjuratio*. The oath-bound confederations of the German North displayed archaic traits bound up with a minor development of the knighthood which was largely missing from the South-European countries. To be sure, here, too, sworn fraternities could be newly created for the purpose of political integration and the usurpation of power from the lord of the city. However, here such revolutionary movements could receive a special stamp from their link with protective corporations which had originated in great numbers in the North and in England.

Such northern protective associations had not been created primarily for the purpose of influencing political conditions. Initially they were substitutes for attachment to a clan with its protective guarantees for the members, an attachment missed with special frequency in the early medieval city. The services to the individual lost by the family were taken over by these protective societies including: help in case of personal injury or threat; aid in economic distress; the settling of disputes and exclusion of feuds between fraternity members by means of peaceful conciliation; the physical protection (banking) of moneys of the members (particularly in England); and the provision of social occasions for fraternization by holding periodic feasts—a practice continued from pagan times. In their function as insurance associations the protective associations even took care of the individual's funeral and the participation of the fraternity in the funeral ritual guaranteed salvation of his soul through good deeds and secured for him indulgences and the benevolence of powerful saints through shared expenses. It goes without saying that such protective associations also represented joint economic interests.

While the city unions in northern France were primarily formed as oath-bound confederations for peace without other corporate attributes, the Nordic and English city unions regularly bore the character of a corporation. In England the commercial corporation monopolizing retail trade within the city was typical. The majority of German commercial corporations were specialized in terms of particular branches of trade as, for example, the often powerful corporation of woolen drapers and the corporation of retailers. Outside these contexts the guild was also developed into a form organizing foreign trade—a function of no concern here.

Contrary to current belief the cities did not originate in the guild corporation but the guild emerged in the context provided in the proto-city. Furthermore, the guild corporation suceeeded in obtaining dominion in the city only to a limited degree (in the North, especially England as *summa convivia*). As a rule "families" by no means identical with the guild corporations managed to obtain dominion for themselves. The corporations were also distinct from the *conjuratio*, the oath-bound civic confederation.

It should be noted that the guilds were by no means the only type of civic corporation. Besides professionally neutral religious associations there appear also purely economic, professionally staffed corporations. Movements toward religious unification and the creation of *confraternitates* accompany guild-political and purely professional economic movements, intersect with each other in manifold manner. They even played a significant though varying role among the handworkers. The fact that the oldest demonstrable corporation of handworkers in Germany, the Bed-Blanket Weavers in Cologne (1180) is older than the corresponding weavers' association does not demonstrate the priority of professional aims for the origin of the associations but rather their basic character. However, the development of the weavers' guild permits the supposition that unions of free handworkers, at least outside Italy, established the authoritative form of the association with handworkers as members and the master at the top.

In other fraternities one may discern the beginning of a significant later type of corporation. As in the last generation in Russia one could still find Jewish workshops which produced articles for ritualistically and religiously correct Jews customarily beginning work only after reading from the Torah rolls, so in numerous guild workshops it was customary to begin work only after religious observance. This was by no means a disguise for strong material interests, as illustrated by the fact that the oldest conflicts of journeyman associations arose not over work conditions but over religious etiquette such as the rank precedence in processions. This demonstrates how thoroughly the social estimates of clanless burghers were interpenetrated by religious elements. It is indicative, too, of the vast difference presented by such a social situation to one with taboo-closed castes which might have prohibited communal fraternization.

By and large the socio-religious fraternities stood in close personal union with official professional associations, the merchant corporations, and artisans' guilds. The order in which the various associations came into existence in the particular case is of no importance. The professional associations did not generally split away from the burgher community as is often believed, though this did occur at times. On the other hand it is also true that artisans' guilds are older than the *conjurationes*. But the artisans' guilds must not be conceived as the forerunners of the *conjurationes* since they appear throughout the world even where no burgher community has ever been found. As a rule, they had indirect effects. They certainly facilitated alliance of the burghers once they became accustomed to protecting their joint interests by means of free unions. They provided models for the fusion of the various lines of authority in the hands of outstanding personalities schooled in such unions and hence able to consolidate the leadership of civic confederations by means of their social influence.

The step of outstanding personalities from leadership of the free unions to leadership of the civic community was a natural development confirmed by further events. Even in the North rich burghers who were interested in the independence of the traffic policy participated actively alongside the nobility in the formation of the *conjuratio*. They supplied it with money and bound the remaining mass of their members to it by oath and duty. Obviously the *Richerzeche's* competence to grant civic rights is a vestige of such formations.

It should be noted however that wherever in addition to the nobility, associations of gainfully-employed burghers participated in the movement to establish the autonomy of the civic community, usually only merchant corporations are involved. Under Edward II in England the small obstinate burghers complained that the rich merchants, the *"potentes"* demanded obedience from them and from the guilds and levied taxes by virtue of their usurped powers. Equivalent development certainly occurred in city fraternizations originating in usurpation. For as the revolutionary usurpations met with repeated successes in the large cities, the political manorial lords who founded new cities or were in a position to grant privileges to existing ones hurried voluntarily to grant rights to the burghers without waiting for the formation of formal unions. By such sponsorship they hoped to retain private control over events while granting no more concessions than necessary, thus the amount of such free bestowals of rights varied greatly.

A product of such successes was the universal spread of the civic unions. An event of particular importance emerged to confirm these developments. Whenever they carried sufficient weight against the city founders due to property or social rank, actual or intended settlers often managed to secure charters confirming the grants of municipal law. The burghers of Freiburg received a charter grant of the same law as Cologne. Numerous South German cities were chartered with the law of Freiburg. Some Eastern cities received the law of Magdeburg. Thereafter in case of disputes the city whose law was granted was appealed to for interpretations. The wealthier the settlers desired by the city founder, the more considerable the concessions the city founder was forced to make. The twenty-four *conjuratores fori* in Freiburg—to whom Berthold of Zeehringen vowed the preservation of the liberties of burghers in new cities—play an equivalent role to the *Richerzeche* in Cologne. To a considerable degree such wealthy settlers are granted personal privileges and at first they conduct the government as consuls.

The establishment of the citizenry as a "corporate body" headed by an administrative organ like the German council was among the things granted by princes and manor lords at the foundation of cities or yielded later. The right to form a council was an especially significant liberty of the burghers who claimed the privilege of autonomously appointing its members. The right was not obtained without resistance. As late as 1392 Frederick II prohibited all city councils and mayors appointed by the burghers without consent of the bishop. In the same period the bishop of Worms claimed for himself and his deputy the chairmanship in the council and the right to appoint its members. Toward the close of the twelfth century, in Strassburg a council consisting of aldermen representing the citizens and five ministerial officials replaced the bishop's administration. In Basel the bishop managed to prohibit the council after it had first been established even though, as Hegel assumed, it had been approved by the Emperor himself. In numerous south German cities the town magistrate appointed or confirmed by the lord remained actual head of the city. Only by purchasing the office were the burghers able to free themselves from this control.

In nearly all the documents of the city, beside the magistrate the mayor increasingly appears and in the end generally assumes first rank. In contrast to the magistrate he was always a representative of the citizens. His office originated in usurpation, not in lordly service. Due to the social stratification of many German cities, the mayor becoming ascendant in the sixteenth century was usually not a representative of the clans. The clans had their counterpart to the mayor in the *scabini non jurati* of Italy who were the counselors and representatives in the large cities in the early period. The mayor as steward of the occupational associations belongs to the later period.

In the beginning, active membership in the burgher association was bound up with possession of urban land which was inheritable, saleable, exempt from compulsory services and either rent-free or charged only with a fixed amount. However, urban land was taxable for civic purposes in a manner very characteristic of Germany. Later other kinds of property were subject to taxation, especially money or monetary metal. Townsmen not possessing land originally only enjoyed the patronage of the city regardless of their position.

The right to participate 'in urban offices and in the council underwent multiple changes. Before turning to this, the general question should be raised as to why civic development did not start in Asia but in the Mediterranian basin, later in Europe. An answer is already provided so far as the growth of an urban community is bound up with the emergence of the city fraternizations. In China the magical closure of the clans, in India the closure of the castes eliminated the possibility of civic confederations. In China the clans as bearers of the ancestor cult were indestructible. In India the castes were carriers of a particular style of life upon the observance of which salvation and reincarnation depended. Ritualistically, thus, the castes were mutually exclusive. The ritualistic obstacles to fraternization were more absolute in India than in China where subjection to the clan was only relative. The barriers grow more weak as one moves into the Near East.

Military Competence of the Citizen as a Basic Component in Occidental Development

Still another complex of factors must be considered to account for the origin of the urban community in the Occident: characteristics of the urban military composition and especially its socioeconomic foundation. The Near East and Egypt in ancient centers of civilization faced the need to regulate river traffic and develop an irrigation policy. To a lesser degree this was also the case in China. Royal bureaucracies were developed to carry out the regulation of river traffic and execution of irrigation policy with the consequent establishment of a process leading toward the bureaucratization of the entire administration. This permitted the king through his staff and revenues supplied them to incorporate the army into his own bureaucratic management. "Officers," and "soldiers" and the army recruited by a compulsory draft equipped and fed by the despot became the foundation of his military power. The result of these trends was the separation of soldiers from ownership of the means of warfare and the military helplessness of the subjects.

No political community of citizens could arise on such a foundation for there was no basis for military independence of royal power. The burgher was not a military man.

Things were different in the Occident where until the time of the Roman Empire the self-equipped army was retained whether it was a peasant militia, an army of knights, or a burgher militia. The individual conscript thus, enjoyed military independence. The principle is already implied in Chlodwig's position with respect to his army that the lord of a self-equipped army is dependent upon the good will of its members. His power rests exclusively on their voluntary obedience. While he is more powerful than any individual member or small group, he is powerless against all the associations taken together or even the majority of them if they unite. The lord lacks the compulsory bureaucratic machine which is blindly obedient because of its complete dependence. He cannot have his way if his top officers unite against him for they are not only independent militarily and economically, but the lord even has to recruit his own administrative officers, dignitaries, and local officials from their ranks.

Military associations of self-equipped soldiers have always taken shape in the Occident just as soon as the lord approached them with new economic demands, particularly monetary payments. Only in the Occident did the "estates" originate from such associations. They were also a fundamental component in the origin of the corporate, autonomous urban communities.

To be sure, the guilds in China and India and the "brokers" of Babylon possessed financial powers which permitted them to bring pressure on the king and which compelled him to take them into account. However, regardless of how rich they were, this did not enable the urban residents to unite and effectively oppose the city lords in a military manner. In contrast to this, all *conjurationes* and unions in the Occident, beginning in early Antiquity, were alliances of urban strata which were eligible for military service. In the decisive hour they were able to take up their own arms and fight for their interests.

Chapter 3

The Patrician City in Antiquity and the Middle Ages

The Nature of the Patrician City

IN MOST civic formations the citizens' assembly, in Italy called the *"parlámento,"* was the highest official, sovereign body of the community, for both leading dignitaries and urban land-owners participated in the *conjuratio.* This was frequently set down formally. In early times the dignitaries were actually completely dominant, but soon qualification for office and service in the council was even formally reserved for a limited number of patrician families. From the beginning it was commonly understood rather than explicitly set down that they were qualified for the council. Where this was not the case the emergence of the patrician was a natural development since as a rule only such persons participated in the council and discussed the common management of affairs who could spare the time from their economic activities. This appears clearly in England where participation in the administrative affairs of the city was at first felt to be a burden and accepted only as a public duty. In the early Middle Ages the burgher had to attend the standard meetings *(Ding)* of the year. Those citizens without specific political interests, however, stayed away from the unscheduled meetings. The management of affairs was quite naturally delegated to those who were respected because of their wealth and eligibility for military service, characteristics in turn resting upon property and military power.

Documents concerning the progress of the Italian *parlámento* show that these mass-meetings as a rule represented only audiences which either approved the proposals of the dignitaries by acclamation or rioted against them. In the early period such *parlámenti* never permanently or decisively influenced elections on measures of civic administration. Often the majority of the members of such assemblies was made up of persons economically dependent upon the dignitaries. The *popolo* later arose as a body independent of the influence of the dignitaries, displacing the unruly burgher assemblies. It accompanied the formation of a smaller assembly consisting of representatives of a strictly circumscribed stratum of qualified burghers. The competition of the two structures is evident in the fact that the summons of the old *parlámento* against which Savonarola warned the people of Florence, marked the revival of the tyrannies and the overthrow of the *popolo*. These were counter revolutions.

Though not always in accord with formal law, the burgess of the city arose as a status group led by a special clique of dignitaries. It will be necessary to discuss their peculiarities later. The central position of these dignitaries had two possible consequences: either these notables might manage to develop a strict, legal monopolization of city government, or their power could be weakened or overthrown by a series of revolutions. These notables who managed to monopolize city administration may be described as a patriciate and the period of their influence as patrician government.

The patriciate of various places was not uniform in its characteristics. The only common element was its socio-political power which rested on landed property and an income not derived from its own trade-establishments. The relevance of land for defining the patriciate flows from its role in medieval styles of life in which the formation of estates sustained the way of life proper to the knights. The knighthood's style of life implied qualification for the tournament and for the holding of fiefs. So far as they achieved these qualifications the patricians were equal in status with the non-urban knights. At least in Italy but also in the majority of cases in the North only those strata were considered to be a patriciate which possessed equality with rural knights. When nothing else is known of the particular case this is to be *assumed a priori* for any city with "families" displaying a knightly style of life. To be sure fluid transitions to other forms must be recognized. In several extreme cases the patrician government developed around a specifically urban nobility. This was especially true where in accordance with ancient traditions civic development was determined by commercial colonial policy. The classic example is Venice.[1]

Monopolistically Closed Patrician Dominion in Venice

The development of Venice was initially determined by an increasing localization produced by the liturgical character of late Roman and Byzantine public economy. The policy also led to a localization of the recruitment of soldiers, beginning in Hadrian's reign. The soldiers of local garrisons were increasingly recruited from the resident population. In practice such soldiers were furnished by the estate owners out of their dependents *(coloni)*. The *tribunes* as commanders of the *numerus* were subordinates of the *dux*. The tribunate was a formal liturgical duty but simultaneously a privilege of the local estate-owning families from the circles of which they were supplied. The honor was in fact hereditary in certain families, while until the eighth century the *dux* was appointed by the Byzantine Empire.

It may be seen that families supplying *tribunes* constituted a military nobility. This military nobility formed the core of the oldest urban patriciate. With the decline of the money economy of the Mediterranian area and increasing militarization of the Byzantine Empire, the power of the tribunal nobility replaced that of the Roman *curia* and *defensores*. In a manner similar throughout Italy, the first revolution (726) which led Venice toward city formation was directed against the current iconoclastic government and its officials. The permanent victory won by this first revolutionary

---

1. Heinrich Kretschmayr, *Allgemeine Staatengeschichte*, I Abtl. Geschichte der Europäischen Staaten, 35 Werke, Geschichte von Venedig, I. Bd. (1905); Ernest Mayer, Italien. *Verfassungsgesch.*, 2 Bde. 1909; B. Schmeidler, *Der Dux und das commune Venetiarum* (v. 1141-1229), 1902; Walter Goetz, *Die Entstehung d. ital. Kommunen im früh. MA* (S.B. Bayr. Ak. d. Wiss., Phil.-hist. Abt., Jg. 1944 Heft 1).

wave was the right of election of the *dux* by the tribunal nobility and the clergy. Soon afterwards the struggle began of the doge[2] with his adversaries: the nobility and patriarch. The conflict was to last for three centuries during which time the doge attempted to establish a hereditary patrimonial city-kingdom. Both the nobility and the patriarch opposed his "taking ways" *("eigenkirchliche" Tendenzen)*, his attempt to consolidate power in his own hands.

However, the doge was supported by the empires of East and West. The acceptance of the son of the doge as co-regent, a device quite in accord with antique tradition, to disguise hereditary appropriation of the position, was favored by the Byzantine Empire. The dowry of Waldrada, niece of the German emperor, afforded the last *Candiano*[3] the means to enlarge the number of his foreign vassals and at the same time to augment the personal bodyguard upon which since 812 the regime of the doge was based. The thoroughly urban and at the same time royal-patrimonial character of the rule of the doge stands out at the time in sharp relief.

The doge was simultaneously lord of a large manor and a great merchant; he monopolized the mail dispatch between the Orient and the Occident which passed through Venice; after 960 he also monopolized the slave trade because of the clerical censorship imposed on it. The doge dismissed and appointed patriarchs, abbots, and priests despite the protest of the church. He was head of jurisdiction, although restricted by the confederate principle of the *Ding*[4] which penetrated into Venice under Franconcian influence.

Still the doge as judicial superior was able to appoint judges and annul contestable verdicts. He conducted the administration through court officials and vassals and, in part, through the aid of the church. The help of the church was particularly desired by the doge as an instrument in Venetian foreign policy. The doge not only had disposition over his domain through nomination of a co-regent but in one case he also had disposition in his will over court property which was not separated from public property. He equipped the

---

2. The change of name of the commune head from dux to doge marks the movement from Imperial Rome to the Middle Ages.

3. Doge Pietro Candiano IV (959-976). Cf. Kretschmayr, op. cit., pp. 401, 436.

4. Actually Dinggenossenschaft—The community as the whole group of legal associates.

fleet out of his private means, entertained troops of soldiers, and disposed over villein labor which artisans owed the *Palatium*.[5] He even arbitrarily increased villein service at times, clearly, however, as a last resort due to growing pressures of foreign policy. That this was going a step too far is shown by the victorious revolt it occasioned in 1032.

The artisans' revolt against the doge in turn played into the hands of the nobility which was ever alert to opportunities to break down the power of the doge. As is always the case under conditions of military self-equipment, the doge was superior to every individual family and to most groups of families, but he was not superior to an alliance of them all. At the time, as today, the alliance held the last word. Thus, as soon as the doge approached the clans with increased financial demands he touched an interest sufficiently basic to bring the alliance about.

Thus the reign of the urban nobility residing in the *Rialto* began under rather democratic legal forms. Its first step was the prohibition of appointment of the doge's son as co-regent. Such a blow at hereditariness (as in Rome) might well have been described as the "first principle of the Republic." After an ambiguous ("standestaat-liches") interim period during which rights and duties were distributed between the doge and the commune, as elsewhere between the sovereign and feudal lords, the terms of the elections settled the issue. The doge was formally demoted to the status of a salaried official, strictly controlled by restrictive formalities. His social position became one of *primus inter pares* in the corporation of noblemen. It is correctly observed by Lenel[6] that the power position of the doge which was formerly supported by his foreign contacts, was restricted by the new foreign policy. The Council of Sapientes (as indicated by events in 1141) gathered foreign policy into its own hands.

It cannot be too emphatically stressed that it was the financial needs of a militant colonial and commercial policy which made the participation of the patriciate in administration unavoidable. In the

5. The Palatine Hill in Rome on which Augustus had his house.

6. Walter Lenel, *Die Entstehung der Vorherschaft Venedigs an der Adria* (Strassburg: 1897) and *Venezianisch-Istrische Studien* (Strassburg: Trübner, 1911).

same manner, the financial needs of princely wars under conditions
of a money economy established the growing power of the estates
on the continent. The Chrysbullon of Emperor Alexius[7] marked
the end of the commercial reign of the Greeks and the origin of
the commercial monopoly of the Venetians in the East. The Venetians, in turn, promised maritime protection and frequent financial
loans to the Eastern Empire. An increasing part of the public, clerical, and private wealth of the Venetians was invested in various
economic enterprises in the Greek empire: in commerce; in *ergastria*
of all kinds; in public leases; in landed property. The war power
of Venice developed for its protection allowed it to participate in
the war of conquest of the Latins by which she acquired the famous
three-eighths (*quarta pars et dimidia*) of the Latin Empire. In accordance with the orders of Dandolo, doge of Venice (1343-54), all
colonial conquest was legalized in the name of the commune and
its officials rather than in the name of the doge. The elimination
of the power of the doge was thereby made final.

Public debts and permanent financial expenditures by the commune were self-evident concomitants of this foreign policy. These
financial obligations, in turn, could only be covered through the
means of the patriciate. The only financially qualified group was
one sector of the old tribune aristocracy, doubtlessly strengthened
by new nobles who because of urban residence were in a position
to participate in commerce and to make profitable investments in
the typical manner by lending *commenda* and other working capital. The patriciate, thus, was able to concentrate both monetary
wealth and political power in their hands. The domination and
monopolization of power by the Venetian patriciate parallels the
dispossession of the doge. In the country, by contrast, there was
an increasing loss of political rights. Until the twelfth century
the original *tribune* dignitaries from the whole *ducáto* nominally
attended the *Placita* of the doge. In reality this terminated with
the formation of the *commune Venetiarum*[8] appearing in the documents in 1143. After this, the council and *sapientes* elected by the
cives and to whom the doge pledged his oath of allegiance appear
to have been exclusively large landlords residing on the *rialto* and

7. Presumably the Chrysbullon of Emperor Alexius I, May 1802. Cf. Kretschmayr, op. cit., I, 333.

8. Weber, *Wirtschaftsgeschichte,* p. 274.

having economic interest in the over-seas use of capital. The separation between a "large" (legislative) and "small" (administrative) council of *dignità* can be found in all patrician cities after 1187.

The political exclusion of the civic assembly of all landlords whose acclamation continued to be formally secured until the fourteenth century; the nomination of the doge by a small electoral college of nobles; the limitation of the selection of officials to families eligible for participation in the council; the formal closure of the citizen's lists (carried out from 1297 to 1315; the so-called Golden Book) were to be sure major events in Venetian history but for the standpoint here represent only a continuation of developments the details of which are of no interest.

The clear predominance in Venice of families participating in trans-oceanic political and economic opportunities facilitated the monopolization of power in patrician hands. The constitutional and administrative techniques of Venice are famous, for under strict control of noble families a patrimonial state-tyranny by the patriciate was developed which extended over a large continental and maritime area. The discipline of the patricians was unshaken for like the Spartans, they held the entire means of power under a more strictly preserved official secrecy than can be found anywhere else. In the beginning this was explained by the solidarity of internal and external interests of the patricians made evident daily to every member interested in the huge monopolistic gains of the association. This solidarity forced the obedience of the members under the collective tyranny. Technically this was accomplished through a number of devices: 1. through competitive separation of powers; 2. through competitive division of work; 3. through short time appointments to office, and 4. through a system of controls. Competing official authorities were instituted in the central offices and nearly all the different boards in the specialized administration were simultaneously furnished with jurisdictional and administrative power. Thus they were largely forced to compete for competency. This was reinforced by the division of work between officials recruited from the nobility. Different officials were in charge of jurisdictional, military and financial administration. Moreover, in addition to making appointment to office of a short term, since the fourteenth century a political court of inquisition "council of the ten" was established. While it was originally organized to review

individual cases of conspiracy it became a permanent office for the
investigation of political offences and, eventually, the watchdog
over the entire political and personal behavior of the nobility.
Frequently it even annulled decisions of the "great council." It
held a kind of tribunal power. Its mode of execution in quick,
secret procedure secured its paramount authority in the community.
A terror to the nobility, it was by all odds the most popular office
with the subjects who, being excluded from political power, were
provided in the "council of ten" with their only effective channel
for successful complaint against noble officials. In this respect it
was much more effective than the Roman jury trial.[9]

The monopolization of power in Venice represents an especially
pure and extreme case of patrician civic development. Its influence
diffused over the entire Italian continent and since it was increasingly maintained by mercenaries in favor of the commune it was,
thus, in favor of the patriciate. However, from the beginning it was
accompanied by another phenomenon. Even apart from the pay for
the troops and replacement of the fleet and war materials, the
mounting expenses of the communities had led to their dependency
on the financing patriciate. It also led to a deep-going change in
the administration. In their struggles against the doge the patriciate found a peculiar occidental accomplice in a strengthened
church bureaucracy.

It was no accident that the weakening of the doge's power was
simultaneous with the separation of the state and church in the
course of the Investiture dispute. The Italian cities profited by the
separation, for until then the strongest support of patrimonial and
feudal elements was the power they had of establishing their own
churches *(Eigenkirchenrecht)*. Even in the twelfth century, churches
and cloisters replaced and made superfluous the secular power
apparatus by farming out the administration in foreign colonies. The
Investiture dispute changed all this for as a consequence of their
disengagement from political power, the churches and cloisters were
excluded from administration.

However, the political neutralization of the churches necessitated
the creation of salaried lay officials. At first this was only for foreign
colonies but this development was temporarily halted in Dandalo's
time. The system of short-term appointments was based not only on

9. Max Weber, *Rechtssozologie*, p. 465.

political considerations, but also on the desire to allow as many persons as possible to receive their turn for these appointments. The limitation of access to government to a stratum of nobles, the unbureaucratic and strictly collegiate administration of governing capital-cities, presented barriers to the emergence of a purely professional officialdom. This was inevitable from the character of a government by notables.

Patrician Development in Other Italian Communes

Even at the time of the rule of the nobility in Venice the development in other Italian communes took a different course. In Venice the monopolization and closure of the guild of urban nobles against newcomers was successful. At first acceptance of new families into the circle of those eligible for the "great council" occurred of course, only through decision of the nobility as to their political merit. Later even this was abandoned. Also in this connection the nobility excluded all feuds between its members as a device for mutual safety.

The need for external closure and internal pacification of the nobility was not felt with the same intensity outside Venice. Nowhere else was the monopolization of trans-oceanic commercial opportunities so critically central to the very existence of the nobility as a whole as well as to the economic standing of the individual noble. As a consequence of feuds raging everywhere within the ranks of the patriciate even in the period of their unbroken rule the nobility was forced to grant consideration to the remaining strata outside the dignitaries. Furthermore the feuds between the families and deep mutual distrust of the large clans for each other excluded the creation of a rational administrative structure in the Venetian manner.

Thus, for centuries in other communes families which were especially wealthy in land and clientele confronted each other with alliances of numerous less wealthy families. Such "parties" attempted to exclude the opposing families and their allies from the offices and economic opportunities of the city administration. When possible they excluded their rivals from the city. In a manner similar to Mecca at any given time at least one part of the nobility was decreed ineligible for office and perhaps even banned from the city itself. However, in contrast to Arabian courtesy, the nobles of the Italian communes often outlawed their opponents and subjected their property to sequestration until a sudden change of the political situation led to a reversal of political fates.

Interlocal interest-communities were a natural product of these practices. The formation of the parties of the Guelfs and Ghibellines however, was also partly due to imperial politics. In the large majority of cases the Ghibellines were sibs of old crown vassals or adherents of them. For the rest and more permanent part they were created by the class interest between competing cities, especially within cities with parties of nobilities interlocally organized. These interlocal parties, particularly that of the Guelfs, were substantial associations with statutes and matriculation fees. In the case of a levy imposed upon the knighthood of individual cities, this assumed the form of quotas similar to the German matriculations for the march against the Romans.

Although the trained knighthood was decisive for military activities, even in the period of patrician domination the non-military burgher had become indispensable for the financing of wars. Such non-military burghers were in the position of third parties occasionally able to secure advantage from the competition of the nobles. In Italy and in some bordering areas their interest in the rational administration of justice on the one hand and the mutual jealousy of noblemen's parties on the other permitted the peculiar emergence of a noble professional officialdom taking shape, so to speak, in the vacuum created by party competition. The administration of the *podesta* replaced the original controversial administration by "consuls" drawn from the local aristocracy and formally elected, but in fact monopolized by a few families.[10]

The origin of the *podesta* occurred in the very period of the most intense conflicts of the communes with the Staufic Emperors. These conflicts had intensified the need both for internal union of the city and for financial provision. The period of its greatest perfection fell in the first half of the thirteenth century. The *podesta* was usually appointed in a strife-torn community for a short time with

10. Though later meaning any magistrate, *"podesta"* initially had a special meaning in the Italian communes. The *podesta* was an administrator brought in from outside the city—neutral with respect to its party wars. He was a kind of arbitrator.

highest judicial powers. The institution has some of the properties of an emergency legislative investigator or perhaps better arbitrator. The *podesta* was an elected official with a fixed salary which was relatively high compared to that of the consuls. He was a nobleman elected by the counselors (aldermen, senators) or as was typical for the whole of Italy, a board of notables designated for that purpose. Often his appointment was negotiated with his home community which had to approve it and which was occasionally requested to designate a candidate for the post. The appointees themselves often demanded hostages as insurance of good treatment, bargained for conditions like a modern professor, and refused unattractive offers. The *podesta* had to bring along his knightly following and especially subsidiary persons consisting not only of subalterns but also of men versed in jurisprudence such as assistants and deputies. The *podesta* often brought his entire staff and had to cover their expenses from his own funds.

In compliance with the purpose of his appointment, the *podesta's* essential task was the maintenance of public safety and order, especially the peace of the city. While he only occasionally had charge of the military force he always had control of jurisprudence. He performed all his duties under the control of the council. His influence on legislation was limited. In principle not only was the *podesta* personally held responsible for his actions but so, too, intentionally, was the locality from which he was called. On the other hand, the communes supplying a *podesta* placed great importance on having their burgher officiate in as many outside positions as possible.[11] Hanauer rightly assumes that this was due to both political and economic reasons. High salaries secured away from home certainly constituted a valuable prebend of the local nobility. But perhaps the single most important property of the institution of the *podesta* is the emergence of a noble professional officialdom represented by it.

Hanauer[12] proves that for the fourth decade of the thirteenth century alone in sixteen out of sixty cities seventy persons occupied two, and twenty occupied half a dozen or more different positions of *podesta*. Frequently the *podesta* formed a life-long career. For

---

11. Placement of one of the nobles of a city as *podesta* elsewhere could have political and economic advantages.

12. G. Hanauer, *Das Berufspodestat im 13. Jahrhundert* (Publication of the Institute for Eastern Historical Research) Vol. 23 (1900).

the hundred years of their main significance, Hanauer estimates that there were 5,400 available positions as *podesta* in roughly 60 communes. On the other hand, there were noble families which continually had new candidates at their disposal. But the administrative significance of the *podesta* does not stop with the official, for in addition a large number of assistants had to be trained in law. Significant, too, is the fact that a part of the nobility was being trained for a purely objective administration strictly controlled by public opinion. Other incidental consequences emerge: in order that the administration of justice be made possible for a foreign *podesta*, the law had to be codified, rationally elaborated, and interlocally balanced. With a concern for principles the possibility emerged of an interlocal applicability of the law. In this case it led to rational codification of the law and especially to the propagation of Roman law.

Royal Restriction of Civic Oligarchy in England

The *podesta* was a phenomenon primarily limited to the Mediterranean area. Some parallels can be found in the North as, for instance, in Regensburg in 1334, when native burghers were excluded from the office of burgomaster and a foreign knight was appointed who was then succeeded in office only by other foreign burgomasters for a hundred years. This was a period of relative peace in a city formerly torn by family feuds, wars, and banished noblemen. However it was not typical of the North.

While in Venice, without discontinuity an urban nobility developed out of the rule of notables and while the rule of a patriciate spearheaded the development in the remaining Italian communes, the emergence of a closed city patriciate also occurred in the North but on a different foundation and from contrary motives. The development of the English civic oligarchy presents an extreme case.

The power of the king was especially important for English developments though this power did not confront the city as strongly in the beginning as later, not even after the Norman conquest. After the battle of Hastings, William the Conqueror did not try to take London by force. Knowing that for a long time possession of the city had been decisive for the English crown, he succeeded in winning the homage of the burghers through concessions and contracts with them. For although the bishop and "portreeve"[13] appointed by the king represented the legitimate authorities to which the Charter of the Conqueror made reference, the voice of the London patriciate carried a decisive weight in nearly every election of the Anglo-Saxon kings. The burghers even subscribed to the interpretation that without their voluntary consent the English king did not rule over the city. Even in Stephen's[14] time they met to ratify the kingship. However, immediately after swearing allegiance the conqueror built his tower in London. Thereafter the city like any other was in principle subject to tax obligations according to the conqueror's whim.

During the Norman period in England and as a result of the unification of the Empire the military importance of the cities declined. The period is characterized by the decline of threats from the outside and the rise of great feudal barons, who built their fortified castles outside the cities. By this practice the barons set in motion the process of separating feudal military power from the burghers in a pattern characteristic of the Occident outside Italy. In contrast to Italy English cities almost completely lost dominance over the countryside which they had possessed in the form of city marks. The cities were transformed into economic corporations. The barons, for their part, began to found cities by granting privileges which varied tremendously from case to case. But there are no reports from England of fights of urbanites against the king or against urban noblemen. Nor are there any reports of usurpations during which the castle of the king or some other urban noblemen was eliminated by force so that he was forced, as in Italy, to transfer it out of the city.

From England, furthermore, there are no reports of a town militia forced to fight the lord and compelling him to grant the right to autonomous jurisdiction with elected officials replacing the judges appointed by the king. Nor are there reports of charters won by cities and bodies of law codified. To be sure, special city courts arose in England by virtue of royal decrees which were able to grant the burghers a rational court procedure without duels. At

13. Highest magistrate of a port.
14. Stephen of Blois (-1154), succeeded by Henry II, Plantagenet.

times, such courts rejected the innovations of the royal trial, especially the jury. However the creation of law remained in the hands of the king and royal courts. The king granted a special judicial position in order to retain the city on his side against the power of the feudal nobility. To this extent the English cities, too, profited from the typical conflicts of the feudal period.

However, more important than the judicial privileges volunteered by the king was the autonomy won by the cities in fiscal administration, a fact confirming the superior position of the king. To the royal mind up to the time of the Tudors the city was important as an object of taxation. The privileges of the burghers the *gratia emendi et vendendi* and the traffic monopolies had their counterpart in the liability for taxation specific to the burghers. Since tax collection was farmed out the richest royal officials were, naturally, next to the burghers the most important entrepreneurial recipients of this rent. The burghers gradually succeeded in excluding their competitors, for a lump sum renting from the king the right to collect civic taxes *(firma burgi)*.[15] Moreover, by means of special payments and gifts they were able to secure further privileges, the most important being the election of the sheriff.

As will be seen later, despite parties with pronounced seignioral interests which repeatedly appear among the urbanites, purely economic and financial interests were decisive for the constitution of the English city. Indeed, the *conjuratio* of continental urbanites is also to be found in English cities, but it followed the formation-pattern of a monopolistic guild. Moreover, in England it does not appear universally, being absent, for example, from London. In numerous other cities the guild became decisive for union of the city because it guaranteed fiscal payments. Like the Richerzeche in Cologne the English guild often bestowed the civic rights. In *mediatized* cities the guild often secured its own jurisdiction over its members, but as guild members rather than burghers. Nearly everywhere the guild was actually, though not legally, the governing association of the city.

Here as in other areas the burghers were restricted to those who paid taxes to the king (duties for protection, guard and judicial service, and assessment). Not only was citizen status withheld

15. Max Weber, *Wirtschaft und Gesellschaft*, p. 799; Jul. Hatschek, *Englisches Staatsrecht*, I, 35.

from some urban residents but some classes of non-residents had civic rights. Adjoining land owners, the gentry, as a rule belonged to the burgher association. In twelfth century London nearly all large nobles, bishops, and officials of the countryside were members of the community and by virtue of their town houses they were residents. London, in fact, was the seat of the king and the authorities, a phenomenon parallel to the Roman Republic but also in plastic deviation from its circumstances. Any individual not in a position to assume the burden of taxes of citizenship, but who only paid royal taxes from time to time was excluded from the stratum of active burghers. So too, particularly, those persons without property were outside it. All privileges of the city rested on an arbitrarily interpreted royal or lordly endowment.

In one respect civic development in England took a quite different course from that of Italy. When the concept of the corporation was finally admitted into English law, the cities became privileged corporations within the estates system. The executives of this corporation possessed individual rights derived from acquisition of a special legal title in somewhat the same way that individual rights were appropriated as privileges by individuals and commercial corporations. There was a fluid transition from the privileged "company" to a guild or corporation. The special position of the burghers as a legal estate consisted of a bundle of privileges which they secured within the national federation of estates which was of semi-feudal and semi-patrimonial character. Citizenship did not flow from membership in a political alliance but was external to the association.

At first the cities were compulsory associations encumbered by liturgical obligations to the king, different from those of the villages. In numerous cities founded by the king and manorial lords an equality of rights and limited autonomy based on special privileges prevailed for resident burghers accoutred with landed property. The first private guilds were recognized through royal privileges and accepted as guarantees of financial responsibility. Eventually, the development was completed, with endowment of the city itself with the right to form a corporation.

London developed into an urban community in the continental sense. Henry I permitted the residents to elect their own sheriffs. Since the end of the twelfth century the commune as an association of burghers was recognized by King John and dealt with through its heads and mayor, who was elected like the sheriff and the *scabini* (jurymen). From the early thirteenth century the *scabini* were united with the same number of elected counselors to form a council. The farming of the sheriff's office for Middlesex by the commune established its dominion over the surrounding districts. By the fourteenth century the office of mayor of London bore the title of "lord."

Despite occasional beginnings toward formation of political communities the majority of remaining cities became compulsory associations with special privileges and carefully regulated autonomous corporate rights. The development of the guild will need to be discussed later, but it may be pointed out that the guilds did not alter the position of the cities. The king mediated the dispute as to whether the constitution of the guilds or of the notables would prevail. The cities continued to owe the tax assessment to the king until the development of the parliamentary estates established collective protection against arbitrary taxation. This was a protection which no city or combination of cities could have attained by their unaided power. Meanwhile the rights to active citizenship were hereditary for members of the corporation. In some associations it was possible to purchase membership. Though the difference was one primarily of degree rather than of kind, some peculiarities of English urban development arose from its peculiar law of corporations for the concept of the territorial corporation did not arise in England.

The special development of the English concept of corporation was anchored in the growth of the royal administration whose development was never interrupted and even further extended after the succession to the throne of the Tudors. The political integration of the country and the unity of its law rested on this power. One effect of the presence of an ever-mounting royal power was that economically and politically interested parties oriented themselves with respect to it rather than to the individual, closed, urban community. Economic opportunities, social advantages, and guaranteed monopolies as well as remedial action in case of infringements upon their privileges were expected from royal power rather than from the city.

On the other hand, the kings were financially in utter dependency on the privileged strata for the conduct of administration. They were afraid of these strata, hence, the political strategy of the king aimed at control of the central parliament. At bottom the kings tried to influence civic composition and the composition of individual urban councils only in the interest of parliamentary politics and by supporting the oligarchy of notables. For their part the urban notables expected from the central administration the guarantee of their monopolies against unprivileged strata.

In the absence of a central bureaucratic machinery and in consequence of the centralization of royal power, the kings were dependent on the collaboration of the notables. Hence the apparent paradox, in England the power of the burghers was established primarily for a negative reason rather than because of their own military power. The negative reason was the inability of feudal administration to maintain permanent dominion over the country without the constant support of economically powerful notables. Such notables, in turn, could be kept in check only by building up a counter-force.

In the Middle Ages military power of the large majority of English cities was comparatively unimportant. The financial power of urban burghers was another story. This financial power of the urbanites was manifest in the influence of an estate of privileged urbanites within the estates-system of "commons" in the parliament. Every economic interest found outside economic exploitation of local monopolies centered in it. Here, for the first time, an inter-local national estate of burghers appeared. The increasing power of this stratum in the ranks of the justices of peace and within parliament—their power in a state composed of estates of notables—obviated the growth of strong political independence movements in the individual communes. It also established the urban-commercial character of the English city oligarchy.

Thus, it was the inter-local rather than local interests of the burgher patricians that formed the basis for political unification. Roughly until the thirteenth century the development of English cities paralleled the German; after this they increasingly turned into a dominion of thé "gentry." This rule of notables in England was never again broken up in contrast to the relative democracy of continental cities. Offices such as those of aldermen originally based on yearly election were increasingly occupied for life. Such civic

offices were often distributed by co-optation or patronage of neighboring manorial lords. However for reasons already sketched the
kingly administration supported the oligarchy of landed aristocrats
in the dependent cities.

Dominance of the Political Patricians and Guilds
in Northern Europe

Civic development in Northern Europe was different from
that either of England or Italy. In this area the development of the
patriciate took its point of departure from differences in the economy and estates present at the time of origin of the burgher-
associations. This was also true for newly founded cities.

From the beginning the twenty-four *conjuratores* at Freiburg
were privileged financially and politically: they possessed tax immunities and were appointed as consuls. Yet in the majority of
newly founded cities as well as in many Northern maritime cities,
though the merchants naturally inclined toward a plutocracy, the
formal limitations upon qualification for the council were only
gradually brought about. The plutocracy was ensconced roughly
as follows. The objective need to keep experienced men in the
council and habituation to the practice of following the advice of
the council regarding its own succession led to the reduction of the
once-free nomination to co-optation. The council was surrendered
to a fixed circle of families. It should be remembered that such a
development can occur even under modern conditions. Despite
the suffrage of the burghers the supplementation of the senate in
Hamburg was about to take a similar course in recent times. The
details of the trend in Hamburg cannot be pursued here but, in
any case, similar tendencies have appeared everywhere. Only the
extent to which they were elaborated in a formal legal manner was
unique.

Families monopolizing eligibility for the council could easily
maintain this control so long as no strong opposition interests were
organized among the excluded burghers. However as soon as a
conflict of interests arose with the outsiders or as soon as the latter's
self-reliance, fostered by wealth and education and availability for
administrative work increased to a point where they could no longer

ideologically tolerate exclusion from power, the possibility of new city revolutions was at hand.

As soon as the situation in the Northern cities was ripe for further revolutionary movements once again sworn unions of citizens became their bearers. The guilds either supported these new revolutionary unions or were identical with them. In this connection it is important not to identify the term "guild" either exclusively or even primarily with the "guild of artisans." The movement against patrician families was by no means an action of artisans. The variable success of the guild revolutions could lead, in extreme cases, to a composition of the council exclusively of guild members. In this case citizenship itself was based on membership in a guild.

For the first time with the rise of guild rule was there general participation of the "burgher class," in the economic sense of the term, in civic administration. Wherever guild rule achieved genuine success the city correspondingly embarked on the highest development of its external power and the greatest achievement of its internal political independence.

The similarity of events here with the "democratic" development in the ancient city is obvious. Beginning in the seventh century B.C. most of the ancient cities of noblemen experienced the sudden rise to political and economic power of broad strata striving for democracy. Though the ancient polis arose from different foundations, similarities were present, but before examining these, it is useful to compare the ancient patrician city with the medieval one.

Charismatic Clans of Antiquity

At least in Troy and Mycenaea, the Mycenaean culture of the Greek motherland presumed a patrimonial kingship of oriental character though of lesser dimensions. The building programs they sustained, unprecedented up to the classical period, are inconceivable without the yoke of socage imposed upon the subjects. An administration employing its own written script for calculations and keeping a registry in Egyptian manner, thrived on the frontiers of the Hellenic cultural area from the Orient to Cyprus. It was a commercial and warehouse administration with patrimonial and bureaucratic features. In contrast to it, later, still in the classical period of Athens, administration was conducted almost completely verbally without writing. The writing system, in fact, the entire socage-based culture disappeared without a trace.

The ship passenger lists of the Iliad contain the names of hereditary kings who rule over large areas. Such areas include numerous localities later known as cities but which might well have simply been castles. The disposition of rulers over such "civic" localities is shown by Agamemnon who was prepared to give one to Achilles as a fief. Their structure is partly illustrated by Troy where old men from noble houses exempt from military service because of their age acted as advisors to the king. From the same source the structure of administration is indicated, for in Troy Hector was war king while Priam had to be fetched even for the contracting of treaties. Only one document is mentioned which may have been written. Otherwise every circumstance excludes the possibility that administration rested on socage and a patrimonial kingship.

Kingship rested on clan charisma.[16] However, Aeneas, a foreigner to the city, was promised the office of Priam if he would kill Achilles. Kingship was conceived as an office-like "honor" rather than as a possession. The king was leader of the army, participating with the nobles in the court. Since he was equipped with the kingdom he was thought to be representative to the gods and human beings. However the degree to which his right to lead is an affair of personal charisma is shown by the Odyssey where the power of the king is repeatedly attributed to personal influence rather than orderly authority.

---

16. The concept of "charisma" was taken by Weber from the vocabulary of early Christianity where it referred to a "gift of Grace." It was used first by Rudolf Sohm in his *Kirchenrecht*. It refers to the ground for leadership, the basis of authority. Authority is charismatic when it rests on devotion to the specific and exceptional sanctity, heroism or exemplary character of an individual person and of the normative patterns or order revealed or ordained by him. For continuing social order a critical problem lies in maintenance of social order beyond the death (or loss of charisma) of the charismatic leader. One form of securing continuing order occurs through the reassignment of charisma from the individual to the structure in which he operates. If this structure is a clan and charisma is assigned to the individual by virtue of his headship of the clan one may speak of "clan charisma" or, as Weber frequently does "gentile charisma" (charisma of the gens). See Max Weber, trans. by A. M. Henderson and Talcott Parsons, *The Theory of Social and Economic Organization* (New York: Oxford University Press, 1947) p. 328.

Also at this period of Greek history oversea military expeditions have the character of follower-like adventures rather than conscriptions. The comrades were even called *hetairoi* in the manner of the armies of the Macedonian kings. In fact, as Odysseus illustrates, the absence of the king for many years was no source of serious upset. While Odysseus was away in Ithaca there was no king at all. Odysseus trusted his house to a mentor with no connection with the kingship. The actual warfare of the army of knights consisted in the individual combat of warrior heroes with ordinary foot soldiers playing a minor role.

In some parts of the Homeric poems the urban political market is mentioned, though the *Ismaros* of the polis could mean "castle." But in any case it is not the castle of an individual but of the *Kikones*. In the market elders of the notable families qualifying by wealth and military power, sat on Achillies' shield and held court. The people in attendance responded to the speeches of the parties with applause. In the market the complaint of Telemachus was an object of discussion by the militarily eligible notables. The discussion was regulated by a herald. The circumstances show that land and shipowners were present who with the king and noblemen went to war in their chariots. King Laertes' withdrawal to his estates is tantamount to his retirement.

As among the Germans, the sons of aristocratic sibs join as follower-adventurers *(hetairoi)* of the hero, in the *Odyssey* of the prince. Among the Phäaken[17] the nobility claimed the right to compel the people to contribute to the expense of hospitality gifts. Free peasants are never mentioned but it is also true that nowhere is it maintained that all residents of the flat country were regarded as copyholders or vassals of the urban noblemen.[18] The case of Theresites proves that even the common conscript who does not go to war in a chariot occasionally dares to speak up against the lord. This, to be sure, was taken as rank insolence.

The king's function as war leader is clear enough, but he also performs domestic chores. He builds his own bed and ditches his garden. His war comrades steer the boat themselves. On the other hand the purchased slave may hope to obtain a *"kleros."* As yet

---

17. *Odyssey* 6. 259, 293.

18. This is quite true for the Homeric poems. It should be noted, however, that *Hesiod* (8th century B.C.) would provide the evidence for such a free peasantry.

there was no difference between purchased slaves and clients receiving the lease of land, a distinction very pronounced later in Rome. A patrimonial household economy satisfies all wants. The Greeks used their own ships for piracy. The trade of the time was pacific, but it was still in the hand of the Phoenicians. In addition to the market and urban residence of the nobility two other important phenomena were to be found. The *agones* (contest) which later dominated the whole range of life arose from the knightly concept of honor and military teaching of the young on the drill ground. Its external organization appears in the funeral cult of war-heroes (Patrocles). Already in Homeric times it dominated the style of life of the nobility. The second major phenomenon of the time is the appearance, despite the deistic demonology of the time, of completely unrestrained relationship to the gods. The poetic licence practiced toward the gods in the Homeric epics was painful to Plato later. Such secularity could only arise in consequence of migrations, especially trans-oceanic migrations during which there was no chance to live with old temples and graves. Thus influences from an early period continue along with others arising later. This also appears in other things. For example, while the noble cavalry of the historic patrician polis is absent from the Homeric poems, the combat of hoplites, arising later with the disciplined organization of common soldiers in rank and file, is conspicuously mentioned. Thus, widely differing periods left their imprint on the poems.

Apart from the case of Sparta and a few others, in the classical Greek period kingship resting on clan charisma remains only in fragments and reminiscences. When it does appear it is always in the form of a kingship over an individual polis. As a form of clan charisma it is equipped with sacred authority. However, excepting for the Spartan and Roman traditions only honorary privileges remain to the charismatic clan kingship as against the nobility. In fact, the nobles are sometimes described as kings.

The Greek examples show that the king owes this power to his horde of treasure gathered in middle-man trade either by trading himself, imposing controls, or granting protection to such trade in return for monetary fees. Knightly warfare prevailing at the time rested on the military independence of the nobles who maintained their own chariots, ships and followers. It shattered the war monopoly of the kings. In the period following the time of the large oriental empires, Egyptian as well as large Hethitic (Canaanite) imperial concentrations of power were disintegrating, while other later empires such as the Lydian were as yet non-existent. Thus the kind of political configuration which the Mycenaean represents in miniature, the state of the Oriental kings resting on trade monopolies and socage services, broke down. The collapse of the economic foundations of royal power prepared the ancient world for the so-called Doric migrations by providing prosperous but militarily weak social aggregations which "invited" pillage. At this time the migrations of militaristic sailor-knights began to the coasts of Asia Minor. Homer did not yet conceive the possibility of such settlements since during his time strong political associations did not exist on the Asiatic coast. However the entry of the Hellenes into active trade had already begun.

The Ancient Patrician City as a
Coastal Settlement of Warriors

From early historical writings the structure of the typical patrician city of antiquity may be discerned. It was fundamentally a coastal city. Until the time of Alexander and the Wars with the Samnites[19] no polis was further removed than a day's journey from the sea. Outside the area of the polis, life was organized in villages "koroi" with labial political associations of tribes "ethne." By its own initiative or by enemies a polis could be disbanded whereupon it was said to have been "dioikoized" into villages. On the other hand the process of synoecism was the real or fictitious basis of the city. Such synoecism consisted in the "joint settlement" of noble families in or around a fortified castle as a result either of royal command or agreement.

Such compulsory or voluntary settlements were also known in the Middle Ages. Moreover it was not absolutely essential for families to settle into the new combinations on a permanent basis. Like the medieval families, those in antiquity continued to reside in part in country castles (as for example in Eleusis) separate from the urban residence. As a rule the families of notables possessed at least

---

19. Samnium was an ancient country of central Italy whose people were allied to the Sabines. The Samnite Wars were wars between the Romans and Samnites 343-290 B.C.

villas in the country. Dekeleia, for example, was the castle of a noble family. Many of the Attic villages and some of the Roman *tribes* were named after castles. The areas of the gods were divided into towers.

Nevertheless, despite these ties to the countryside the point of gravity of the nobility was in the city. The lords of the manor, financiers of trade, and creditors of the peasantry, the political and economic masters of the country constituted the *astoi*,[20] the noble families residing in cities. Moreover, the actual resettlement of the country nobility in the city was progressive. In the classical period the castles of the country were dismantled. The necropolis (cemetery) of the notable families was always in the city.

According to one interpretation, the most essential element in the constitution of the polis was the fraternization of noble families in a cultic community.[21] In institutional terms, the formation of the city into a new cultic community took the form of the replacement of the *prytaneum*[22] of individual families by a joint *prytaneum* of the city in which members took their meals jointly. In antiquity this did not imply as in the Middle Ages, that the *conjuratio* of the burghers adopted a saint for the city when it became a commune, but more importantly it implied the origin of a new local commensal (table or meal) community. The common church which everyone in the Middle Ages joined was absent. To be sure, in addition to local deities there were always gods revered on an interlocal basis, however the cult of the individual clans excluded outsiders as one of the most fixed everyday cult forms impeding fraternization in the name of an interlocal god. This was reversed in the Middle Ages.

The cultic table-community of the ancient patrician city was almost as severely restricted as to membership as the cults of India.

20. Max Weber, *Gesammelte Aufsätze zur Sozial-und Wirtschaftsgeschichte* (1924), pp. 116, 122, 217.

21. This idea is the central contribution of the study of Fustel de Coulanges, *The Ancient City* (Garden City: Doubleday Anchor Books, 1956). The critical element in the formation of the ancient city was found to be the invention of a new more comprehensive religious structure permitting and confirming the confederation of existing social elements into the new unity of the city.

22. In ancient Greek states and cities the *prytaneum* was a public hall housing the official community hearth. The *prytaneum* of Athens, for example, was the place where the hospitality of the city was extended to honored citizens and ambassadors.

Only in the absence of magical taboo-barriers was fraternization possible. But the enduring principle remained that *only* from members of the clan would the clan spirits accept sacrifices. The principle also applied to associations. From the early period to later times in classical Greece the phyles and phratries represented associations, membership in which qualified the individual to be a member of the city. They were fraternal religious associations resting on the cultic union of the polis.

There is no doubt that the phratries reach back to the remote periods of the polis. Later they became cultic associations retaining only residues of their ancient functions. In Athens, for example, they retained control over judgments of qualification of children for war service and the related capacity for inheritance. They must originally have been military associations corresponding to the "men's house" or "warrior barracks."[23] The name of the phratry *(Andreion)* was preserved in the Doric warrior states and in Rome *(curia* equals *coviria)* for the sub-division of the military community whose association helped form the polis. Community meals *(syssitia)* or the military mess of the Spartiates, the segregation of qualified warriors from their families for the duration of their entire military service, and communal warrior-asceticism of the boys in military training were aspects of the general type of education received by companies of young men in the original warrior associations. Except for a few Doric associations radical semi-communistic militarism was not preserved in historical times. Even in Sparta itself the rough execution of communistic militarism only occurred with the destruction of the nobility and military expansion of the Spartan *demos* which made it necessary to secure the discipline and status equality of all warriors. By contrast in other cities the normal phratries of the noble class *(gene oikoi)* were alone in possession of the right to rule (the documents of the *Demotioniden* prove this for the old clan having its castle in Decelea). In Athens it was still

---

23. Students of contemporary ethnology and of pre-history have reported the appearance of an association or secret society of the qualified warriors of the tribe from areas as remote as heroic Greece and contemporary Polynesia and Melanesia. Such a secret warrior society has almost always had its barracks or club house magically off-limits to all women and carefully guarding its magically qualifying warrior rituals which have at times included head hunting and magical cannibalism. Because of his conception of the role of power, including military power, for social organization, Max Weber repeatedly took it into account in his sociological studies.

true in the Draconian code[24] that the "ten best men" of the phratry, that is the most powerful ones because of their wealth, were designated to undertake the vendetta.

In later urban constitutions the phratries are dealt with as subdivisions of the *phyles* (of the three old *tribes* in Rome) into which the ordinary Hellenic city was divided. The term "phyle" is technically associated with the polis; the word for "tribe" is *Ethnos*. The tribe did not persist as a subdivision in the city. In historical times the phyles become artificial divisions of the polis created for the purpose of alternating public service,[25] structuring elections and occupancy of office as well as providing a basis for the organization of the army and distribution of revenues from public property or booty and conquered countries (like the booty from the destruction of Rhodes).

The three typical phyles of the Dorians were artificially created as indicated by the very name of the third, Pamphyles corresponding to the Roman tradition of the *tribe* of the Luceres. Originally the phyles may have arisen out of compromise social arrangements between resident urban warriors and others entering the city by conquest. This may possibly be the source of the two Spartan royal families which had unequal ranks, corresponding to the Roman tradition of the original dual kingship. In any case, the phyles were originally personal rather than territorial associations. The chieftains, "kings of the phyles" were hereditary leaders by virtue of clan charisma, becoming elective later.

Every participant in the army of the polis was a member of the phyles and phratries, *tribes* and *curia*, in the capacity of active or passive citizens. Only the nobles were active citizens participating in the offices of the city. At times, thus, the designation of urban burgher is identical with "tribal comrade." Without doubt membership in the nobility was originally tied to the clan charisma of the office of district chief. With the advent of chariot warfare and castle construction "nobility" became a property of the knights. Under the kingship the rise of the new aristocracies must have been

---

24. Draco was an Athenian legislator commissioned with the task of codifying the laws (about 621 B.C.) to meet the exigences of politico-economic *crisis*. The code of laws was noted for its rigidity.

25. In Athens each division held office for five weeks. As were all rationally created social divisions in the early period the phyles were cultic associations.

as much facilitated by the conversion of bearers of the life-style of the knights into a stratum of fief holders as was true in the Middle Ages.

A significant feature of the period was the fact that only a member of the patriciate *(Patricius, Eupatride)* was qualified as a priest or official to communicate with the gods of the polis by sacrifice or consulting the oracle *(auspicia)*. Corresponding to its extra-urban origin the patriciate had its own gods differing from those of the polis; the private cults of the patricians were located at their ancestral seats. In addition to clan charisma, priesthood also appeared. In contrast to almost the whole of Asia there was no priestly monopoly of communication with the gods. Urban officials were also authorized to do so. Also aside from a few small interlocal sanctuaries like Delphi, the priesthood was not independent of the polis, but priests were appointed by the polis.

No independent hierarchy had control of the Delphic priesthood. At first it was under the disposition of a neighboring polis. After the destruction of this polis in the course of holy wars several neighboring communities united to form an Amphictyony which assumed control of Delphi. The political and economic power of the large temples, which were landlords, owners of *ergasteria*, money lenders to private persons and to states, and bankers holding the military chest in deposit and serving as deposit banks in general—did not change the fact that the polis was and became, in fact, ever more complete master over the property of the gods and benefices of the priests in the Hellenic mother country. In the colonies the power of the polis in religious concerns was complete.

In Hellas the final consequence of the dominance of religion by the polis was the auction of priestly offices as a device for staffing them. The rule of the military nobility was decisive for this development which was completed through democracy. The priesthood and holy laws and magic norms of all kinds were instruments of power in the hands of the nobility. As in Venice the nobility of the polis was not necessarily closed. A few burgraves with their clients *(gens Claudia)* moved into the cities in small groups like the *gentes minores* in Rome, though this was more frequent in the early period. The nobility was not a purely local territorially-based community. Even in the classical period Attic noblemen such as Miltiades possessed large foreign dominions. As in the Middle Ages interlocal relations existed within these strata. By nature the property of the nobility was predominantly seignorial. The services of slaves, bondsmen and clients, to be discussed later, supplied its economic basis. With the disappearance of bondage and clientage property remained only as agricultural real estate.

Parallels appear between the Greek patriciate and that of other places and times. In Babylonia for example the patriciate faced a situation similar to the Greek disappearance of bondage and clientage when the property of Babylonian trade-houses (Egibi) was distributed as the documents indicate, after existing for many generations. There, too, urban and rural landed-property, slaves, and cattle were registered as main assets. In Babylonia, in the Middle Ages and in Holland the source of the economic power of the typical urban nobility was a direct and indirect product of trade and shipping. In most of these areas and in others qualification for trade and shipping was accepted as in accord with patrician status. It was generally true in Rome, being forbidden only for the senators. In Rome as in the Orient and in Europe in the Middle Ages, urban residence was sought precisely for sake of its economic opportunities.

Moreover in most areas and times with the accumulated wealth won from urban economic activities, the patricians practiced usury against rural freeholders who did not participate in political power. Enormous debt servitude and the best rent-producing land (the Attic *pedia*) accumulated in the hands of the *astoi* in contrast to the hill-sides (the location of the *Diakrier*)[26] occupied by farmers not producing wealth. To a large extent the seignorial power of the patriciate originated in such urban economic chances. Except for the old bondsmen produced by seignorial and bondage rights, the indebted peasants were either utilized as semi-serfs or taken directly into villein service. The slave market grew in importance. Indeed nowhere, not even in Rome, did the free peasants completely disappear from the patrician state. In Antiquity they were perhaps even more numerous than in the Middle Ages. The tradition of the Roman wars of the estates indicates that the status of the free peasants did not rest upon seignorial right but on a quite different incompatible basis.

26. Max Weber, *Gesammelte Aufsätze zur Sozial-und Wirtschaftsgeschichte*, pp. 134, 152.

Free holders *(Agroikos, perioeci, plebs)* not belonging by blood
or military training to resident urban nobles were at the noble's
mercy because of their exclusion from political power and because
of the severity of the law concerning debts. Also exclusion from
political power carried with it exclusion from active participation
in the strictly regulated and limited administration of law. Thus
the free holder could obtain legal rights only by giving presents to
or entering into client relationship with a nobleman. At the same
time the peasant of the patrician city had considerable inter-local
freedom to choose a domicile and obtain land as the case of Hesiod's
family shows. This was in sharp contrast to the later hoplite-based
city and even more so to radical democracy. Free resident urban
artisans and merchants not belonging to the nobility were in a situation similar to the "Muntmannen" of the Middle Ages. As long as
he had power the Roman king seems to have been a patron to
them like the patrician of the early Middle Ages. At times traces of
liturgical organizations of artisans appear. Perhaps the Roman military artisan-centuries have this origin. This cannot be determined.
Nor can it be determined whether the artisans were organized as
guest-tribes as was regularly the case in Asia and in Israel before
the exile, but in any case, there is no evidence of a ritualistic separation in the manner of the Indian castes.

Contrasts with the Medieval City

Even in a purely external sense the stereotyped numbers of
phyles, phratries and noble families in the structure of the patrician
city of Antiquity appears in contrast to that of the patrician city
of the Middle Ages. This is underlined by the fact that they primarily formed military and religious divisions. Such divisions are explained by the fact that the ancient city was primarily a warrior
community and in that respect similar to the *Hundertschaft* of the
Teutons. Such military associations constituted the very foundations
of the ancient city, explaining its structural difference from the
medieval patrician city.

There were also differences in the surrounding world out of
which the properties of the ancient patrician structure arose. The
medieval patrician city arose within large patrimonial continental
empires and in opposition to their political power. The patrician

cities of Antiquity arose on the sea coast in the neighborhood of peasants and barbarians. In the one instance the patrician city sprang from city-kingship; in the other, from a feudal-dominated or episcopal city.

Despite such differences formal similarities also appeared whenever political conditions were similar. It has been seen how the Venetian principality which was dynastic and patrimonial was formally transformed through the prohibition of nominating a coregent and the transformation of the office of doge into the head of the corporation of notables. Outwardly this corresponds to the transformation of the city kingships of Antiquity into a yearly municipal council. The original importance of the nomination of a co-regent, which was strongly emphasized by Mommsen[27] is evidenced by a number of things: (1) the role played by the *interrex*[28] in Rome; (2) the residues of former nomination of successors and colleagues which implied the nomination of the dictator by the council as a preliminary condition for their legal installment and co-optation, the admission of candidates and creation of new officials by the old ones; (3) the original restriction of the role of the Roman community in political affairs to acclamation; (4) the election only of those candidates proposed or (later) admitted by the magistrate.

The transition of the Hellenic city kingship to a yearly municipal council under the control of the nobility deviates more extensively from the Venetian development than did the course of events in Rome. Again city constitution outside Venice in the Middle Ages shows important deviations from Venice. Basically, thus, the patrician city comprises a range of phenomena which vary around a common core.

In Greece the patrician nobility replaced the Homeric council of the aged who were unfit for military service. The new council was often composed of the heads of clans. Examples are found in the patrician senate of the early Roman period and the Spartan

---

27. Theodor Mommsen, *The History of Rome* (Glencoe: Free Press, 1957); *Corpus inscriptionum latinarum* (15 vols. Berlin: 1863-1932); *Römisches Staatsrecht* (3 vols. Leipzig: 1871-88).

28. Persons holding supreme authority during an interregnum.

council of *gerōchoi*[29] (gerontes). This gerontic council was not simply a council of old men but of noblemen entitled to honorific presents from their clients. Still another example of patrician organs is the Attic council of the prytan.[30] The equivalent body was elected by clans in Naucratis. Corresponding situations appear in the Middle Ages without the consistent schematism produced by the sacred character of the clans.

The administrative organ of the patrician city could also be a council of former officials like the Areopagus and the Roman senate of historical times. The Areopagus and historical Roman Senate have only modest parallels in the Middle Ages where, at times, former burgomasters and counselors are admitted to a kind of honorary membership to meetings of the council. Again the military as well as sacred character of ancient magistry gave its administration a more enduring impact than the offices of the Middle Ages. There were always a few noble families in mutual rivalry, but also, at times a single family like the Bacchiadae in Corinth[31] at times held power and simply rotated the offices among its members. As in all government by notables including that of the Middle Ages the number of officials of the clan-based polis remained small. Where the nobility persisted over time as in Rome this remained true.

Once the patriciate had developed, other similarities emerge between those of the Middle Ages and Antiquity. Feuds between the clans, the exile of defeated clans and their counter-attack in force, wars of resident knights of the city against each other (as in the example of the Lacedaemonian war in Antiquity) all make their appearance. In both periods the countryside was outside the law. Whenever they could the cities of the Middle Ages and Antiquity took other cities under clientage. The cities of the *perioeci*,[32] the localities of the Aratites later under the rule of Harmodius, and numerous communities subject to Athens and Rome find their parallel in the Venetian *terra firma* and the cities subjugated by Florence, Genoa, and others. Such satellite cities were subject to the mother city and administered by its officials.

---

29. Gerontocracy—a governing body of old men.
30. Council or senate supplied by one of the ten sections of Athens during the presidency of that section. Such a section presided for five weeks.
31. The Bacchiadae was a ruling family of Corinth from 926-657 B.C.
32. "Dwellers around," inhabitants of the countryside, in Sparta.

The Economic Structure of the Patrician City

Economically the clans of Antiquity and the Middle Ages formed self-sufficient units living by independent means. In both periods knightly style of life and not descent alone decided membership in the clan. The medieval clans comprised families of former government officials and, in Italy, free vassals, knights, and land owners who had accumulated sufficient wealth to maintain a knightly style of life. In Germany and Italy some of the clans had castles outside the city. When battles broke out with the guilds they withdrew to their country castles from which for long periods they attacked the cities which had expelled them. The best known example is the clan of the Auer in Regensburg.

In Italy strata observing a knightly style of life within the feudal or ministerial association were known as "magnates" and "nobili" proper. Later, when the guilds took over civic government, knightly families without castles were largely forced to remain in the city and submit to the new government and even take up military service against the magnates. There were two possible lines of development from here. Either non-knightly families could gain entrance into the nobility by purchase and transfer of their residence outside the city or noble families could undertake mercantile activities on their own on a capitalistic basis, abandoning their mode of life as rentiers. Both alternatives were taken. However, on the whole, the first tendency dominated since it implied the social ascent of the family.

In the Middle Ages when cities were newly founded by political or manorial lords no knightly families joined these settlements. They were, thus, directly excluded when the struggle of the guilds against the nobility occurred. The further East and North one goes the more frequent was this phenomenon on economically virgin land. In Sweden foreign-born German merchants participated in the founding and military staffing of cities. This also occurred in Novgorod and was generally frequent in the East. In the early civic period in this area the patriciate and mercantile class are really identical. Their importance will be discussed later.

Circumstances were quite different in the old cities which tended to develop a strata of persons living from their independent means as nobles and exercising leadership over the patrician clubs. However, it should be noted that even in Antiquity a real mercantile patriciate can be found especially on colonial territory as in cities like Epidamnus.[33] Thus the economic quality of the patriciate was fluid and can be characterized only in terms of the point around which it gravitated. This point of gravity was rentiership.

It cannot be too often re-iterated that the urban residence of the nobility had its economic cause in urban economic opportunities. The exploitations of these opportunities in every case produced the power of the patriciate. Neither the ancient Eupatride patrician nor the medieval patrician was a merchant. Nor was he a wholesale merchant in terms of the modern concept of the merchant as an entrepreneur in charge of a counting house. To be sure he was quite often a partner in such enterprises, but in the capacity of ship-owner or one who holds a benefice in commendam.[34] At times the patrician participates in an enterprise as a silent partner or money lender for risks at sea, leaving the actual work to others such as the voyage and carrying out negotiations. The patrician is in partnership only with respect to risks and the profit though he may at times enter as a casual merchant in the intellectual management of the enterprise.

All important forms of business of early Antiquity and the early Middle Ages, especially the *commenda* and sea-loan were tailored to the existence of such money-lenders. They invested their wealth in concrete individual enterprises and usually in numerous ones to distribute risks. Each enterprise was carried on a separate account. Every imaginable transition can be found from the patrician to pure business man. The traveling merchant receiving money on the basis of limited liability *(commenda* capital) from the capitalist for occasional enterprises, could use his gains to become manager of a large house operating with capital obtained for limited liability and which had its own foreign agencies.

The blurring of the lines between noble and merchant was certainly a developmental product of particular importance. It entered the picture with special frequency in the period of guild rule when the nobility was forced to join the guilds in order to participate

---

33. A colony of the Corcyraens.

34. A benefice in commendam is a fief or estate or other economic opportunity granted by a feudal superior. When held in commendam it is held until the appointment of the regular intendent.

in city administration while the burgher remained a guild member even though he was no longer an active entrepreneur. The name *"scioperati"* for the great merchants' guilds in Italy emphasizes this point. This was also especially typical of large English cities, particularly London. The struggle for self-government by the productive burghers who were organized into guilds appears in the opposition to the election procedure for community representatives and officials. As long as election procedure was in the hands of local city districts (wards) and their representatives the power position of the resident urban nobility prevailed. The struggle increasingly led to the attempt to shift election procedure into the hands of the guilds (liveries). The increasing power of the guilds is shown by the growing dependency of all civil rights on membership in the professional associations. Finally, Edward II established guild membership as the basic principle determining London citizenship. The election of the communal council was carried out according to city wards until 1351 and re-introduced several times (1383) but finally abandoned in favor of election by guilds.

However with compulsory guild membership for every burgher —King Edward II became a member of the Linen Armourers (merchant tailors)—the importance of the active merchants and tradesmen continued to decline in favor of the rentier. Inevitably and with characteristic irony as the guilds become the sole avenue to civic power forces formerly outside the guilds penetrate them and transformed them from within. Theoretically membership in the guild was acquired only through apprenticeship and initiation. Actually membership was increasingly obtained through inheritance and purchase. With few exceptions the relationship of the guilds to their nominal business was reduced to fragments. Economic and social tensions split the guilds apart as the guild was transformed into a purely electoral association of gentlemen with access to communal offices.

As is true of all sociological phenomena patrician types everywhere show great fluidity, a fact that should not prevent ascertainment of the typical elements. Both in Antiquity and the Middle ages the point of gravity for the patrician was not found in activity as a professional entrepreneur but as a rentier and casual entrepreneur. In the statutes of the cities on the Upper Rhine the expression "venerable idler" was the official designation for members of the gentleman's chamber in contrast to the guilds. In Florence the large merchants of the *arte di Calimata* and the bankers were members of the guild rather than the nobility.

In Antiquity the exclusion of entrepreneurs from the nobility was a matter of course. However, this did not mean that, for example, the Roman Senators did not include any capitalists. In early antiquity patricians including old Roman patricians acted as capitalistic money-lenders to the peasants. Later senatorial clans served as money lenders for political subjects. Nevertheless in ancient and medieval cities families considered to be noble were forbidden the role of entrepreneur.

Because of a circumscribed status etiquette which was occasionally legal, the kinds of investments made by the patricians varied greatly but the contrast to those of the true entrepreneur remained. Whoever too noticeably crossed the line separating the two forms of economic behavior, property investment and capital profit, forthwith became a philistine in Antiquity—he identified himself as a man without knightly manners in the Middle Ages. Inasmuch as the old knightly families sat with the guilds-men on the same bench in the council, thus physically with entrepreneurs, they were denied equal rank with the landed gentry in the later Middle Ages. Practically it was not "greed for gain" as a psychological motive that was prohibited. The Roman nobility and medieval families were as eager for gain as any other historic class. Rather the rational business-like form of economic procedure or systematic economic activity identify the class as burgher like. If the Florentine *Ordinamenti della giustizia* through which the rule of the nobility should have been broken up were consulted as to the identifying properties of a family belonging to the *nobili* (in terms of which it lost its political rights) the answer would be: All families to which knights belong are to be identified by an aristocratic style of life. This was also the kind of life style that in Antiquity brought about exclusion of candidates from manufacturing.

According to Machiavelli the effect of the Florentine *ordinamenti* was to force those noblemen who wished to remain in the city to accommodate themselves to the life styles of the burghers. A knightly life conduct was, thus, still the primary "status" characteristic of the patriciate. Descent from a family once occupying offices and possessing honors was a political property important for the formation of the charismatic nobility. Such descent claims were conceived as evidence of office competence. This was true for the sherif families in Mecca, for the Roman nobility, and the families of tribunes in Venice. Restrictions on access to office varied in elasticity. They were less rigid in Venice than in Rome, where the *homo novus* was not formally excluded from office. However when ascertaining eligibility of a person for council an office investigation sought to ascertain whether a member of his family formerly occupied a seat in the council or one of its offices. The Florentine *ordinamenti* sought to determine whether a knight appeared among the ancestors of the family of an office candidate. With increasing population and the growing importance of a monopoly of the civic offices the exclusiveness of the estates increased.

References have been repeatedly made in the previous pages to a period during which the old charismatic noble clans lost their legally privileged positions and were forced to share or completely yield power to the *demos* of Greece, to the *plebs* of Rome, to the *popolo* of Italy, to the *liveries* of England, and the *guilds* of Germany. So far as the patriciate was to retain power it had to occupy the same status. It is to this series of events we must now turn.

Chapter 4

The Plebeian City

The Revolutionary Nature of the "Popolo" as a Political Association

THE MANNER in which the rule of patrician families was shattered shows strong parallels in the Middle Ages and Antiquity. These parallels are especially close if the large Italian cities are taken as characteristic for the Middle Ages, where the destruction of the patriciate was a development flowing from its own intrinsic nature—that is, it occurred without the interference of nonurban powers. In Italian cities after the origin of the *podesta* the next decisive stage in urban development was the emergence of the *popolo*.

Like the German guilds the *popolo* was economically composed of varied elements ranging from artisans to entrepreneurs. Initially the entrepreneurs led the fight against the noble families. While the entrepreneurs created and financed the sworn fraternities against the nobility the artisans' guilds provided the necessary manpower for battle. Once the revolution had succeeded the guild often established its own representative at the head of the commune to consolidate its gains. After the recalcitrant nobility had been exiled, Zürich (in 1335) was ruled by the knight Rudolf Brun and a council consisting of equal representatives of the remaining knights and constables, guilds of entrepreneurs, salt and cloth merchants, goldsmiths, and small tradesmen. The burghers of Zürich had consoli-

dated into so solid a unity that they were able to withstand the
siege of the Imperial Army.

In Germany the sworn confederation of guildsmen was ordinarily a temporary phenomenon. The city constitution was either
transformed by the reception of the guild representatives into the
council or by the absorption of the burghers including the nobility
into the guild. The sworn confederation assumed permanent guild
form only in some cities of Lower Germany and the Baltic region.
However, even here it was of secondary importance compared to
the professional association as shown by the composition of its board
which was made up of the guild masters of separate associations.
In Münster in the fifteenth century no one could be imprisoned
without approval of the guild. The guild could, thus, function as
a protective association against legal actions of the council. Furthermore, the council was assisted administratively by guild representatives either in all or in important matters. Nothing could be accomplished without consulting them. The protective association was
comparatively more powerful in Italy than in the North.

Distribution of Power Among the Social Classes
of the Medieval Italian City

The Italian *popolo* was a political as well as an economic phenomenon. As a political sub-community it had its own official,
finances, and military organization. In the truest sense it was a state
within a state. At first it was a conscious, illegitimate, and revolutionary political association. It formed to counteract the presence
of a settlement of families in the cities forming an urban nobility
and practicing the knightly style of life based on an extensive
development of economic and political power. The association of
the *popolo* opposing them rested on the fraternization of professional associations *(arti* or *paratici).*

The *popolo* took form in a number of places at approximately
the same time: Milano, 1198; Lucca, 1203; Lodi, 1206; Pavia, 1208;
Siena, 1210; Verona, 1227; Bologna, 1228. Formed as a special association it assumed the name of *"societas," "credenza," "mercadenza,"*[1]
"communanza" or, simply, *"popolo."* The highest official of such a

---

1. Max Weber, *Wirtschaftsgeschichte,* p. 205.

political sub-community in Italy was usually called *capitano popoli.*
He was a salaried official elected for a short period, usually a year.
In the manner of the *podesta* he was often called from another community bringing his own office staff along. The *popolo* supplied him
with a *militia* recruited either from the city wards or guilds. In
the manner of the *podesta* he often resided in a special people's
house with a tower, the fortress of the *popolo.* In financial administration the *capitano* was assisted by guild representatives *(anziani*
or *priori)* functioning as a special board elected from the city
wards for short terms of office.

Such elected officials of the guilds *(anziani* or *priori)* participated directly in the decisions of the *commune.* They claimed the
right to protect the populace before the court, to contest decisions,
address applications to the communal authorities and even directly
participate in legislation. When the *popolo* achieved full development it had its own statutes and financial bills. At times it even
established the principle that decision of the commune could become
effective only if confirmed by it.

Once the legal institutions of the *popolo* assumed shape, laws,
to be effective, had to be established in the statutes of the *popolo*
as well as of the commune. Where possible the *popolo* attempted
to win acceptance of its statutes among those of the commune. In
a few cases it even obtained priority of its own statutes over those
of the commune *(abrogent statutis omnibus et semper ultima intel-
ligantur* in Brescia). Beside the jurisdiction of the *podesta* appeared
that of the *mercanzia*[2] or *domus mercatorum* embracing the affairs
of the market and trades, constituting a special court for the affairs
of the merchants and manufacturers. It often obtained universal
importance for the populace.

In the fourteenth century the *podesta* of Pisa was compelled to
declare under oath that he and his judges would never interfere in
disputes of the populace. At times the captain attained a jurisdiction
competing with that of the *podesta.* In some instances he was even
able to reverse the *podesta's* verdicts. He was often granted the
right of presiding over meetings of the communal authorities with
power to convoke and dismiss them. Occasionally the captain had
authority to summon the citizenry of the commune and to execute

---

2. Max Weber, *Gesammelte Aufsätze zur Sozial-und Wirtschaftsgeschichte,*
pp. 368, 442.

the decisions of the council if the *podesta* failed to do so. Additional powers of the captain included the right to proclaim and remit the ban, to control, as co-administrator, communal finances, and to dispose of property of exiles. While the captain's official rank was lower than that of the *podesta*, he was often as a *capitanus populi et communis*, or in Latin a *collega minor* the more objectively powerful official of the two. This finds confirmation in the fact that the captain also had disposition over the military power of the commune, particularly when it was made up of mercenary troops whose maintenance could only be covered from tax-assessments of rich citizens.

With the full success of the *popolo*, formally the nobility had only negative privileges, the offices of the commune were open to the populace; the offices of the *popolo* were not reciprocally open to the nobility. If insulted by the nobility, the populace was privileged in law suits. At times only the decisions of the *popolo* concerned the entire citizenry. Often the nobility was explicitly excluded from participation in communal administration either temporarily or permanently.

The best known of these arrangements is the *ordinamenti della giustizia* of Giano delle Bella of 1293. Beside the captain who was commander in chief of the guild militia, the *gonfaloniere della giustizia* was a purely political official appointed on a short term basis. The *gonfaloniere* protected the populace, prosecuted and executed trials against the nobility, controlled observance of the *ordinamenti*, and commanded a special people's militia of 1000 men which was drawn by lot and subject to immediate call. The political justice of the *popolo* system with its system of official espionage, its preference for anonymous accusations, accelerated inquistorial procedures against magnates, and simplified proof (by "notoriety")[3] was the democratic counterpart of the Venetian trials of the Council of Ten. Objectively the *popolo* system was identified by: the exclusion of all members of families with a knightly style of life from office; obligating the notables by pledges of good conduct; placing the notables' family under bail for all members; the establishment of a special criminal law for the political offences of the *magnates*, especially insulting the honor of a member of the populace; the

---

3. Guilt by rumor or "guilt by association" in the language made popular by senator McCarthy.

prohibition of a noble's acquiring property bordering on that of a member of the populace without the latter's agreement.

The Parte Guelfa assumed the government of the *popolo*. Party statutes were treated as a part of the city's law. Only individuals registered with the party could be elected to office. The party's power apparatus has already been discussed.

Since the party was basically supported by knightly military forces it may be assumed that the *ordinamenti* could not really destroy the social and economic power of the nobility. As a matter of fact within ten years after these Florentine class laws had been copied by numerous Tuscan cities, the feuds between noble families broke out once again. Small plutocratic groups remained continuously in possession of power. Even the very offices of the *popolo* were nearly always occupied by noblemen, since noble families could be expressly accepted as part of the populace. The rejection of the knightly style of life was only partially effective. To avoid the ban it was only necessary to guarantee political obedience and register with a guild.

The basic social effect of the rise of the *popolo* was the fusion of resident urban families with the *popolo grasso*—strata distinguished by possession of university education or capital wealth. "*Popolo grasso*" was the name given the seven high ranking guilds embracing: judges, notaries, bankers, merchants of foreign cloth, merchants of Florentine woolens, silk-merchants, doctors, merchants of spices, and merchants of furs. Originally all officials of the city had to be elected from these groups into which, in the time of democratic crisis, the nobles entered. Eventually, after several additional revolutions the fourteen *arti minori* of the *popolo minuto* (small tradesmen) obtained some access to power. After the revolt of the *Ciompi* in 1378, artisan strata not belonging to the fourteen guilds obtained a temporary share in government. They did so as an independent guild association. Only temporarily and in a few places such as at Perugia in 1378 did the small burghers succeed not only in excluding the nobility but the *popolo grasso* from participating in the *priori* council. Characteristically the impoverished strata of industrial citizens regularly enjoyed support of the nobility in their counter-attacks on the *popolo* in the same manner as the later *tyrannis* was established with mass support.

As early as the thirteenth century the nobility and such lower strata frequently withstood together the attacks of the burghers. Economic factors determined the strength of the support. Wherever the putting-out system was fully developed the interests of small artisans collided sharply with those of entrepreneurial guilds. Count Broglio d'Anjano[4] has proven that the development of the putting-out system occurred so rapidly in Perugia that in 1437 one individual entrepreneur maintained 176 *filatrici* and 28 *filatori*. The situation of the small artisans under the putting-out system was precarious. Foreign workers were in the competition for jobs. Hiring by the day was practiced. Moreover, the entrepreneurial guilds attempted to regulate conditions of the putting-out contract in as one-sided a fashion as the guilds of artisans (like the *cimatori* in Perugia) tried to prevent the undercutting of wages.

However, the industrial strata nowhere obtained permanent political power. Moreover, the proletarian strata of traveling journeymen was completely outside the civic administration. Only with the participation of these lower ranking guilds in the councils of the city did a relatively democratic element appear even though their actual influence was usually unimportant. The custom of setting up special committees of election officials common to all Italian communes was intended to prevent demagogy and political irresponsibility of the election managers, such as appears, so often anonymously,[5] in modern European democracy. However, such committees of election officials made possible a selection of civic officials according to plan and the uniform inclusion of counselors and officials currently officiating. This tended to turn the officialdom into a closed corporation of socially influential families. It was certainly unable to ignore financially decisive strata. Only in times of competition between several families of relatively equal strength and power and in periods of religious agitation could "public opinion" exercise any positive influence on the composition of the offices.

Without occupying any official positions the Medici dominated the city through social influence and systematic manipulation of elections. Against them the *popolo* achieved success only with vehement and continuous blood fights. When all else failed the nobility withdrew from the city and attacked it from their castles. The

---

4. Graf Broglio d'Anjano, *The Venetian Silk Industry and its Organization* (1893).

5. The political "boss" of modern civic party politics.

burgher-army pillaged the castles and their civic-legislation shattered the traditional seignorial constitution of the country, at times through the planned liberation of the peasants.

The *popolo* obtained the necessary instruments of power for crushing the nobility in the guild organizations which from the beginning were utilized by the commune for administrative purposes. Tradesmen were called by guilds to guard duty of the citadel and increasingly as foot soldiers for field service. With progress in military technique, the financial help of the entrepreneurial guilds became indispensable. Jurists, especially notaries and judges and allied professionals such as physicians and pharmacists, provided intellectual and administrative-technical support.

Guild-organized intellectual strata were in leading position among the *popolo.* They played a role similar to the advocates and other jurists in France within "*des tiers.*"[6] The first captains were regularly recruited from the superintendents of the guilds or their associations. The *mercadanza* was a normal first step in the political organization of the *popolo;* their superintendents, the *podesta mercatorum* were frequently the first people's captains. (As E. Salzer[7] rightly emphasized *mercatores* was also here the designation for all urban tradesmen and merchants.) The initial development of the *popolo* was toward organized protection of the interests of the populace before the communal courts, corporations, and offices.

The point of departure for the development of the *popolo* was the frequent denial of legal rights to non-nobles. This may be illustrated by German experience (historically reported for Strassburg) where nobles thrashed purveyors and artisans rather than pay their bills and these little people had no recourse from the law. The personal insults and gangster-like threats of the populace by the militarily superior nobility were effective in denying them their rights. In fact, such events even continued to occur for a century after the formation for its protection of a special association of the *popolo.* The status pride of the knighthood clashed with the natural resentment of the burghers.

In its first form the people's captainship represented a kind of

---

6. Providing the intellectual leadership of the third estate in the French revolutions.

7. Ernst Salzer, *The Beginnings of the Signorie in Upper Italy,* a contribution to Italian Administrative History (Historical Studies, Vol. 14, 1900).

tribune-like right of control and assistance of the populace against the communal authorities themselves. From this point it gradually evolved into a kind of reviewing authority and was eventually developed into a general coordinating authority. The rise of the *popolo* was aided by feuds of the nobles resulting in an injury to the economic interests of the burghers and providing the first occasion for an interference of the officers of the *popolo* in civic affairs. Another factor in the rise of the *popolo* was the personal ambition of some noblemen who sought to set up a tyranny with the assistance of the *popolo*. The nobility was everywhere in a permanent state of anxiety at this possibility. However, because of the divisions within the ranks of the nobility it was possible almost everywhere for the *popolo* to enlist the military assistance of part of the knighthood in its own service. Furthermore, from a purely military point of view, these events provided the occasion for an increasing importance of the infantry at the expense of the cavalry. The overall military situation of the knighthood resting on horsemanship was declining in importance. Rational military engineering techniques were also developing at the expense of knighthood. The *"bombardin,"* appearing for the first time in the army of Florence of the fourteenth century, are the forerunners of modern artillery.

Parallelism Between the Roman Tribunes and Spartan Ephors

Externally, the development of the *demos* in Antiquity is similar to that of the *plebs*. In Rome a special plebeian community developed with officials quite comparable to the officials and special community of the *popolo*. Originally the Roman tribunes were elected superintendents of the four city districts. Ed. Meyer[8] would have it that the nobles were administrators of the corporate cult sanctuary. Since the sanctuary was the treasury, the nobles were also treasurers of the plebs. The populace itself was formed into an oath-bound fraternity, sworn to strike down anyone opposing the tribunes in the conduct of popular affairs. This implied that the tribune was *sacro sanctus* in contrast to the legitimate officials of the Roman community. Similarly the Italian captain of the people

---

8. Ed. Meyer, *Kleine Schriften* (I. Aufl. 1910) I, 373.

did not normally possess the *dei gratia* which the *counsels* as legitimate officials still added to their names.

The tribune lacked legitimate official authority and its related right to communicate with the communal Gods, or to take *auspicia* as well as the most significant right of legitimate authority—the right to punish. However, as head of the plebs the tribune had the power to execute a kind of lynch-law without procedure and verdict against anyone who opposed the execution of his official duties. Such persons could be arrested and executed by throwing them down from the *Tarpeian* rock. As in the case of the captain and *anziani*, the Roman tribune's official authority was a gradual development out of his right to intercede in favor of the populace at official meetings of the magistrates and veto their decisions. Such right of intercession representing the negative power of Roman officials against any authority of the same or lower rank, was the primary attribute of the tribune. As in the case of the captain of the *popolo*, authority evolved from this point into a general power of review. It became the highest internal civic power.

However, the tribune had no military power, for in military campaigns the power of the general was unrestricted. Such a restriction of its area of competence to the city, in contrast to the old official authority, is testimony of the special burgher-origin of the tribune. The political accomplishments of the tribunes were made possible by virtue of their veto power alone. Their veto powers included the right to challenge criminal verdicts, to moderate the law governing debts, to interfere with the administration of justice on market days in the interests of the peasantry, to secure the equal participation in offices, even including the offices of the priesthood and council. Eventually in the course of its last succession in Rome the rule of the plebs was extended to the rural plebiscite. This also occasionally occurred in the Italian communes. This rule established the binding character of the decision of the plebs on the entire community.

In effect the plebiscite was equivalent to the formal degradation of the nobility as occurred in medieval Italy. After the termination of the older struggles of the estates the political importance of the tribuneship was greatly reduced. Like the captain, the tribune was transformed into an official of the community. He even became a part of developing bureaucratic structure. He was elected by the populace alone. However the separation of plebeian from patrician became practically meaningless making room for the development of a nobility based on office and wealth.

In the class struggles breaking out at this time, the old political forces asserted themselves beginning in the times of the Gracchi[9] as instruments in the service of political reformers. Such political reformers headed up the economic class movements of politically demoted burghers hostile to noblemen deriving their nobility from the occupancy of offices. The effects of this revival was the establishment, alongside the military command, of tribunal power as a life-long official attribute of the prince.

Such striking parallels between the medieval Italian and old Roman development appear despite fundamental social, economic, and political differences to be discussed later. Within a city the forms of technical administration available for regulating relations between the estates cannot be altered at will. The forms of political administration obey their own laws and are not to be interpreted merely as a superstructure resting on economic foundations.[10] There is no doubt of the parallelism between the development of the Roman tribune and the medieval Italian captain. The question may quite legitimately be raised, however, whether the Roman tribune had any parallels in Antiquity itself, for so far as is known the formation of a special political association like the *plebs* of Rome or the *popolo* of Italy can not be found elsewhere in Antiquity.

However the observation was already made in Antiquity (by Cicero) that despite apparent differences, phenomena were present which in their inner relations were essentially similar to the tribunate. Such was the Spartan Ephorate.[11] It is essential to interpret this parallel correctly.

In contrast to the legitimate kings, the ephors (superintendents)

9. The Gracchi were a plebeian family of the Sempronian gens. Its most distinguished representatives were the famous tribunes Tiberius and Gaius Sempronius Gracchus.

10. Max Weber's references here are self-evidently opposed to the Marxian analysis of social organization with its treatment of economic production as fundamental to all other social configurations seen as a mere superstructure resting on this basis. Weber's argument is directed against such economic monism. At times influences must be traced from politics to economics and not only the reverse as a kind of one-way street.

11. The Ephors were bodies of magistrates appearing in various ancient Dorian States. At Sparta the body of five ephors were annually elected by the people.

were officials elected annually. Like the tribunes they were elected by the five territorial phyles of the Spartans and not by the three clan divisions. The ephors convoked the burghers' assembly and had jurisdiction over civil and criminal affairs, though perhaps not unlimited jurisdiction in the latter case. The ephors even summoned the kings to their chairs. They held officials accountable for their activities and had power to dismiss them from office. Administration was consolidated in their hands and together with the elected council of the *gerusia*[12] the ephors possessed the substantively highest political power within the districts of Sparta.

Within the urban area of Sparta the kings were restricted to honorary privileges and purely personal influence. During war they exercised absolute disciplinary power which was very severe in Sparta. Only in later periods did the ephors accompany the kings into war. The fact that the ephors were originally appointed by the king, presumably even after the First Messenian War,[13] does not contradict the tribune-like quality of ephor power. It is probable that the first tribunes in Rome also originated in this manner.[14] More important is the fact that the absence of the power of intercession does not contradict the tribune-like character of the ephors, which may be determined from the tradition that in accordance with their position the ephors had to protect the citizens against the kings.

The absence of the power of intercession by the ephors between the people and the kings is to be explained by the unconditional victory of the Spartan *demos* over its opponents. The kings did not have enough internal power to require intercession. The *demos* itself was transformed, originally into a plebeian and later to an oligarchic ruling class holding dominion over the entire country. In Sparta in historical times a nobility was unknown. The polis guarded

---

12. The *gerontes* or elders appearing in Homer and advising the king as well as acting as judges developed in Sparta into a body of fixed number, forming a definite part of the constitution, called the *gerusia*. The council consisted of thirty members including the two kings. The other twenty-eight had to be over sixty years of age. They held office for life and were chosen by acclamation in the general assembly of citizens.

13. Messenia was the name of the rich region of the southern portion of the Peloponnesus. It is impossible to determine the exact date of the first Messenian War but it was some time during the eighth century B.C. The conquest was very critical to the growth of Sparta.

14. One may see parallels in the Public Defender—an official appointed by the court to defend the interests of accused persons unable to afford private counsel.

its seignorial position over the helots[15] against whom war was yearly
declared in order to give their status outside the pale of the law a
religious basis. The political monopoly against the *perioeci* who
were excluded from the military association was as absolute as the
social equality maintained internally among the full citizens. Both
were sustained by an espionage system *(krypteia)* reminiscent of
that of Venice. One of the first acts of the Lacedemonians was the
abolition of the traditionally separated noble way of life distinguished even by its costume. The oath mutually exchanged between
the kings and ephors representing a kind of periodically renewed
constitutional contract seems to be convincing evidence that the
severe restrictions on royal power were consequences of struggle
and compromise. Care must only be exercised since the ephors
seem to have retained some religious functions. However, they became legitimate officials of the commune even more fully than the
Roman tribunes. The decisive features of the Spartan polis, too,
bear the imprint of a rational design imposed upon an ancient
institution.

Complete parallels to the Spartan institutions cannot be found in
the other Hellenic communities. Rather one everywhere finds a
democratic movement of non-noble citizens against the patricians,
which in a number of cases led to the temporary or permanent
elimination of patrician dominion. As in the Middle Ages this neither
implied equality, eligibility to vote and qualification for office and
the council for all citizens, nor did it imply the reception of all
free families into the civic association. In contrast to Rome some
freemen did not belong to burgher associations. There was, rather,

15. The Spartan people formed a military caste. Each citizen was devoted
to service of the state. To carry out this practice it was important that every
citizen be freed from the need to provide for himself and his family. The nobles,
indeed, owned family lands but the common land of the community acquired by
Sparta was divided into lots which were assigned to each Spartan and passed
from father and son—such lots could not be sold or divided. The original inhabitants of the land were dispossessed and reduced to serfdom, cultivating the lands
of their lords. Each year the owner was entitled to receive seventy medimini of
corn for himself, twelve for his wife and a stated portion of wine. All production of the land beyond this was allowed to go to the helots. Though the helots
were not driven, and though they could acquire land of their own, their lot was
hard. They were a menace as well as a necessity to the state and the *Krypteia*
or secret police was instituted to control them. Young Spartans were sent to
the country empowered to kill suspicious helots.

a graduated system of rights: from suffrage to eligibility for office in terms of ground-rents, capacity for military service, and wealth. Such a gradation of citizenship was never completely abolished legally in Athens. Similarly in the medieval city the destitute classes never permanently obtained equal rights with the middle class.

The first stage of democracy consisted in the granting of the right to vote in the people's assembly to all landowners attached to the *demos* and registered in the military association of the phratry. Or, again, the right to vote was granted to the owners of other objects of wealth. Initially decisive for the rise of democracy was qualification for the self-equipped army of hoplite infantry with whose rise the democratic revolution was correlated. As will be seen, the simple gradation of the right to vote was not the most important means for bringing about the democratic revolution. As in the Middle Ages the formal composition of the civic assembly could be arranged in any way one wished and its formal competency measured ever so carefully without in any way destroying the social power of the proprietors.

The evolution of the *demos* assumed variable directions. In some cases a democracy emerged that was externally similar to that of the Italian communes. The wealthiest non-noble strata, reported in the census as owners of money, slaves, *ergasteria*, ships, and commercial and loan capital, acquired access to the council and offices beside the nobility whose status rested on landed property. Normally the bulk of the small tradesmen, retailers, and people of moderate means were legally excluded from office. At times, because of their indispensability they had legal right to office but were factually excluded. If this were not the case, as the process of democratization ran its course, power gravitated into the hands of these very strata. To prevent this, means had to be provided to cancel the economic indispensability of these strata. This was done either through payments of daily allowances or through reduction of the census of offices. Nevertheless, this along with the factual disregard of the class-degradation of the *demos* only occurred in the fourth century in the last stages of Attic democracy. It accompanied the decline in military importance of the hoplites.

In Antiquity the most important consequence of the complete or partial victory of the non-noble for the structure of political

administration was increasing institutionalization.[16] This could take
the form of an organization of the political community on a local
territorial basis.[17] In the Middle Ages even under the rule of the
nobility the division of the urban community into local districts was
already important for the great bulk of the burghers. The *popolo*
elected some of its officials according to city districts. The ancient
city was divided into local districts for the non-nobles, especially for
purposes of distributing statute labor and taxation.

In Rome in addition to the three old private *tribes* composed of
families and *curia* there appeared in time four territorial urban districts also called "tribes." After the victory of the plebs some rural
tribes, were also added. In Sparta four, later five, locality phyles
were added to the three older phyles. The victory of democracy
was identical with the triumph of the *demos* as a local territorially
organized sub-division of the whole area and as the basis for all
rights and duties in the polis. It will be necessary to consider the
practical implications of this change. It resulted in conversion of
the city into an institutionalized territorial corporation rather than
a fraternization of military and noble associations.

Correlated therewith was a changed concept of the nature of
law. The law was transformed into institutionalized form applying
to the burghers and inhabitants of the urban area as such. The residues of older structures have already been mentioned. Simultaneously it increasingly became a rational statute-law rather than an
irrational charismatic judicature.

The beginning of legislation paralleled the abolition of patrician
rule. Legislation initially took the form of charismatic statutes by
the *aesymnetes*.[18] But soon the new creation of permanent laws
was accepted. In fact new legislation by the ecclesia became so usual

16. At times Weber employs the term institutional to mean consciously or
rationally established. This usage is familiar also to us when we speak of something as "instituted"—when, for instance, we speak of the institution of a reform
movement in city politics. It is precisely this type of meaning that Weber intends
for he conceives of an extensive elimination of traditional political structures
replaced by one consciously set up.

17. Henry Sumner Maine, whom Weber found useful on many points, believed that a two-fold shift characterized social development: a change in the
individual's personal legal situation from status to contract; a change in the
organizing principle of the community from kinship to territory.

18. A governor possessing supreme power for a limited time was called an
aesymnete.

as to produce a state of continuous flux. Soon a purely secular administration of justice applied to the laws or, in Rome, to the instructions of the magistrate. The creation of laws reached such a fluid state that eventually in Athens the question was directed yearly to the people whether existing laws should be maintained or amended. Thus it became an accepted premise that the law is artificially created and that it should be based upon the approval of those to whom it will apply.

To be sure this conception did not become omnipotent in classical Antiquity. For instance in Athens of the fourth and fifth century not every decision *(psephisma)* of the *demos* was law *(nomos)* even if it contained general rules. If the decisions of the *demos* were illegal they could be contested by any burgher before a jury *(heliaia)*. At the time, law originated on the basis of a motion of a burgher rather than from the decision of the demos. Contests as to whether the old or a newly proposed law should be followed took the form of a legal dispute before a sworn jury (the *nomothetae)*. This was a long retained residue of the older concept of law. In Athens the abolition of the religious and noble veto power of the Areopagus[19] by Ephialtes[20] was the first decisive step toward the conception of the law as a rational creation.

Democratic development brought with it an administrative revolution. Functionaries of the *demos* or its sub-divisions elected by lot for short terms and who were, at times, removable, replaced the dignitaries ruling by virtue of clan or office charisma. The new officials received only moderate compensations for their services or daily allowances like the jurymen who were also drawn by lot. This short-term occupancy of offices and the very frequent pro-

19. The Council of Elders was a part of the Aryan inheritance of the Greeks. It came to be called at Athens the Council of the Areopagus. Manslaughter in Greece was thought of as a religious offense requiring cleansing. This led to the entry of the state into criminal jurisprudence—by way of the notion that if the individual were impure the wrath of the gods may be called down upon the community. The Council formed a court the proceedings of which were closely associated with the worship of the *Semnai.*

20. In the fifth century B.C. in Athens, Aristides was the leader of the democracy while Cimon had no sympathy with the democratic constitution. After the death of Aristides, Cimon remained the most powerful statesman in Athens, but his lack of sympathy with the democracy made it impossible that he retain power long. Younger statesmen rose, forming a party of opposition against Cimon and the oligarchs. The two chief politicians of this democratic party were Ephialtes and Pericles who began to play a prominent part in the assembly.

hibition against re-election excluded the emergence of the professional as in modern civil service. The official "career" and status honor of the professional were missing. Business was discharged as an occasional office.

For the majority of officials, their duties did not require full-time service. For the poor the revenues from public service constituted only an incidental though desirable income. Of course the highest political positions and especially the military ones, required full-time service. Hence, they could be occupied only by the wealthy. In Athens instead of requiring office security such as bonding, a close inspection was provided for finance officials. However, the positions remained honorary.

The political leader proper, the demagogue of fully developed democracy was formally the leading military official in Athens after the time of Pericles. However, his real power rested not upon law nor office but entirely upon personal influence and trust by the *demos*. Thus the position was not only illegitimate but illegal as well, even though the whole constitution of the democracy was tailored upon his presence. This is comparable to the modern constitution of England based upon the existence of the cabinet, which also does not rule by virtue of legal competence. In different forms, accusation of the demagogue because of mismanagement of the *demos* corresponded to the vote of no-confidence of the English parliament which is also extra-legal. Finally the council whose members were drawn by lot now became simply an executive committee of the demos, losing jurisdiction, but undertaking preliminary discussions of plebiscites (through *Probuleuma*)[21] and financial matters.

Comparative Structure of Ancient and Medieval Democracy

The establishment of rule by the *popolo* had similar consequences in the medieval cities. It, too, ground out enormous editions of city laws and codified the common law and court rules (trial law) producing a surplus of statutes of all kinds and an excess of officials. Four to five dozen categories of officials are to be found

21. Ed. Meyer, *History of Antiquity* IV, 540 (1944); Hermann Bengtson, *Greek History*, p. 184.

in the smaller German cities. In addition to the staff offices of the bailiff and *Bürgermeister* there was a host of specialized functionaries who officiated only occasionally. The office revenues, mainly fees of these functionaries constituted a desirable though incidental income. Furthermore commonly in the ancient and medieval cities, at least in large cities, numerous affairs were dispatched by organizations whose members were elected by lot. Similar affairs today are usually handled by representatives of elected assemblies. In Hellenic Antiquity the activities of these officials included legislation and such political activities as affidavits in the making of federal contracts and the distribution of tribute from the confederates. In the Middle Ages the election and composition of the most important judicial assemblies was often similar. Election by lot was a kind of substitute for the modern system of representation which did not exist at the time. Moreover, in a situation dominated by traditional political rights organized by privileged estates representation is only possible for associations. In ancient democracy the representatives were drawn from cult or state communities and even communities of federal confederates; in the Middle Ages they were drawn from guilds and other corporations. Moreover, only the special rights of associations were represented, not the rights of a district "electorate" as found in the modern proletariat.

In both the ancient and medieval city tyrannies appeared or at least attempts to establish them. In both areas this was a locally restricted phenomenon. During the seventh and sixth centuries B.C. city tyrannies were established in a number of large cities, including Athens. They lasted only a few generations. The civic freedom they represented was normally only destroyed by superior military force. The tyrannies in colonial areas of Asia Minor and especially in Sicily had more permanent effects, partly supplying the decisive form of the city-state until the time of its decay.

The tyrant was the product of the struggle of the estates. At times, as illustrated by the case of Syracuse, the nobility which was threatened by the *demos* helped establish the rule of the tyrant. The primary support of the tyrant came from sections of the middle class and people suffering under the usury of the patricians. The typical class opposition of the ancient world from Israel and Mesopotamia to Greece and Italy appeared between resident urban patricians qualified for military service and engaged in money lending and the peasantry as debtors. Babylonian patricians acquired possession of the entire holy land transforming the peasants into coloni.[22] In Israel debt servitude was an object of regulation in the "Book of the Confederation." From Abimelech to Judas Maccabeus[23] every revolutionary leader found support in fugitive debt slaves on the basis of the promise in Deuteronomy that Israel "shall lend to anyone," which means that the burghers of Jerusalem shall be the creditors and patricians and others shall be their debt servants and peasants.

The class oppositions of Hellas and Rome were similar. Once in power the tyrant surrounded by a political coterie of nobles was supported by the peasantry and sections of the urban middle classes. Tyranny regularly relied upon bodyguards of mercenaries though the military organizations of the citizenry (as shown with the Pisistratids[24]) was normally the first step in the establishment of the tyranny. In actual fact the tyrant often pursued the policy of balancing the estates off against one another in a manner similar to the *aesymnetes*[25] (Charondas,[26] Solon[27]). Apparently the fundamental political alternatives of the time that faced the *aesymnetes* were the re-ordering of the estates or the rise of the tyrants. The socio-economic policy of both aesymnetes and tyrants, at least with respect to the mother country, was the prevention of the sale of peasant lands to the resident urban nobility. They also tried to

22. The coloni were important to the ancient world as transitional strata on the way toward full serfdom. In this instance, the formerly free peasants were transformed into guests in their own land in a state of semi-bondage.

23. The Maccabees were a family of heroes, deliverers of Judea during the Syrian persecutions of 175-164 B.C. They founded a dynasty of priest kings which lasted until 40 B.C.

24. In Athens, Pisistratus organized a new party called the Hill, for it consisted primarily of poor hillsmen from the highlands of Attica, as well as hektemors for whom Solon had done little, and many discontented men, formerly rich, who had been impoverished by Solon's measure cancelling old debts. One day Pisistratus appeared in the agora wounded, saying that he had been attacked by political enemies. The Assembly was packed with hillsmen. A bodyguard of fifty clubsmen was voted to him. Having obtained a bodyguard, the first step was the seizure of the Acropolis, from which vantage point Pisistratus made himself master of the state 561-0 B.C.

25. Governors granted supreme power for a limited time.

26. Charondas, one of the great law givers and codifiers of the seventh century. Charondas was legislator of Catane.

27. Solon the Wise of Athens was the most famous of all.

restrict the immigration of the peasants into the city. In some places the attempt was made to restrict the purchase of slaves, and luxuries, and to control the intermediate trade and grain exports. All these measures implied an essentially philistine economic policy quite corresponding to the urban economic policy of medieval cities still to be discussed.

The tyrants perceived themselves and were perceived as illegitimate masters. This differentiated the entire position of tyrannies religiously and politically from the old city-kingdoms. Regularly the tyrants sponsored new emotional cults like that of Dionysus[28] in contrast to the ritualistic cults of the nobility. As a rule the tyrants tried to manipulate the external forms of the communal constitution to sustain claims of legality. In the wake of their downfall the tyrannies usually left a weakened nobility, forcing it to secure cooperation of the commoners and to make far-reaching concessions to the *demos*. As a matter of fact without the cooperation of the commoners the tyrants could hardly be expelled. Thus the middle-class democracy of Cleisthenes followed the expulsion of the Pisistratids. In other places a merchant plutocracy succeeded the tyrants. The tyrannies, which were aided by economic class tensions, at least in the mother country effected a timocratic or democratic balance of the estates. Thus tyranny was frequently the forerunner of democracy. By contrast, there were successful and unsuccessful attempts to establish tyrannies in the late Hellenic period stemming from a policy of conquest of the *demos*. These were bound up with military interests to be discussed later. Victorious army leaders like Alcibiades[29] and Lysander[30] attempted such conversions. Until the Hellenistic period these attempts were unsuccessful in the Hellenic mother country. Moreover, the military empire-formation of the *demos* disintegrated for reasons to be discussed later. However, in Sicily, the tyrants pursued the old expansionist maritime policy in the Tyrian sea as well as later in

---

28. In the marshes on the south side of the Areopagus, the bacchic god had an ancient sanctuary. Pisistratus built him a new house at the foot of the Acropolis. This represented public recognition of the religion of the oppressed strata.

29. Alcibiades, son of Cleinias, was educated by his kinsman, Pericles, in democratic traditions, but he had no sincere belief in them. He advanced the cause of the democratic party only so long as it suited his private interests.

30. Lysander was a Spartan admiral of unusual ability and boundless ambition. He established the Spartan empire.

the national defence against Carthage. The tyrants relying upon
mercenary armies rather than conscripted burghers and employing
ruthless oriental measures such as the compulsory naturalization of
soldiers and re-settlement of subject populations created inter-local
military monarchies. In Rome in the old republican period the
tyranny failed and the government fell into the hands of a military
monarch arising from within. This occurred in consequence of a
social and economic configuration which will be discussed separately.

The City Tyrannies in Antiquity
and the Middle Ages

The city tyrannies of the Middle Ages were primarily confined
to Italy. The Italian *signoria* was compared by Ernst Mayer[31] to
the ancient tyranny. Like the tyranny, the *signoria* arose predominantly in the hands of a wealthy family in opposition to other members of the estate. It was the first political power in Western Europe
to carry through rational administration (increasingly with appointed officials) while retaining certain forms of the traditional
communal constitution.

However there were also important differences between the
tyranny and the *signoria*. This was especially true so far as the
growth of the *signoria* proceeded directly out of the status struggle,
also because the *signoria* first appeared at the end of the development with the victory of the *popolo* and to a considerable extent
later. Moreover, the *signoria* usually developed out of the legal
offices of the *popolo* while in Hellenic Antiquity the city tyrannies
normally represented only a transitional phenomenon between the
patrician rule and timocracy or democracy. The formal development of the *signoria* was accomplished quite differently as demonstrated by E. Salzer. A whole series of them arose out of the new
offices of the populace and as a product of their revolts.

The people's captain or the *podesta* of the *mercadanza* and
podesta of the *commune* were elected by the *popolo* for increasingly longer periods, even for life. Such high officials elected for
long periods were to be found by the middle of the thirteenth
century in Piacenza, Parma, Lodi, and Milan. By the close of the
thirteenth century the rule of the Visconti in Milan, the Scaliger

31. Ernst Mayer, *Italienische Verfassungsgeschichte*, II, 39.

in Venice and the Este in Mantua were already in fact hereditary.
The extension of the authority of such top officials paralleled the
development toward a life-long occupancy of office which was at
first factual, later legal. Beginning with a purely arbitrary political
penal power, the *seignoria* developed into a general power *(arbit-
rium generale)* issuing orders at will in competition with the council
and the community. Eventually it acquired dominion with power
to govern the city *libero arbitrio*, to occupy the offices, and to issue
orders with legal sanctions.

The development proceeded from two different, but on occasion
coincident, political sources. One was the party rule as such. Of
especial importance was the constant threat to the political and,
indirectly, economic existence of the land-owning estate from the
lower class. The nobility especially was accustomed to war threats,
and the fear of conspiracies which necessitated the installation of
party chieftains with unrestricted power. Foreign wars and the
threat of defeat by neighboring communities or other dictators
were added factors. When such conditions led to the creation of
a special military command the war captain, either a foreign prince
or a condottieri, was the source of the *signoria* rather than the position of the people's captain as party leader.

The surrender of the city into the protective domination of a
prince in the face of external threats often began with narrowly
defined authority of the dominus. However, within the city the
dictator could easily win over the broad lower strata ordinarily
excluded from active participation in the administration since a
change of alliance did not imply any loss while the presence of a
lordly court promised economic advantages. Moreover, the masses
tend to be emotionally responsive to personal leadership. As a rule
the aspirants to the *signoria* employed the parliament as a device
for the transformation of power.

Occasionally when threatened by political or economic opponents the nobility or the merchants seized the *signoria* which was
not at first viewed as a permanent establishment of monarchy. Cities
like Genoa repeatedly imposed severe restriction on powerful monarchs whose domination they accepted. Such limitation involved
limited armies and fixed money payments. Sometimes the cities even
dismissed the *signore* from his position. This was, at times possible
for foreign monarchs as when the king of France was deposed by

Genoa. However such independence as against a *signore* was difficult whenever he took up residence in the city.

It should be observed that both the ability and inclination of
the burghers for opposition declined in the course of time. The
signoria relied upon mercenary armies and increasingly also upon
alliances with the legitimate authorities. Except for Venice and
Genoa, after the forceful subjection of Florence with the help of
Spanish troops, in Italy the hereditary *signoria* constituted the final
form of the city legitimized by imperial and royal recognition.

The decreasing opposition of the burghers to the *signoria* may
be explained by a series of individual circumstances. For one thing
the court of the *signoria* created an interest community for the
nobility and the burghers and the number of persons increased in
time who were interested for social and economic reasons in its
continued existence. Meanwhile, a series of factors was responsible
for the rapid decline of interest in the political fate of the city:
1. the increasing sublimation of needs; 2. the slowing of economic
expansion together with a growing sensitiveness of economically
interested upper burgher strata to disturbances of pacific traffic;
3. the general decline in political aspirations of tradesmen because
of increasing economic competition and mounting economic and
social stability (factors which in turn explain their increased attention to gainful economic activities or the peaceful usufruct of
rents); 4. finally, the general policy of the prince who sponsored
both developments to his own advantage. Large monarchies like
the French and the *signorias* of individual cities, could count on the
interest of the lower strata both in the pacification of the city and
an economic policy which took the small burgher into account.

The French cities were defeated by the kings with the support
of the small burghers who also supported the *signorias* in Italy.
However, more important than anything else was the political phenomenon of pacification of the burghers because of their business
requirements, their relief from military service and their planned
disarmament by the prince. Initially this was not a princely policy.
In fact some princes developed the first rational schemes of recruitment in the cities. However, in accord with the requirements of
the patrimonial army such schemes were soon applied to the recruitment of the poor and resulted in the creation of an army foreign
to the character of the republican burghers' army. The development
of the mercenary army and capitalistic supply of military require-

ments by entrepreneurs *(condottieri)* due to the economic indispensability of the burghers and the necessity for professional military training, all cleared the path for the prince. Even at the time of the free communes these factors were at work paving the way toward the pacification and disarmament of the burghers. The personal political alliances of the prince with the large dynasties were an additional factor, for against any such power combinations the rise of the burghers was doomed to failure. Eventually the economic indispensability of the burghers, the military disqualification of their educated strata, and the increasing rationalization of military technique requiring a professional army combined with the development of a stratum of noblemen, rentiers and prebendaries who possessed economic or social interests in the principle court, provided the *signoria* the chance to develop into a hereditary patrimonial kingdom. Thereby it entered the circle of the legitimate forms of power.

In one particular point which is alone of interest here, the politics of the *signoria* corresponds with that of ancient tyranny: the tendency to break up the political and economic power position of the city as against the country. In a manner similar to Antiquity, it was often with the aid of rural populations that the dictator forced the surrender of city government (in Pavia in 1328). After its victory over the nobility, the free citizenry often broke up the manor and in its own political and economic interests liberated the peasants and sponsored the free transfer of land to the wealthiest purchasers. The acquisition of landed property *en masse* from feudal lords by the burghers and the replacement òf the socage-farm system by the *mezzadria* in Tuscany was carried out under the rule of the *popolo grasso*. The *mezzadria* rested on the consideration that the lord was predominantly a resident of the city and only linked to the country by part-time residence; moreover his part-time tenants were free-holders. However, though they were free rural land-owners the peasants were excluded from participation in political power. As the *mezzadria* was tailored upon the interests of private enterprise, so the urban policy toward the country was adapted to the interests of urban consumers. After the victory of the guilds urban policy was also adapted to the needs of urban producers. When the policy of the prince changed this at all, it was neither immediately nor everywhere. The famous physiocratic policy of the Grand Duke Leopold of Tuscany in the eighteenth century was influenced by certain concepts of natural law and was not, in the first place, a policy of agrarian interests. In all cases the policy of the prince was directed toward a balance of interests and the prevention of sharp collisions and was no longer purely a policy of urbanites utilizing the country as a means to an end.

The rule of the prince often encompassed several cities. However, it did not constitute a uniform state association in the modern sense, created from hitherto independent urban territories. Rather the different cities united under the rule of a lord often had both the right and occasion in semi-autonomous fashion to communicate through ambassadors with each other. Their constitutions were by no means regularly made uniform. They were not demoted to the status of subordinate communities which by virtue of delegation from the state fulfilled a part of the state's functions.

This development only occurred gradually, parallel with the uniform transformation of the modern patrimonial states. Representation by estates, already known by the Sicilian empire during the Middle Ages as well as in other patrimonial monarchies, was almost completely absent in the governmental configurations arising out of city territories. The essential organizational innovations were: 1. the introduction of princely officials employed for unlimited periods apart from criminal officials elected on a short-time basis, and 2. the development of central collegate magistracies for financial and military purposes. Technically the establishment of the administration of the urban prince in a rational manner was aided by the unusual existence in the communities of statistical records of their financial and military affairs. Moreover, the arts of balanced accounts and record keeping were technically developed in the banking houses of the city. Both Venice and the Sicilian Empire had an indubitable effect on the rationalization of administration, although this effect was one of stimulation rather than of adoption.

The Special Position of the Medieval Italian City

The cyclical development of the Italian cities from a subordinate part of a patrimonial or feudal association, to independent rule or rule by their own dignitaries following revolutionary movements, followed by the regime of the guilds, and, in turn, by the *signoria* and finally the return to a subordinate position in a relatively rational patrimonial association—this cycle has no exact counterpart elsewhere in the Occident. City development elsewhere especially omits the *signoria* which when present at all appears only in early traces. The people's captain is paralleled in the area North of the Alps only in some of the more powerful burgomasters.

However, the cycle of city development was universal in one respect. Cities in the time of the Carolingians were of little importance as administrative districts because of peculiarities of the estates structure. In the modern patrimonial state they are again approximately in this situation and are distinguished only by corporate privileges. In the transitional period they were everywhere "communities" with political rights and an autonomous economic policy. The development in Antiquity was similar. Yet neither modern capitalism nor the modern state grew up on the basis of the ancient cities while medieval urban development, though not alone decisive, was carrier of both phenomena and an important factor in their origin.

Despite all external similarities, far-reaching differences appear most easily recognized by comparison of city types in their characteristic forms. However, it is necessary first to clarify structural differences appearing between the medieval cities in a more systematic manner. It is also useful to elucidate the general situation of the medieval cities in the time of their greatest independence which may permit us to discover their specific features. During the period of maximum urban autonomy the cities displayed an exceptional variety of forms and trends.

Variations in the Medieval Urban Community

POLITICAL AUTONOMY

In varying degrees the medieval urban community enjoyed political autonomy and even, at times, pursued imperialistic foreign policies. Correlated with this was the appearance of permanent urban garrisons composed of the city's own soldiers. Such militarily supported city administrations concluded treaties, conducted great wars, and conquered large land areas, at times, held other cities in complete subjection and even won over-seas colonies. Only two

Italian maritime cities succeeded in obtaining foreign colonies. Some
large communities in North and Central Italy, Switzerland, and to
a lesser degree in Flanders and North Germany—the Hansa cities—
not only managed to obtain temporary domination over large territories but to achieve international political importance. The great
majority of cities, however, achieved no general political importance except for dominance over the immediate rural hinterland
and a few small satellite cities. Such was the case for: the cities of
Southern Italy and France; Spanish cities for a short period; French
cities for a longer period. With the exceptions of the few North
German, Flemish, Swiss and South German cities already mentioned,
city imperialism was unknown from the beginning in English and
German cities. This was also true for the greater number of western
German cities except during the short period of the city federations.

Many of these cities had permanent city garrisons (as until late
in France) or they had—as a rule—a conscripted civic militia of
urbanites who defended the walls and had the power in confederation with other cities to carry out the pacification of the land,
destroy robber castles, and interfere in the feuds of the parties of
the empire. However, they never lastingly sought to conduct international politics like the Italian and Hanseatic cities. Most of them
sent representatives either to the estates of the empire or to territorial bodies. Not infrequently because of their financial power they
then won a decisive voice therein despite a formally subordinate
place. The primary example is the English commons which was not
so much a representative of the city communes as of corporate
estates.

However numerous, citizenries did not achieve such rights (the
details from legal history will not be pursued here). On the continent the modern patrimonial bureaucratic states deprived most
of them of their political autonomy as well as their military powers
except for police purposes. Only where, as in Germany, development took a peculiar turn, were some of the city governments
permitted to remain as independent forms alongside the patrimonial
state.

English city development, too, assumed special form because
of the failure of patrimonial bureaucracy to emerge. Within the
rigid framework of the central administration individual English
cities never developed autonomous political ambitions precisely

because they had representation in the parliament. They entered into trade monopolies but not into political confederations as on the continent. They were corporations of a privileged stratum of notables and their good will was financially indispensable to the kings. The Tudors sought to destroy their privileges. However, the breakdown of the Stuarts put an end to this. From that time they remained a corporation with the right to vote in parliament, indeed constituting the "Kingdom of Influence" which the nobility utilized as a voting block won with ridiculous ease to secure a parliamentary majority.

AUTONOMOUS LAW OF THE CITY
AND ITS GUILDS

In full compass, the law of the politically independent Italian and, at times, Spanish and English cities and in considerable measure of the French and German cities was practiced without express or chartered confirmation. In problems respecting land owners, market traffic, and trade, the city courts customarily employed an autonomous law with citizens as jurymen. Such legal establishments originating through usage, through charter, through imitation or bestowal by another city, operated with a specific law common to all citizens. Such city courts increasingly opposed juridical use of irrational and magical means of proof: duels, ordeals, and family-oath. They preferred, rather, the employment of rational evidence, though such city pressure for a rational law must not be represented as a straight-line development. At times the retention of a special trial procedure in city jurisdiction consisted precisely of adherence to older legal forms in the face of rational innovations by royal administration. English cities, for example, did not adopt the more rational king's jury. Or, again, sometimes the cities preserved medieval law against the penetration of Roman law. However, generally, on the continent legal institutions adaptable to capitalism appeared in city-law and their origin is in the autonomy of the interested parties rather than in the Roman (or German) common law.

For its part, the city administration attempted to prevent the guilds and corporations from securing charters without its permission. If this was not possible the cities tried at least to limit the charters of the guilds and corporations to such as would per-

manently restrict their actions to an assigned area. Just as all cities
had to reckon with a political or manorial lord in establishing their
autonomy so, too, for all, outside the Italian, the division of statu-
tory power between the council and guilds was labile and a question of strength.

The rise of the patrimonial bureaucratic state everywhere made
increasing inroads into city autonomy. In England the Tudors were
the first to systematically apply the principle that the cities like the
guilds were corporately organized state institutions for definite purposes with rights which actually cannot exceed the chartered privileges binding only on them as citizens. Any offence against these
restrictions was seized as an occasion in *quo warranto*—to cashier the
charters (as in London under James II). According to this conception the city was not, as we would say, in principle a "territorial
corporation" but a privileged estates organization in the administration of which the Privy Council progressively interfered. In France
in the course of the 16th century city jurisdiction, outside police
matters, was removed and for all financially important acts ratification of the state magistracy was required. In central Europe the
autonomy of the territorial cities was completely destroyed.

AUTOCEPHALY: AN AUTONOMOUS LEGAL
AND ADMINISTRATIVE MAGISTRACY

Few of the cities outside the Italian achieved full autocephaly.
In many non-Italian cities autocephaly was only partially achieved
and then only for lower jurisdiction and normally with the reserva-
tion of appeal to the royal or supreme court. Whenever legal judgment was in the hands of jurors chosen from the burghers, the personal interest of the juridical lord was originally only fiscal. The
city did not find it necessary to appropriate the formal jurisdiction
nor purchase it. The most important thing for the cities was that
they possess a jurisdictional area of their own and a procedure conducted through jurors recruited from their midst. This was carried
through at least for lower jurisdiction and partially for higher jurisdiction in relatively early times. Personal choice of jurors or co-
optation without interference of the lord was achieved by the
burghers to a considerable extent. Important, further, was the attain-
ment of the privilege that the citizen be responsible only to the
court of the city.

The development of the city's own administrative body, the council, cannot be pursued here. That such a structure, accoutered with extensive administrative powers, should appear, at the height of the Middle Ages, was the identifying symbol of the city community in West and North Europe. The manner of its composition varied endlessly depending on the distribution of power between a variety of groups: 1, the patriciate of notables including land-lords, money owners and money lenders, and casual merchants; 2, the city and guild-organized merchants; 3, according to individual circumstances, a great number of traders or (collectively) large retailers and transporters of industrial goods. On the other hand the structure of the council varied in terms of the extent to which the political or feudal lord participated in nominations to it.

The city also remained partially heterocephalous in terms of the distribution of economic power between the burghers and the city lord. At times, because of the lord's money needs, the ransom of his justice was possible. Again the reverse was possible because of the financial power of the cities. However, the financial needs of the city treasury and the money market of the city were not alone decisive if the city treasury did not possess the means of political power. In France under Philip Augustus the kingdom allied itself with the cities (partially also with non-city lords). Already in the 13th century, the intensified money needs of the kingdom led to "parity" shares in the distribution of administrative positions, control rights over the administration of the magistracy, especially in financial administration which interested the king, and confirmation rights over the elected consuls. The power of the king over the cities continued to grow until by the 15th century the king's provost presided over the burgher assembly.

By the Age of Ludovika the offices of the city were completely in the hands of the royal intendant and the financial requirements of the state led to the sale of city and state offices. The patrimonial bureaucratic state transformed the administrative structure of the city into a representative corporation with status privileges, independent only with respect to the circle of its corporate interests, but without meaning for administrative purpose of the state.

The English state, which was forced to permit the city to be autocephalous because the cities were electorate bodies of parliament, ruthlessly disregarded the city once it wished to execute those tasks which our contempory communal associations fulfill through local corporations. The new tasks of the state were carried out either through parish organizations to which not only privileged corporation members but all qualified inhabitants belonged, or other newly created associations. However, patrimonial bureaucracy primarily transformed the magistracy into a sovereign authority alongside the others.

TAX POWER OVER THE BURGHERS
AND TRIBUTE AND TAX FREEDOM
TOWARD THE OUTSIDE

The taxation power of the burghers varied with the efficacy of control by the city lords. In England the cities never acquired full tax powers, but for all new taxes the consent of the king was required. Freedom from tribute and tax obligations toward the outside was also only partially achieved. External tax and tribute freedom was achieved by politically heteronomous cities only when tax obligations were farmed and when the city lord was paid off once and for all or by regular lump sums. When this occurred the city was able to include royal taxes within its own management (*firma burgi* in England). The most complete success in the achievement of freedom from outside encumbrances was realized with respect to duties stemming from personal legal or bondage relations.

After its victory the normal patrimonial bureaucracy taxed city and country from a purely technical point of view. It sought simultaneously to tax production and consumption through a specific city tax, the excise. For all practical purposes the cities were deprived of their autonomous tax powers. In England the corporate taxation of the city signified little since the new administrative taxes applied indifferently to other communities. In France after Mazarin, the king appropriated one half of the urban excise after all city financial operations and taxation were brought under state control. In Middle Europe the organs of the city were transformed into almost pure devices for levying taxes.

MARKET REGULATION: TRADE AND CRAFT POLICY
AND MONOPOLISTIC EXCLUSION POWERS

Every medieval city had a market the supervision of which had everywhere in considerable measure been taken by the council from the hands of the city lord. Depending upon the local power composition, police supervision over trade and production either gravitated into the hands of civic authorities or a professional corporation with extensive powers independent of the city lord. The craft police were competent to exercise quality control over production partly in the interest of enhancing the reputation of the profession but also in the interests of the export trade in some measure in favor of the city consumer. Price control in particular was exercised in the interest of the civic consumer. The craft police also defended the subsistence opportunities of the small burghers; they restricted the number of apprentices and fellows and under some circumstances also the number of masters. Particularly with the decline of subsistence opportunities, movements were set afoot to monopolize master positions for the home-bred, especially master's sons. On the other hand so far as the guilds brought police powers into their hands they attempted to prohibit the establishment of capitalistic enterprises by outsiders or of large-scale enterprises. To this end they sought the prohibition of the putting-out system, the control of capital loans, the regulation and organization of the importation of raw materials. At times the guilds even attempted to control the form of the market.

Above all else, however, the city sought to eliminate competition from the countryside brought under its domination. It attempted to suppress the rural pursuit of trade and to force the peasants to satisfy their needs in the city. It was in the interests of the city also to force the peasants to sell their products only in the city. Moreover, in the interests of consumption and occasionally of industrial use of raw materials, the city tried to prevent forestalling of wares outside the market. Finally, in the interests of city merchants they sought to secure transport and middle-man monopolies and at the same time to win privileges of free foreign trade.

This kernel of the so-called city economic policy varied through numerous compromise possibilities of the conflicting interests. However, its principal features were to be found almost everywhere. At times the direction of the policy was determined by the opportunities for gain apart from the power distribution of the interested parties. Its extension in the first period of settlement brought about a widening of the market; its restriction toward the end of the Middle Ages was accompanied by a tendency toward monopolization. In general, each city had its own policy determined by the peculiar competition and collision of interests. Especially among the foreign-trade cities of the South, city politics assumed the form of a life and death struggle.

After the subjection of the cities, the patrimonial bureaucratic state did not in principle reject the city economic policy. Quite the contrary. The economic flowering of the cities and their industries and the conservation of their populations through defence of the sources of their subsistence lay at the very heart of the state's financial interests.[32] On the other hand the stimulation of foreign trade on the basis of a mercantilistic trade politics represents measures copied, in part, from urban economic politics. By means of friendly capitalistic policies the state sought to synthesize the conflicting interests of the cities which from a subsistence standpoint could destroy the civic associations. To the very end of the French Revolution, the patrimonial state pursued a traditional economic policy except where local monopolies and the privileges of the burghers loomed in the path of increasingly capitalistically privileged and monopolistic politics inaugurated by it. In individual instances, this could lead to drastic disruption of the economic privileges of the burghers. However these represented only exceptional local discontinuities in traditional development.

However, the city's autonomy in economic regulation was lost, and that could have considerable indirect significance. Decisive in this was the inability of the city to bring military-political power into the service of its interests in the manner and measure of the patrimonial bureaucratic prince. Only exceptionally were the cities, like the prince, as associations able to take part in the economic opportunities newly opened by patrimonial politics. In the nature of the case that was only possible for individuals, particularly socially privileged persons. Such proto-capitalists included especially many landlords or members of the higher officialdom but in England as well as in France, besides the king himself, relatively few burgher elements participated in the monopolistically privileged domestic and foreign enterprises of patrimonialism. Occasionally, indeed, cities such as Frankfort participated in a comprehensive manner in risky speculative foreign undertakings. Most cities which did this, how-

32. The sheep must be sheared, but the value of the shearing depends on the quantity and quality of the wool.

ever, ran severe risks, for a single failure could destroy them as important political forms.

The economic decline of numerous cities since the sixteenth century, occurring even in England, was only partially due to the displacement of the trade routes.[33] It was also only partially due to the establishment of the great household industries, resting on labor not belonging to the estates. However, to a far greater extent it was due to the fact that the traditional forms of enterprise organized in the city economy no longer represented the activities where the greatest economic gains were to be made. Like the revolution at one time worked by feudal military technique so, now, revolutionary changes centered in politically oriented commercial and industrial capital undertakings. Even where these were formally located in the city they were no longer sustained by a city economic policy nor borne by local individual burgher organizations.

The new capitalistic undertakings settled in new locations. So far as they required laborers, the entrepreneurs needed other types than those supplied by the local urban community.[34] In England even the dissenters[35] who played so important a role in the development of capitalism did not, in consequence of the Toleration Act belong to the dominant city corporation. The great modern trade and industrial cities of England arose outside the precincts and power spheres of the old privileged corporation. For this reason it

---

33. The Revival of Mediterranean trade in the Renaissance was followed by a wave of civic development throughout inland Europe, and the areas servicing it. With the discovery of the new world and other events, orienting European commerce away from the Near East cities depending on this suffered a severe loss. While it was not an exclusive cause, it certainly contributed to the civic decline of the time.

34. This was made dramatically evident by the phenomenal growth of capitalism in German in the 19th century when Germany was able to take over capitalistic technology at an advanced level without going through the complicated preliminary stages as they appear primarily in England. One of the unexpected assets in the capitalization of German industry was the so-called "backwardness" of its population in an industrial sense. Precisely because it was industrially backward, German labor was directly adaptable to an advanced state of capitalistic technology without a complicated un-learning and re-learning process.

35. Members of a religious body in England separate from the Established Church. While including English Roman Catholics who in the original draft of the Relief Act of 1781 were styled "Protesting Catholic Dissenters," in practice it was restricted to "Protestant Dissenters" referred to in sec. ii of the Toleration Act of 1688.

frequently displayed archaic elements in its judicial structure such as the retention of the old land courts. The court farm and court leet remained in Liverpool and Manchester until modern times, though the landlords were re-baptised as legal lords.

RELATION OF THE MEDIEVAL CITY
TO NON-CIVIC STRATA

From the specific political and economic peculiarities of the medieval city flowed also its relation to non-civic strata. In individual cities this led to very different portraits. Common to all was the economically organized opposition to extra-city political, status, and landlordly forms—market against *oikos*.[36] This opposition must not be interpreted simply as an economic struggle between political lords or landlords and the cities. To be sure, such a struggle emerged naturally whenever the city in the interest of extending its power incorporated politically or manorially dependent persons over whom the master retained control. Such persons were either admitted within the city walls or accepted as external citizens of the burgher association. At least in the Nordic cities this latter expedient was soon made impossible by princely organizations and the prohibition of the king.

The economic development of the city, however, was in principle contested merely in its political aspects. Everywhere, as was often the case, the economic interests of the master came into collision with the traffic policies and monopolistic tendencies of the cities. And inevitably the feudal war organization headed by the king could only view the development of autonomous fortresses within their territorial spheres with considerable distrust. Except for short intermissions the German kings were never without suspicion of the cities. By contrast, the French and English kings were often quite friendly to the cities in which they found an ally in their opposition to the barons as well as financial significance.

The tendency of the market economy to dissolve manorial and indirectly feudal structure did not necessarily assume the form of a "struggle" of the cities against other interests. Rather communities of interests often dominated wide areas of life. The political and manorial lords were extremely anxious for the money tribute they

36. In other words, the most fundamental of oppositions is located between market and household economies by Weber.

levied on their tenants. The city provided the latter a local market
for their products and therewith the possibility of paying their traditional taxes in money instead of service or natural products.
Similarly it provided the lords the opportunity to sell their income
in kind rather than to use it themselves. Such income in kind could
be sold on the local market or into foreign commerce which was
increasingly provided with capital. Of these possibilities the political
and manorial lords made energetic use by insisting upon money
payments from their peasants. Moreover they implemented the
tenants own interests in increased production, awakened through
the market, by creating enlarged economic units. Such units could
furnish large shares of natural produce, the surplus of which could
be sold on the market by the lords themselves.

The more local and inter-local traffic developed, the more was
it possible for political and manorial lords to increase money income
out of different forms of tribute made possible by this traffic. This
appears in relatively clear form in the German West in the Middle
Ages. From the point of view of their founders the establishment
of cities was a business undertaking for increasing the opportunities for money income. Because of economic self-interest still in
the time of the Jewish persecutions in the East, especially in Poland,
the establishment of many cities by the nobles was carried out.
Such "cities," the inhabitants of which often had to be counted by
hundreds, still in the 19th century often consisted of up to 90%
Jews.

This specific medieval North European city foundation was also
factually an acquisitive "business"—as we shall see, in sharp opposition to the military fortress establishment represented by the ancient
polis. The conversion of almost all personal and material claims by
the lordly and legal masters into rent claims resulted in legal and
extensive actual economic freedom of the peasant. This occurred
everywhere that the city was weak. As a consequence political and
landlordly income in the territories of intensive city development
could increasingly be constituted out of market sales of peasant
products or out of peasant taxes or, in general, from other sources
existing in an exchange economy, rather than out of the use of
service duties or, in the manner of the ancient *oikos* (household)
economy, out of the imposition of household requirements directly
on them. Hence the lord and to a lesser degree his dependents

increasingly participated in the requirements of the money economy. In general the conversion from household to money economy was conditioned by the sale of landed estates to city burghers who transformed them into a rational economic form of possession. This process was restricted wherever the fealty organization of the owners of noble estates was under a form of escheatment excluding the urban patriciate. This was primarily the case everywhere north of the Alps.

In any case no conflicts occurred between the political or feudal lords and the cities purely on the basis of the money economy as such. A purely economic collision only occurred where in order to increase their income the lords sought to enter economic production on their own. This, of course, was only possible where suitable labor power was available for such use. Where this occurred the struggle between the cities and these industrial production activities of the lords also flared out. In modern times it was precisely within the patrimonial bureaucratic state that such conflicts developed with great intensity. By contrast, this was not an issue in the Middle Ages. The abolition of the old manorial organization and the subjection of the peasants took place without any struggle as a result of the penetration of the money economy. Such was the case in England. Elsewhere, to be sure, the cities consciously and directly furthered the development. As we have seen, this was true in the power sphere of Florence.

The patrimonial bureaucratic state sought to equilibrate the interest oppositions of the nobles and the cities. However, since the patrimonial bureaucracy wished to use the nobles for its service as officers and officials it also stipulated the impermissibility of the purchase of noble estates by non-nobles.[37]

The City and the Church

In the Middle Ages the conflicts between ecclesiastical and especially monastic landlords and the cities were often more severe than those between the cities and secular feudal lords. Outside the Jews, the priesthood was the only alien body within the city after the separation of State and Church in the Investiture struggle. As spiritual estates the property of the priests enjoyed extensive tax

---

37. This, of course, was primarily true for Prussian dominated Germany.

freedom and immunity, thus being outside the sphere of official actions and of the civic magistracy. Also as an estate the priests were freed from military and other personal duties of the burghers. At the same time through continual endowments by pious burghers their encumbrance-free possessions swelled, and, in turn, the number of persons immune to civic liabilities.

Moreover, in their lay brothers the monasteries had labor power without obligation to support a family and which could be utilized to destroy outside competition if, as frequently occurred, the cloister developed its own industry. Moreover the monasteries and foundations, quite like the *Vakuf*[38] in Medieval Islam, took possession precisely of the permanent sources of money rent in the Middle Ages: market buildings, sale establishments of all sorts, slaughter houses, mills, which were, thus, not only exempt from taxation but independent of the economic policy of the city. Often the monasteries had monopolistic control of these rent sources. Even in military respects the immunity of walled cloisters could be significant. Furthermore ecclesiastical law with its prohibition of usury was a general threat to city business. Against the accumulation of landed possession in the dead hand[39] the city sought to ensure itself through prohibitions even as the princes and nobles through amortization laws.

On the other hand religious foundations and especially the possession of pilgrimage places with indulgences provided extensive opportunities for economic gain for the urban trade. Moreover, so far as they were accessible to the burghers, foundations provided places for old age (asylum, charitable homes etc.).

The relation between the priesthood and the monasteries, on the one hand, and the citizenry, on the other, were, therefore, toward the end of the Middle Ages in no way so completely unfriendly that these factors alone could at any moment result in an

38. *Vakuf* was land held by religious foundations in mortmain. It was very important in the Ottoman Empire (found also among the Arabs) where before recent reforms it comprised two-thirds of all the property. At conquest, the sultans transformed one-fifth of the land into *vakuf*. Private necessity was responsible for its enormous extension. As elsewhere in the Middle Ages, land was given to the church to make its transfer to the owner's heirs secure. It was rarely given absolutely. The general administration of the *Vakuf*, except that belonging to non-Moslem foundations, was in the hands of a special department, the *Evkaf*.

39. In law, *mortmain* the condition of lands or tenements held without right of alienation as by an ecclesiastical corporation.

"economic resolution" such as the Reformation. The ecclesiastical institutions and cloisters were in no way as inviolable for the city community as one might assume from Canon Law. It has been correctly observed that precisely in Germany after the power of the king receded following the Investiture struggle, the foundations and cloisters lost their most interested protector against the power of the laymen. In many instances the city council came under jurisdictional guardianship of the old type under the bailiff, by pressuring them under most diverse pretexts and names to accept guardians and attorneys for the management of administration. The latter then conducted administration in accord with the interests of the burghers.

The status position of the clergy within the burgher organization was most various. In part it was legally quite outside the city corporation. However, also, where this was not the case, it formed —with its ineradicable status privileges—an inconvenient and unassimilable foreign body. The Reformation put an end to this within its sphere. However, the cities which were soon brought under control by patrimonial administration, derived no benefit from this.

In this last respect the development in Antiquity was quite different. The further back one shifts attention, the more similar appears the economic position of the temple in Antiquity to that of the church and especially the monastery in the early Middle Ages. This is particularly true with respect to the Venetian colonies. However developments in Antiquity did not take a course similar to that of the Middle Ages, toward an increasing separation of state and church and mounting autonomy of the area of religious dominion. Quite the reverse. The noble city families took possession of the priesthood as a fee and power source. Ancient democracy politicized them completely, transforming priestly positions into prebends which were ordinarily auctioned. It destroyed the political influence of the priesthood and took economic administration into the hands of the community. The great temple of Apollo in Delphi or that of Athena in Athens were treasure houses of the Hellenistic state, deposit banks for slaves, and a part of them remained large land owners. However, the economic competition with burgher industry did not come into the picture in the ancient city. A secularization of sacred property did not and could not occur. However in fact, though not in form, the "secularization" of temple-oriented

THE PLEBEIAN CITY [195]

trades was carried out in incomparably more radical form than in the Middle Ages. The absence of the monasteries and autonomous organizations of the church as an inter-local organization was the essential reason for this.

The conflict of the citizenry with the manorial powers was known in Antiquity as in the Middle Ages and in the beginning of modern times. The ancient city had its peasant politics and an agrarian policy which destroyed feudalism. However, the dimensions of these politics were much greater and their significance for city development so heterogeneous as compared to the Middle Ages, that the difference between the two areas clearly appears. It is necessary to examine this general configuration.

Chapter 5

Ancient and Medieval Democracy

The Three Main Types of Occidental Cities

THE ECONOMIC opposition of citizens to non-citizens and their life styles did not provide the medieval city with its historical peculiarities. Rather this was due to the location of the city within the total medieval political and social organization. It is in these respects that the typical medieval city was most sharply distinguished from the ancient city. The medieval city, in turn, may be divided into two sub-forms with continuous transitions between them but which in their purest forms variably approximate ancient city forms. The South European city, particularly of Italy and South France, despite all differences, was closer to the ancient polis than the North European city, that is of North France, Germany, and England. It is necessary, thus, once again to compare ancient medieval city types and, on occasion, others.

The patrician knights of Southern European cities owned castles and land outside the city quite in the manner of Miltiades in Antiquity. The possessions and castles of the Grimaldi, for example, stretched far along the coasts of Provence. In the North this was rare and in the typical Middle European and North European city later it was absent. On the other hand, forms such as the Attic *demos*, resting on civic gratuities and rent distributions conditioned on pure political power were almost completely missing from the medieval city. To be sure, parallel to the Athenian distribution of gains from the Laureion[1] mines is the medieval and even modern community share in the profits from civic properties. But these are incidental to the main configuration.

Class Oppositions in Antiquity
and the Middle Ages

The opposition of the lower strata to others was very sharp and the ancient city recognized the economic differentiation causing it as a paramount danger. Thus all parties, though by different means, sought to forestall the emergence of a class of individuals descended from the families of full citizens which had been economically ruined, leaving them in debt, without property, and unable to equip themselves for military service. Such a stratum could become a prop to a tyranny which would promise redistribution of land, release from indebtedness or support out of public means. Its members would demand grain dispensations, gratuitous feasts, spectacle circus games and direct contributions from public funds, or admission to feasts. Equivalent strata were not unknown in the Middle Ages. They are found in modern times in the Southern United States where the "poor white trash" confronted the slave-holding plutocracy. In the Middle Ages strata of nobles, declassed through indebtedness, as in Venice, were an object of concern as in Rome in the time of Catiline.[2]

However, despite some parallels such strata played a much less important role in the medieval city, particularly in the democratic states. They did not form the starting point for the kind of class struggles appearing in Antiquity. From early Antiquity class struggles arose between city-domiciled patricians as creditors and peasants as debtors along with dispossessed debt slaves. The *civis proletarius*, descendant from a full citizen, was typically declassed. In later times it was the indebted Junker like Catiline, who confronted the propertied strata as leader of a radical revolutionary party. The

1. On the silver mines of Laureion cf. Max Weber, *Gesammelte Aufsätze zur Sozial-und Wirtschaftsgeschichte*, p. 18; Ettore Ciccotti, *Greek History* (1st Edition 1920), p. 98; Hermann Bengtson, *Greek History*, p. 153.

2. Lucius Sergius Catilina (c. 108-62 B.C.) was a Roman politician and conspirator.

interests of negatively privileged strata of the ancient polis were essentially those of debtors and consumers. In fact, this configuration of interests in the territories of the ancient city was correlated with a recession of the kind of city economic policy addressed to the expansion of productive interests typically forming the cardinal point of democratic city politics in the Middle Ages.

The guild-like "subsistence politics" of an urban economic character which was present in the early period, also receded with the rise of ancient democracy; at least those aspects concerning production did. So far as civic populations were involved the fully developed Hellenic democracy as well as the fully developed Roman dominion of notables recognized beside trade only consumers' interests. The prohibition of grain export appearing in the ancient polis, the medieval city, and in mercantilistic state politics did not suffice in Antiquity. In fact, direct public provision for grain imports dominated economic policy. Friendly grain-supplying princes at Athens provided a primary occasion for revision of the citizens' register in order to exclude the unqualified. After crop failures in the granaries of the Pontus, Athens was forced to remit the tribute of the confederates. This is evidence of the extent to which political efficiency rested on the price of bread. Direct grain purchase by the polis also occurred in Hellenic territory. The most extreme example of the imposition of grain tributes on the provinces for provisioning the citizenry appears in the last days of the Roman Republic.

The typical medieval needy person was the poor artisan, the craftsman without work; the typical needy persons, the proletarian, of antiquity was the person politically declassed because he no longer possessed property. In Antiquity the specific means to meet the needs of the proletariat were through great public works such as instituted by Pericles. However, the considerable role of slave labor in the economy prevented their entry into the crafts.[3]

---

3. So far as the advantages of public works were preempted by wealthy citizens through slaves, they were lost to needy de-classed citizens. In an equivalent manner, the slave owners of the pre-Civil War American South prevented an economy by non-slave owning white farmers. Eighteen percent of the farms were in plantations and yet able to dominate the entire economy pressing the non-slave owners into the condition of "poor white trash." In recent times, an equivalent preemption of advantage occurs when farm subsidies in America redound to the advantage of large farmers and middlemen.

To be sure, in the medieval cities, too, there were some permanent slaves. Moreover, in the Mediterranean maritime cities slave
trade persisted to the end of the Middle Ages. Furthermore,
a continental city like Moscow, before freeing the serfs, could
retain the character of a large Oriental city of the time of Diocletian. Moscow represented a place where rents from possessions
in land, slaves, and office income were consumed.

However, in the typical city of the medieval Occident the
economics of slavery declined until it lost all importance. The
powerful guilds could not tolerate the work of slaves, paying personal tribute to a master in competition with free crafts. Precisely
the reverse was true in Antiquity where increase in wealth invari-
ably signified increase in ownership of slaves. Every war increased
the number of captives swelling the slave market. Such slaves were
in part pressed into the personal service of the owner.[4] In Antiquity
possession of slaves was one of the essential requirements of the
style of life of the full citizen. In times of chronic war the full
hoplite was as little able to dispense with the work of slaves as the
knight of the Middle Ages was able to dispense with that of the
peasant. Anyone forced to get along without slaves was a proletarian (in the ancient sense) under all circumstances.

Eminent households of the Roman nobility used slave labor in
quantities for personal service—it being required by the extensive
functional division of labor of such households. To a considerable
extent slaves were also required for the productive needs of the
oikos economy. Nevertheless, food and clothing for slaves was
largely purchased. In Athens the household economy resting completely on a monetary foundation was the norm; it became dominant for the first time in the Hellenistic East. It is especially
noteworthy that Pericles in response to the requirements of the
craftsmen supplied his needs whenever possible by purchase in the
market rather than through the economy of his household. At
the same time a considerable portion of the industrial production
of the city was in the hands of independently established slaves. As
already noted, in the *ergastria* beside unfree workers free craftsmen
and traders appear. The co-existence of slaves and free craftsmen

4. That is, in the sense that their service was consumed as a part of the owner's
style of life rather than used by the owner for productive purposes.

may be seen in the mixed piece-work on the Erechtheion.[5] Slave competition, thus, made itself felt on work patterns both socially and economically. The full exploitation of slaves in Hellenic territory fell in the blossom-time of democracy.

The Ancient Democracy of Small Peasants; The Medieval Democracy of Professional Traders

The coexistence of slave and free labor apparently destroyed all possibility of the development of guilds in Antiquity. Presumably, in the early days of the polis—it cannot be ascertained for certain—there were beginnings of industrial organizations. But from all appearances they were organizations of the old militarily important war craftsmen—such as the *centuriae fabrum* in Rome or the *Demurgi*[6] of the Athenian status struggle. However the beginnings of a political organization of craftsmen disappeared under democracy. Under the conditions of the social structure of the economy it could hardly be otherwise. To be sure, the ancient craftsmen could join together with slaves in a mystery community (as in Hellas) or into a *collegium* (as later in Rome). However, they could not belong to an organization claiming political rights like the guilds of the Middle Ages.

The *popolo* of the Middle Ages was organized on a guild basis in contrast to the patricians. In classical Antiquity precisely under the dominion of the demos all traces of guilds were lacking. Ancient

5. The first Greeks who won the Pelasgic acropolis were probably the Cecropes. Other Greek dwellers in Attica won the upper hand, conquered the acropolis and brought with them the worship of Athena. The God whom the Cecropes worshiped, Poseidon Erechtheus, was forced to give way to the goddess. The dethroned deity was not banished. Erechtheus, in the shape of a snake, was permitted to live on the hill of Athena, and the oldest temple, built for the goddess, harbored the god as well. These are the ideological correlates of political and economic activities reviewed by Weber. The public works intended in part to provide work for free craftsmen, also provided public recognition to the previously suppressed cythonian deities. Meanwhile, the appearance of slaves on these projects meant that much of the economic advantage deriving therefrom was being preempted by the rich.

6. Under the rule of the kings and the aristocracies in Athens, the free population fell into three classes: the *Eupatridae* or nobles; the *Georgi* or peasants who cultivated their own farms and the *Demurgi* (public workers) who lived by trade and commerce.

democracy was not organized by guilds but by *demes*[7] or according to tribes[8] which were conceived spacially and indeed (formally) territorially. Naturally the sub-division of the city into quarters was common not only to the cities of Antiquity and the Middle Ages but to the Oriental and East Asiatic cities as well. These served as the foundation for a political organization based on local communities and, above all, its extension to the entire political area—including the surrounding countryside—under the domination of the city. This area was reduced to sub-divisions of the city in a manner unknown in the Middle Ages and the cities of all other areas. The *deme* divisions were closely identified with village boundaries historically formed or created *ad hoc*.

The *demes* were under the supervision of *Almende* and locality authorities. This cannot be overemphasized as the unique foundation of the city constitution of the ancient democratic polis. On the other hand industrial organizations as constituents of the city appear only in early Antiquity and then alongside status corporations. They were important for election purposes as in Rome the *centuriae fabrum* beside the *centuriae equitum* in the old military classes. An equivalent role was possibly played by the *Demurgi* in Athens at the time of the pre-Solonic status compromise. Such structures may have originated in voluntary decisions—as was certainly the case for the political composition of the very old *Collegium mercatoris* of the professional god Mercury in Rome. Or they could have emerged from liturgical associations formed for military purposes. Originally, to be sure, the ancient city supplied its needs through socage service by the burghers.

In the ancient world isolated guild-like phenomena were to be found. The cult organization of the dances of Apollo in Miletus, for example, while unknown as to content was sufficiently important to lead to the designation of the year after its organizational head. This organization finds its closest parallels in the guilds of the medieval North or in the guilds of magical dancers among the American Indian tribes, the magicians (Brahmans) in India, and the Levites of Israel. However one should not think of it as a guest tribe of professional ecstatics. In historical times it was, rather, a club of notables

7. The territory of the tribe was called a "deme."

8. Weber refers here to the *tribus* organized later in Rome on a territorial basis, hence equivalent to the *demes*.

qualified for participation in the Apollo processions, thus closely corresponding to the *Richerzeche* of Cologne. The one point where the comparison breaks down is the typical ancient—in contrast to the medieval—identification of the special cultic community with the dominant political association.

When, in late Antiquity in Lydia, colleges of craftsmen with hereditary masters appear which seem to have taken the place of the phyles, they were certainly developed out of tribes of great craftsmen. They are more reminiscent of Indian than Occidental developments. In the Occident the division of craftsmen according to professions first re-occurred in the late Roman and early medieval *officii* and *artificii* of manorial handicraft.

Later in the Middle Ages, city handicraft workers appeared, producing for the market but being personally obligated to and dependent upon a lord. When such craftsmen appear in associations it was clearly by the lord who formed them into liturgical organizations for ease in collection of dues. Besides these associations which disappeared in time there were also unions of handworkers organized for monopolistic economic purposes. The latter played a decisive role in the insurrections of the citizens against the patricians.

In ancient democracy none of this was to be found. Liturgical guilds which may have existed in the early period of city development cannot be traced apart from the military and plebeian associations of Rome. They only appear (or re-appear) in the liturgical states—the monarchies of late Antiquity. To be sure, free associations did appear in the time of classical democracy; moreover they involved all possible life spheres except those of a guild-like character. They are of no further concern here. To have achieved the economic character of guilds, great masses of unfree handworkers could not have existed. This may be seen from the events in the medieval city which could not permit the distinction between free and unfree members to stand. The persistence in the medieval city of a distinction between free and unfree persons would have destroyed political efficacy and would have had important economic disadvantages as will soon be seen.[9] Ancient democracy rested on a burghers' asso-

9. To illustrate: political efficacy of the citizens depended in some measure on the fact that they established themselves as a guild of legal associates. The persistence within their ranks of a distinction between free and unfree urbanites would have destroyed this. Moreover, it would put the free citizen into an impossible position if he could not enter into full contractual relations with others

ciation of free citizens. This property determined its entire political orientation. Free guilds or similar unions emerged precisely at the time the political role of the ancient polis came to an end.

The possibility that unfree industrial workers and free semi-citizens (the enfranchised, metics) would be repressed, expelled or effectively circumscribed was not present in the democracy. Tendencies of this sort appear clearly in the status struggle, especially at the time of the lawmakers and tyrants. They disappeared with the victory of democracy. The extent to which slaves of private lords were used beside free citizens and metics in public construction and state production of goods in the very period of the dominion of the demos clearly demonstrates that the lords were not willing to forego the profit they represented and had the power to prevent their exclusion. Otherwise they would certainly not have been used[10]—at least for state activities.

Furthermore the crafts of free full-citizens were not sufficient for major state needs. In this is revealed the basic structural difference between the fully developed ancient and medieval city, the one under the *demos*, the other under the *popolo*. In the ancient democratic city dominated by the hoplite army, economically competent craftsmen played practically no political role. In the Middle Ages resident citizen entrepreneurs *(popolo grasso)* and small capitalistic craftsmen *(popolo minuto)* played the politically central role. Such strata had no significant role within the ancient citizenry. Ancient capitalism was politically oriented toward the state production of goods, construction, outfitting of ships and state credit (important in Rome as early as the Punic Wars), state expansion and booty in slaves and land, the imposition of tribute and provision of privileges for the purchase of and loaning of money on estates and land, trade and traffic to subject cities. It was also true for ancient democracy that so long as they remained the core of the hoplite army the peasants were interested in military land acquisition for settlement purposes. Resident city-domiciled small burghers, however, were dependent directly or indirectly on tribute extracted

---

because they were unfree. Or, again, it could be highly destructive to the city economy to have a resident unfree individual suddenly recalled by the lord to the country-side in order to extract his earnings in the city.

10. One is reminded of the reaction of American labor to the importation of coolie labor in the 1880's by the transcontinental railroads.

from dependent communities, state buildings, income from theatres, Heliasts' pay,[11] and grain distribution extracted by the state from its subjects. A guild politics in the medieval manner was quite impossible in view of the position of the landed strata which made up the hoplite army in the period of its victory in the time of Cleisthenes and in Rome in the time of the status compromise of the *decemviri*.[12] Such a policy could not arise because of the dominant consumption interest in cheap supplies. The later sovereign Hellenic *demos* influenced by interested parties of urban residents no longer showed any interest therein or the possibility for such.

The political goal and means of democracy in Antiquity were fundamentally different from those of the medieval citizenry, as revealed in manifold structural differences. If in the Middle Ages the patricians did not disappear completely but were forced to enter the guilds, this put them in a position to be outvoted, formally losing part of their influence. Often, of course, the reverse occurred and the guilds, quite in the manner of the London liveries, were set in course toward development into gentlemen's corporations. Such events always signified the mounting importance of inner-city burgher strata interested directly in trade and manufacture in the modern sense.

When in Antiquity in place of or beside the old personal patrician organizations, the phyles and phratries, the division of the city areas into *demes* or *tribes* occurred and when these bodies and their representatives held exclusive political power, it had a twofold significance. First it shattered the influence of the patricians. The power of the patricians resting on loans and debt foreclosures was largely destroyed since it could no longer reach full force but could only operate in small individual demes. Since property was registered and taxed in the individual deme this signified far more destruction of the political power of large possessions than, today,[13] the incorporation of East German estate areas (enclosures) into the

---

11. A radical measure of Solon which became the corner-stone of Athenian democracy, was the constitution of a court of all the citizens. Panels of judges were enrolled by lot so that the poorest burgher might have a turn. People sitting in sections as sworn judges were called the *Heliaea*.

12. The *decemviri* were members of a commission or council of ten men in ancient Rome appointed to prepare a system of laws and exercising absolute powers of government.

13. Before 1918.

village communities. Moreover the reduction of the entire city territory into *demes* involved replacement of all council and administrative positions with their representatives, as occurred in Hellas or in the organization of the *comitia* according to tribes (31 rural and 4 urban) as was carried out in Rome. At least the original intention was to establish the preeminence of the peasantry rather than city inhabitants. The intention was not to promote the political assent of the urban industrial citizenry like the *popolo* but of the peasants. From the beginning in the Middle Ages commercial strata were bearers of democracy; in Antiquity in Cleisthenes time the peasantry was the foundation of democracy.

Developmental Differences
Between Hellas and Rome

In the nature of the case the peasantry was permanently important only in Rome. In Athens membership in a *deme* to which one had once belonged was a hereditary quality independent of residence, land possession and profession—it was like one's relation to the phratry and extended family into which he was born. A family of a *deme* such as the Paeanian[14] from which Demosthenes derived remained for centuries legally assigned to its *deme*, obligated for its duties and drawn by lot for its offices regardless of whether his residence and property remained in the *deme*. As a matter of fact the *demes* assumed the character of local personal associations of burghers as did the phyles. In Athens burghers actually present in the territory of the ecclesia not only were favored by their presence but formed the majority of the formally rural *demes*.

Things were different in Rome, though a similar principle seems to have been valid for the four old city tribes. However the later rural tribes included only those domiciled and owning property therein. With the loss of property or purchase of new property elsewhere one changed his tribe. The Gens Claudia, for example, in time lost membership in the tribe named after it. The result was emphasized by an enormously more expanded area than in Athens. Only those city resident tribe members, actually present at the *comitia* were favored. In specific contrast to Athens only rural landowners holding properties of such size that the management of their

---

14. Demosthenes' father was an Athenian citizen of the deme of Paeania.

estate could be left in the hands of hired labor counted for political purposes. City administration was thus in the hands of landlords. After the victory of the plebs large and small landlords dominated the Roman *comitia*. One basic difference between Athens and Rome is located in the dominance of the city dwelling landed noble families in Rome, the dominance of the demagogue in Athens.

The Roman plebs was not a *popolo*, a union of craft and trade guilds. The point of gravity was in the estate of rural landowners qualified as hoplites. As a rule only resident city members of this estate dominated politics. Nor were the plebeians small peasants in the modern sense nor a peasantry in the medieval sense. They were landowners qualified for military service. Though belonging to the flat country they were no "gentry" but a "yeomanry" which at the time of their ascent preserved the property and style of life of a middle class of farming burghers. As time went by the influence of city domiciled rent collectors mounted while the total population of urban craftsmen remained without influence.

The Roman office nobility always rigidly preserved this state of affairs. So much so that the Gracchi[15] were far from changing this or wanting to introduce a "democracy" of the Hellenic type. The character of the Roman army composed of peasants made possible the domination by large city-dwelling senatorial families. By contrast Hellenic democracy appointed the executive council by lot and destroyed the veto power of the Areopagus, which was composed of former officials comparable to the Roman Senate. The Roman Senate, on the other hand, remained the primary organ of the city and the attempt was never made to change this. During the great expansion period the command of the troops always remained in the hands of officers from the city nobility.

Like all specifically ancient social reformers, the Gracchi party

---

15. Tiberius and Gaius Gracchus were agrarian reformers. They sought to limit the possibility of domination by the nobility by agrarian laws dividing up the great landed estates among free citizens dispossessed by the patrician class. Tiberius Gracchus (162-133 B.C.) was elected tribune in 134 B.C., and immediately revived the old Licinian land laws under which no individual was permitted to hold more than five hundred jugera with two hundred and fifty additional jugera for each of two sons. A triumvirate was appointed to carry these laws into effect but their work was halted by the assassination of Tiberius by the patricians. In 123 B.C., Gaius Gracchus (153-121 B.C.) repeated the attempt of his brother. The Agrarian laws were supplemented by a corn law making grain available to the citizens of the capital at a low price.

of later republican times wished to re-institute the military power of the political organizations, to prevent declassing and proletarization of rural land owners as well as their being bought out by large owners, to strengthen their number and re-establish the self-equipped citizen's army. It was, thus, primarily a rural party. In fact in realistic hope to succeed the Gracchi sought the support of the knights against the office nobility. Such knights formed a capitalistic strata interested in public loans and public supplies, being excluded from participation in office because of their economic activity.

Pericles' construction policy is justly conceived as serving for the employment of craftsmen. Since construction was financed by the tribute of the confederates, they were the ultimate source of economic opportunities. However, as proven from inscriptions, joint labor of metics and slaves shows that such opportunities were by no means open only to craftsmen who were full citizens. In Periclean times "unemployment payments" proper of the lower strata were sailor's pay and booty, particularly booty from piracy. For this very reason the demos was readily won for war. Economically declassed burghers were expendable and had nothing to lose. On the other hand an economic politics oriented around production is quite unknown as a decisive element for the whole ancient democratic development.

Military Orientation of Interests in the Ancient City

As in the case of the medieval city, the primary orientation of ancient city politics was around the needs of city consumption. However the rigidity of policy was much greater in Antiquity since it was impossible for cities such as Athens and Rome to provide for their grain needs through private traders alone. To be sure there were also occasional traces of an ancient city production policy as when profiteering was sanctioned for some important forms of exports. However, these phenomena were incidental rather than central; ancient economic policy was not primarily concerned with industrial production nor was the polis dominated by the concerns of producers.

Particularly in the old maritime cities policy was determined by the interests of landlords and knights in sea trade and piracy, the foundations of their wealth. Later policy was determined by the interests of the stratum of hoplite free-holders which developed only in the early democracy of Mediterranean Antiquity. Finally, ancient city politics was determined by the interests of money and slave owners, on the one hand, and of small burgher strata on the other. Both were interested, though in different ways, in state needs and booty. These latter strata break down into large and small capitalists, renters, warriors, and sailors.

Ancient city democracy was different from the medieval in these respects due to factors already present at the founding of the city. They were not only geographic but military and cultural. At the time of its establishment the ancient Mediterranean city was not influenced by the presence of technically advanced extra-city military and political powers. The ancient city was itself the bearer of the most highly developed military technique. This was initially true for the ancient patrician city with its knightly phalanges; it was true, later, for the democratic city resting on the disciplined hoplite army. It is not without significance that where medieval cities display military parallels, as in the case of the early medieval South European maritime city-states, extensive developmental similarities to the civic formations of Antiquity appeared as well. As in Antiquity, the initial aristocratic composition of city organization in the South European cities was determined by the aristocratic character of military technique. In fact these maritime cities and next to them the relatively poor inland cities dominated by resident patrician landlords (such as Bern) with subject areas, showed least development toward democracy.

In contrast to such relatively unimpeded dominance by the city of its hinterland, the industrial inland cities, particularly of North Continental Europe, were located in a social context dominated by the military and official organization of the kings and their castle-dwelling knights who were spread over the inland plains. Inland and in North Europe the cities were established by concession of these manorial and feudal military and official powers. Increasingly, the establishment of the city was not a product of political or military concern, but a product of the economic motives of founders desiring income from market tolls, traffic charges, and taxes. The establishment of the city was an economic rather than a military affair. Where military interests were present at all they tended to recede in importance. The autonomy enjoyed by the city of the Occidental Middle Ages was the product of quite other factors than those of the Ancient city. It was achieved by default of the non-urban power holders who did not yet possess a trained body of officials able to meet the administrative needs of the city to the extent required by the economic development of the city. It was to the advantage of the extra-city powers to permit the free economic development of the city.

Early medieval princely administration and justice were oriented to the position and status of its bearers. They did not have the form of a technical knowledge with the predictability and studied rational factuality necessary for the full exploitation of city trade and commerce. At first the interests of the power holders were exclusively in money income. When the citizens demanded freedom to conduct their affairs, it was probable that the extra-city power holders would grant this. In fact, they viewed any interference with the economic opportunities of the burghers of their own city foundations, established in competition with other power holders, as a threat to their own sources of revenue. The competition of the extra-city powers, especially that between royal power, the large vassals, and the hierocratic power of the church redounded to the advantage of the cities. At the same time within this competition access to the money power of the city burghers could provide decisive advantage to the power concerned. The cities were often in position to be courted by the various powers. Indeed, the more unified the organization of the political structure, the less was the political autonomy of the city apt to emerge. For all feudal powers beginning with the king viewed the development of the cities with extreme distrust. Only the lack of a bureaucratic office apparatus and their monetary requirements forced the French Kings after Philip Augustus and the English Kings after Edward to rely upon the cities. Similarly the German Kings sought support from the bishops and church property. After the Investiture Struggle, which terminated with the loss by the German kings of this support, there ensued a short period during which the Salic kings also favored the cities. However, as soon as the means of financial power were sufficient or as soon as territorial patrimonial administrators had developed their own office apparatus, the kings once again sought to destroy the autonomy of the cities.

Medieval city autonomy rested on different conditions from those

of Antiquity. The more typical the ancient city, the more its ruling strata, its capitalists, and even its burghers were politically and
militarily oriented. The self-equipped, disciplined hoplite bore the
brunt of the struggle against the noble, displacing him militarily as
well as politically. The consequences of the displacement were very
extensive. At times it led to the complete destruction of the nobility
as in Sparta. At other times it resulted in the formal displacement
and status restriction of the noble, freeing the demand for rational
and more available justice, personal legal protection, and relaxation
of the rigidity of the debt law while the actual place of the noble
in other spheres was untouched as in Rome. At times this displacement led to communal fusion of the nobles in the *demos* and to timocratic tendencies as in Cleisthenes' Athens. So long as the rural hoplite was decisive in the city there was a strong inclination to retain
the authoritative institutions of the patrician state.

The degree of institutional militarization was variable. The
Spartan hoplite dominion transformed all land belonging to the
warriors and the unfree individuals domiciled on it into community
property, granting claims to land rent to each militarily qualified
warrior. No other polis went so far. In contrast to the reversion of
land to the sib, the free alienability of property was widely diffused.
To be sure there were residues still retained later of the restrictions
on the alienation of warrior's property and on the hereditary land
of members of the city guild. However, this did not occur everywhere and was later generally dispensed with. In Sparta land accumulation was not in the hands of men but in the hands of women.
It so fundamentally transformed the economic foundation of the
Homoioi that of the well over 8000 full citizens qualified for war,
finally only a few hundred remained. Contributions to the *Sysites*[16]
on which full citizenship rested became difficult.[17] In Athens the

16. The public mess.

17. In the end the small lots which meagerly supported the Spartans were
gathered into large estates and the lots of the citizens disappeared. There has
probably never been a case of as complete an attempt to militarize a total community. Shortly after birth, the child was brought before the elders who decided
whether it would be raised or exposed. After the seventh year, the training of
boys was undertaken by the state—consisting mostly of physical exercise with
some music and literature. From his 20th year dated the Spartan's liability for
military service. He always ate at a public mess, *Sysites*. At thirty, he achieved
full citizen's rights and duties. Spartiates were debarred by law from trade.
Wealth was derived from landed property consisting in an annual return made

reverse process occurred with the carrying through of freedom of land sale in connection with the democratic conception of parcelling corresponding to increasing requirements of garden culture. In Rome still another alternative appears where freed alienation of land from the time of the Twelve Tablets had quite different consequences, leading to the destruction of the village composition. In Hellas hoplite democracy disappeared wherever the point of gravity of military power shifted to sea-power (in Athens since the downfall of Cronion). From that time rigorous military education began to decline beside authoritative institutions and the city fell under the domination of the *demos*.

The Dominance of Peaceful Economic Interests in the Medieval City

The medieval city knew nothing of such purely militarily conditioned philosophy. The victory of the *popolo* rested primarily on economic foundations. The medieval inland city was economic in character. The powers in the feudal Middle Ages were not primarily city kings or nobles. Unlike the nobles of antiquity they had no interests in peculiar military technical advantages offered only by the city. Apart from the maritime cities with their navies, the cities of the Middle Ages were not the bearers of a special military technology. While in Antiquity the hoplite army and its training and military interests moved to the center of city organization, most civic privileges in the Middle Ages began with the reduction of civic military service to garrison duty. Economically the urbanites were increasingly concerned with peaceful gains through trade and industry, the lower strata of the city most of all, as shown by the political opposition of the *popolo minuto* to the upper strata in Italy.

The political situation of the medieval citizen shows him on the way toward becoming an economic man *(homo oeconomicus)*, while in Antiquity in the blossom-time of the polis which preserved

by the helots, who cultivated the plot of ground allotted to the Spartiates. However, despite such attempts to equalize property, differences in wealth emerged —as Weber indicates. Land accumulation becoming possible for the women undermined this warrior communism. The law of Epitadeus removed the legal prohibition on the gift or bequest of land. The number of citizens, 8,000 at the beginning of the 5th century, had sunk to less than 1,000 in Aristotle's time. It decreased to 700 in 244 B.C.

the military technique of the war-band, the political situation of the citizen was reversed. The ancient citizen was a political man *(homo politicus)*. As we have seen in the North European cities the ministerials and knights were often excluded from the city. Non-knightly landlords played a role as simple city subjects or patrons, at times organized by guilds, but as gardeners and vine cultivators they had no important political role in city politics. As a general rule dominance of the countryside was not an objective of medieval city politics. The typical medieval city was hardly in a position even to dream of launching on a course of colonial expansion.

Negatively Privileged Status Groups as Bearers of Rational Economic Technology in Antiquity

With this we reach a very important point in the comparison of status compositions of the ancient and medieval city. Apart from slaves, already discussed, the ancient polis contained a number of social strata which were known only in the early Middle Ages or not at all or which only appear outside the city. Counted among them are: 1, bondsmen; 2, debt slaves; 3, clients; 4, enfranchised individuals. As a rule the first three strata belong only to the period before the hoplite democracy, declining to residual significance later. The enfranchised, on the other hand, play an increasingly important role in late Antiquity.

THE BONDSMEN

As a social formation patrimonial bondsmen appear primarily in conquest territories of the ancient polis in historical times. However they must have been very widely diffused in the early feudal period of city development. While they vary widely in detail, throughout the world, strata of bondsmen have been similar in fundamentals. The ancient Greek bondsmen were not in principle different from those of the Middle Ages. Wherever they appear bondsmen have primarily been utilized economically. In its full development a stratum of bondsmen was retained in Hellenic areas where city organization was not carried through. In Italy and in cities with an unusually rigid military organization bondsmen represented a part of the state[18]

18. Such were the helots of Sparta.

rather than a possession of individual masters. Outside these areas in
the time of the hoplite dominion the stratum of bondsmen almost
disappeared. They reappeared in Hellenistic times in the occidental-
ized areas of the Orient subjected under city organization. Large
land areas retaining their tribal composition were allotted to cities
whose burghers formed a Hellenic (or Hellenized) garrison in the
interest of semi-autonomous kings. However such initially purely
political bondage of non-Hellenic tribal peoples (ethnē) had a quite
different character from the patrimonial dependents of the dawn
epoch and no longer belong to the representation of the autonomous cities.

DEBT SLAVES

As sources of labor power debt slaves played a very significant
role in ancient times. They were de-classed burghers. Their situation
formed the special social problem of the old status struggle between
urban-dwelling patricians and rural-dwelling hoplites. In the legislation of the Hellenes, in the Twelve Tables, in debt legislation, in
the politics of the tyrants, the many compromise solutions to the
problems of declassed rural-dwelling peasant strata are advanced.
The solutions varied. Debt slaves were not bondsmen, but free
former landowners who had been sentenced with family and land
into lasting enslavement. Or again they may have voluntarily assumed this status to avoid public auction. With special frequency
they were utilized as farmers on the land of their creditors. The
danger they represented is indicated by the commandments in the
Twelve Tablets which prescribed that debtors were to be sold outside the land.

CLIENTS

The clients must be distinguished both from debt slaves and
bondsmen. They were not, like the latter, despised subjects. They
constituted the loyal following of a lord to the degree that a legal
suit between a lord and client was a religious sacrilege. His contrast
to the debt slave is revealed in the fact that the economic exploitation of the client relationship by a master was held to be improper.
Such clients were personal and political but not economic means of
power for the master. They stood in a relation of fidelity to the

lord over the content of which no legal but a customary code ruled, the violation of the precepts of which was thought to have sacred consequences (the breaking of faith was an infamy).

Such clientele stemmed from the time of knightly struggles and noble dominion representing, originally, a personal following of the lord which was taken into battle, obligated for gifts, for support in time of need, and, perhaps, occasional labor service. The lord, in turn, provided them with land and represented them before the court and authorities, but as the language of the Middle Ages indicates, they were not servants. Nor were they, like the later ministerial persons, of knightly type and rank, but small people with tiny peasant holdings—a plebeian stratum of possessors of war fiefs. The clients did not share in the landed possessions of the local community and therefore in the military organization. They were (in Rome through the *applicatio*) in a protective relation to a patrician family head *(pater)* or endowed by a king with equipment and land (technically in Rome, *adtribuere*). Ordinarily this relation was inherited from their ancestors. This was the old meaning of clientage. Precisely like the *Muntmannen* of the nobility of the Middle Ages under equivalent circumstances in Antiquity numerous small peasants voluntarily entered clientage to secure legal representation. In Rome this was the source of the later free forms of clientage. By contrast the older forms of clientage gave the master nearly unlimited power over the client. Still in 134 B. C. Scipio as commander-in-chief summoned his clients into service. During the civil wars the coloni (small lease holders) of the large landowners took their place.

In Rome the clients were authorized to vote in the military assembly and according to tradition (Livy) were an important source of support of the patricians. Removal of legal restrictions on clients, however, is nowhere probable. The triumph of hoplite technology also transformed the military significance of the clients and in later times clientage was only retained as an institution establishing the social standing of the masters. In Hellenic democracy, on the other hand, the institution was completely destroyed. The medieval city knew the institution only in the form of the so-called *Muntwaltschaft*, the domination of the full citizen over the semi-citizen to whom he extends protection. The system of legal clientage vanished along with patrician domination.

THE ENFRANCHISED

The ancient city also included a stratum of enfranchised persons. Their number and role were significant. They were economically important. From inscriptions carefully examined by Italian researchers, it is evident that about half of the enfranchised were of the feminine sex. In this case enfranchisement must have served the purpose of validating marriage arrangements worked through ransom of the betrothed. In general archival materials show an especially large number of enfranchised persons who had been house servants, owing their freedom to personal favor. The apparent total number of such individuals is probably deceptive for precisely these categories of enfranchised persons had the greatest chance of inscriptural recording. In this connection Caldomini's assumption is quite plausible that the number of enfranchised household servants increased in times of politico-economic trouble and declined in times of comparative economic prosperity. A reduction of chances for economic gain led the lords to restrict the household and at the same time to shift the risk of bad times onto the slave. The same circumstances should have encouraged the slave to rebel against his duties to the master. The agrarian writers mention enfranchisement as a device for securing excellent economic service. A master would often enfranchise a house slave rather than use him as a slave because, as Strack indicates, he then only had limited liability for him.

However, other phenomena must have been at least as important as a source of enfranchised persons. The slave whom the master had set up in independent business in return for fees was in position to exploit his economic opportunities for the accumulation of money toward the purchase of his freedom. This was also the case for Russian bondsmen. Moreover the service and fees possible to a master from an obligated enfranchised person must also have played a decisive role in the growth of the stratum.

Initially for generations the enfranchised remained in a patrimonial relation to the lordly family. The enfranchised person owed the lord not only service and fees which were often quite steep but his very inheritable position which, as in the case of the unfree of the Middle Ages, could be a source of extensive extortion by the lord. Besides he was bound through personal obligation to the most varied forms of personal obedience which validated the social position of the master and enhanced his political power. The consequence of this was, for example in Athens, that the enfranchised were completely excluded from civic rights and numbered among the metics. In Rome the power of the office nobility was never broken; though equated with the plebeians, the latter were restricted to the four city tribes. The nobility made this concession out of fear that they might constitute the basis for tyranny.

In the attempt to set up a tyranny the Censor Appius Claudius[19] undertook to distribute the freedmen equally throughout the tribes thus giving them practical control of elections. This characteristic composition cannot with Eduard Meyer[20] be taken as the attempt to create a "periclean" demagoguery. The Periclean domination did not rest on enfranchised individuals who in Athens were excluded from civic rights by democracy. Periclean democracy rested, rather, on the interests of the guild of full citizens in the political expansion of the city. Ancient enfranchised individuals, on the other hand, were by and large free business men, *homines oeconomici* who, in contrast to the full citizens of ancient democracy, were closer to the economic citizenry of the Middle Ages and modern times. Therefore it must be denied that a people's captain would have been able, with their help, to set up a Periclean democracy. This is shown by the failure of Appius Claudius. In Rome the peasant army was normally dominated by the city office nobility and this remained the decisive factor.

It is useful to clarify the place of the enfranchised further since they represent the stratum in Antiquity standing most close to the modern bourgeoisie. Nowhere did the enfranchised have full access to the city offices and the priesthood; nowhere did they enjoy full

---

19. Appius Claudius was elected censor in 312 B.C. During his censorship he retained office for five years despite the lex *Aemilia* which limited the office to 18 months. He filled vacancies in the senate with men of low birth and even, at times, the sons of freed men. He abolished the old free birth, freehold basis of suffrage and enrolled the freedmen and landless citizens both in the centuries and in the tribes, distributing them through all the tribes to give them practical control of the elections. In 304 the landless and poorer freedmen were limited to the four urban tribes and the effect of Claudius' arrangement was annulled. See Mommsen's appendix to his Roman History (vol. i); also the treatises by W. Siebert (1863) and F. D. Gerlach (1872). .

20. Eduard Meyer, *Wirtschaftliche Entwicklung des Altertums* (1895); *Geschichte des Altertums* (3rd ed. 1909).

connubium with these strata. At times, to be sure, in case of necessity they were called to arms. However, they were not permitted to take part in military exercise (the gymnasium) and the administration of justice. In Rome they were not permitted to become knights and almost everywhere their legal situation was somewhat less favorable than that of the free. Their special legal situation had the economic significance of excluding them from the governmental and politically conditioned emoluments of the burghers, especially land acquisition and profits from the ownership of mortgages. Land rent remained the characteristic monopoly of full citizens precisely under democracy. In Rome where they were second class citizens, their lack of qualification for knightly honors signified that they were excluded (at least as entrepreneurs) from tax farming and state supply which were monopolized by the knightly stratum. They confronted the knights as a kind of plebeian bourgeoisie. Such things meant that as a stratum they were withdrawn from the specific type of ancient political capitalism; they were sent on a course of development toward a relatively modern type of burgher business.

Thus the enfranchised were the most important bearers of those economic forms which best display a character corresponding to modern petty capitalism. Under the circumstances, however, it signified the accumulation of wealth in a middle class in contrast to the typical *demos* of full citizens in the Hellenic city which monopolized politically conditioned rents: state rents, daily allowances, mortgages, and land rents. The industrial schools of slavery operating under the possibility of the achievement of freedom were as powerful an incentive for rational economic conduct on the part of the unfree in Antiquity as it has been in modern Russia.[21] The ancient demos, on the other hand, was militarily and politically occupied. As a stratum of persons with purely economic interests within the cult community of Augustus as Bringer of Peace, the emancipated were pacifistically inclined.[22] The honor of "Augustus" es-

21. Weber is referring to 19th century Russia.

22. When Caesar defeated Pompey in Civil War he was not for a moment ready to surrender his power. The empire extended from London to Damascus with frontier garrisons stretching along several thousand miles. An unquestioned master was needed if the civil wars were to end. Neither the citizens' assembly nor the senate were competent to rule this broad area. The senate was composed of a group of jealous and ambitious nobles who had long been severed from direct

tablished in this cult corresponds somewhat to our title of "Purveyor
to His Majesty the King."[23]

As a special stratum, the enfranchised were known only in the
pre-city period of the Middle Ages. Within the cities the serfs forming part of the inheritance of the lord, partly or completely disappeared in accordance with the principle that "city air makes men
free." An important factor were the city privileges granted by the
emperor forbidding the retention by the lords of hereditary claims
on city burghers. The process manifest from the earliest times of
city growth reached its full development under the domination of
the guilds. While in Antiquity a guild organization comprising full
citizens, freed men, and unfree craftsmen would have been impossible in principle as the political foundation of the city as a military
organization, by contrast the medieval guild composition was carried
through precisely by ignoring non-urban status differences.

---

responsibility to the people. Caesar forced the government to grant him a temporary dictatorship and immediately set about to make it permanent. He tried
to develop a mystical cult of his own divinity as a device of absolute monarchy
but proceeded with too much haste and when his intentions became known to
the senate he was murdered. After thirteen years of civil war Augustus again
succeeded in acquiring complete control of the empire but he shrewdly saw
the danger of offending the nobles. He set aside extraordinary honors and titles
and worked through traditional magistracies. He used the proconsular office
over the border provinces and for control of the army and the tribunician
power for controlling legislation. The senate could then safely be permitted to
continue as an administrative body in control of the government of pacified
provinces which had no armies. In fact Augustus established a monarchy distributing only enough offices and authority to keep the senate content. Around
12 B.C. his Caesarist tendencies took shape. In the provinces, assemblies were
already holding festivals in the worship of the deities "Roma" and "Augustus"
and temples were erected to them. There were to be no temples in Italy—in
fact, a few were erected—but the "genius" of Augustus was to have a place with
the public Lares, and the new cult was to be in the hands of a select group of
enfranchised individuals in each city. The imperial cult helped smooth the
path of government in the oriental provinces and among the freedmen in Italy.
It also helped keep the heterogeneous elements of the army loyal.

23. For two centuries the cult was confined to canonized dead emperors,
though Caligula and Domitian invited the title of *Deus* while living. Diocletian
connected the cult to Mithraic religion which was powerful among the eastern
troops of the empire. He called himself representative on earth of the "Uncon-
querable Sun." His successor Constantine recognized as legal the religion of his
Christian subjects. In all these formations the monarchy was by-passing the older
social strata which had been politically and militarily inclined, establishing itself
on a foundation of the more purely economically oriented and peaceably inclined
elements such as represented by the enfranchised.

Contrasts of the Ancient Polis as a Warrior's Guild
to the Commercial Inland City of the Middle Ages

To summarize: from the time of the creation of hoplite discipline the ancient polis was a warrior's guild. Wherever the city carried on an active territorial politics it was inevitably pressed in greater or less degree into a course similar to that of Sparta: the creation of a trained hoplite army out of the citizens. In the time of their expansion Argos and Thebes had contingents of warrior virtuosos. In Thebes these were formed from groups bound by ties of personal friendship. Cities which possessed no such troops but only had burgher hoplites like Athens were often forced to defend their lands. Everywhere following the downfall of the patricians, burgher-hoplites formed the decisive class of full citizens. Neither in medieval Europe nor elsewhere were analogous strata to be found.

Sparta was not the only Hellenic city with the character of a permanent military camp. From the first, the hoplite polis underwent an increasing closure against the outside in contrast to the relative freedom of immigration in Hesiod's time. Moreover there were extensive restrictions on the alienation of military lots.[24] However, these arrangements decayed very early in most cities and there were smooth transitions to armies of professional soldiers or to navy service which moved into the foreground in the maritime cities. However in such cases, too, military service was decisive for political dominion and the cities retained the character of military guilds.

In view of the restriction upon the number of citizens it was precisely the radical democracy of Athens which pursued a fantastic expansion politics aimed at encompassing Egypt and Sicily. The citizenry dealt as it chose with the individual. It dominated the economy, being especially concerned with the squandering of inherited warrior shares (the *bona patria vitaque* of Roman interdiction formula), divorce, bad relations between son and father, mishandling of elders, Asebia, Hybris. In short, any relation which could endanger military and civic discipline or which could bring the disfavor of the gods down upon the polis was sternly punished despite the famous certification of Pericles in Thucydides' funeral oration that

24. The land lots assigned to the warriors as a fixed inalienable basis of his support, discussed above.

Athens permitted every individual to live as he wished.[25] In Rome similar development led to the establishment of the censors. In principle there can be no talk of personal freedom and so far as it occurred in fact it was secured through the power of resistance of the burgher yeomanry. Economically, too, the Hellenic polis had unconditional power of disposition over individual wealth. Still in Hellenistic times, for indebtedness individuals and property were pawned to creditors.

The burgher remained primarily a soldier. Beside water wells, the market, office buildings, according to Pausanias, a gymnasium belongs to the city. It was nowhere lacking. Most of the citizen's time was spent in the market or gymnasium. His personal requisition by the ecclesia to jury service, service in the council, administrative service in rotation and, above all, to military campaigns for decades, summer after summer, were in Athens in classical times a formation hardly historically paralleled in any other culture before or after.

The polis of democracy laid its hands upon any considerable aggregation of burgher wealth. The liturgies of the Trierarchy,[26] the hierarchy outfitting and provisioning the commanders of war ships, the requisitions for great festivals and processions, the forced loan in case of necessity, the Attic institution of Antidosis, transformed all burgher accumulation of wealth into a liability. The ab-

---

25. "Our form of government does not enter into rivalry with the institutions of others. We do not copy our neighbors, but are an example to them. It is true we are called a democracy, for the administration is in the hands of the many and not of the few. But while the law secures equal justice to all alike in their private disputes, the claim of excellence is also recognized; and when a citizen is in any way distinguished, he is preferred to the public service, not as a matter of privilege, but as the reward of merit. Neither is poverty a bar, but a man may benefit his country whatever be the obscurity of his condition. There is no exclusiveness in our public life, and in our private intercourse we are not suspicious of one another, nor angry with our neighbor if he does what he likes; we do not put on sour looks at him which, though harmless, are not pleasant. While we are thus constrained in our private intercourse, a spirit of reverence pervades our public acts; we are prevented from doing wrong by respect for authority and for the laws, having special regard to those which are ordained for the protection of the injured as well as to those unwritten laws which bring upon the transgressor of them the reprobation of the general sentiment." Pericles Funeral Oration Thucydides, *Peloponnesian War*, Book II, Ch. 37.

26. The trierarchs in Athens had the duty of outfitting triremes for public service.

solutely arbitrary Kadi-justice of the people's court (civil processes before hundreds of legally untrained jurymen) endangered the formal legal certainty of the law so greatly that the very continued existence of its power constitutes a marvel like the very strong dramatic action accompanying each political failure. This operated as destructively as another important circumstance, the mass desertion of slaves which caused the institution to shrivel up. On the other hand democracy increasingly farmed out supply, construction and tax collection to capitalists.

A pure national capitalistic class such as developed in the knightly stratum in Rome did not appear in Hellas. Most Greek cities sought quite the reverse, through concessions and inducements to intensify the competition of the foreign merchants since the single city territory was too small to offer adequate opportunities for gain. Property in land, and particularly slaves, who paid tribute to the lord or who were used as laborers (Nikias), besides ships and capital shares were the typical investment forms of burgher wealth. Conjoined to these in ruling cities[27] were opportunities for investments in foreign mortgages and property. Such foreign investments were only possible when the local land monopoly of the ruling burgher guild had been broken. Earnings from public lands, which in Athens were farmed or assigned to the Attic cleruchy,[28] and access by Athenians to property in subject cities was the essential aim of maritime dominion. During the democracy, as earlier, land and human possessions played the decisive role in the economic situation of the burgher. War, which sustained all these property relations, was chronic; in contrast to the knightly war of patrician times it rose to extraordinary heedlessness. Almost every victorious battle was accompanied by the mass slaughter of prisoners. Every conquest of a city ended with the death or enslavement of its entire population. Each victory led to an intensification of the slave traffic. A *demos* in which such events predominated could not possibly move in the direction of free economic activity resting on a rational methodology.

From the earliest period of its development the citizenry of the Middle Ages was set upon a different course. The nearest parallels

27. For example like Athens in the time of its dominance of the confederation.

28. In Ancient Athens a citizen who received an allotment of land in conquered foreign territory, but retained Athenian citizenship was known as a *cleruch*.

to Antiquity were provided by the maritime cities: Venice and Genoa, where wealth depended on over-sea colonial power. The point of gravity was located in the latifundia, a plantation or manorial type of possession on the one hand and in commercial privileges and trade settlements on the other, not, however, in a cleruchy dependent on military pay or upon endowments of the mass of the citizens from tributes as in Antiquity.

The industrial inland city of the Middle Ages was far removed from ancient city types. To be sure with the victory of the *popolo* the entrepreneurs of the major guilds were often extraordinarily militaristic. However the elimination of competition, domination of the street or the toll freedom of the street, trade monopolies and staple rights played the decisive role in their activities.

Within the medieval city, the meaning of landed possessions was transformed as a consequence of its victory against the surrounding world and the transformation of party dominion within the city. Especially in Italy the landed possession of the former or enemy party provided the dominating party with an opportunity for farming of the land by officials of the political administration or for making direct gains from its sale. Furthermore each victory over a foreign community increased the conquered land at the disposal of the victorious citizenry and thereby the possibility of earnings from such land. However, the radicalism of the transformation of possessions is not to be compared to the vast property revolutions accompanying each revolution or victorious foreign war in the late period of the ancient city. And despite such phenomena in Italy, land possession no longer stood in the foreground of economic expansion interests.

Under the domination of the guild the medieval city was pressed in the direction of industry on a rational economic model in a manner alien to the city of Antiquity throughout the period the independent polis. In Antiquity all this was changed only with the disappearance of city autonomy in late Roman times and with the destruction of the opportunity for economic gains by means of military expansion. To be sure, there were individual cities in the Middle Ages, such as Florence, in the armies of which artillery was first established and which was the bearer of military progress of the time. Moreover the citizens' summons of the Lombards against Frederick I signified an important technical military innovation.

However the knightly army remained equal to the city army in all essentials and in the conquest of the countryside it was superior. The citizens had sufficient military strength to sustain the integrity of the inland city but not to serve as a basis for economic gain. The seat of highest militarism did not lie in the cities which were in process of developing rational economic means.

Four great power formations were undertaken by the ancient polis: the Attic confederation, the Sicilian domain of Dionysus, the power sphere of Carthage, and the Roman-Italian Empire. The Peloponnesian and Boetian confederations may be ignored since their power positions were ephemeral. Each of these formations rested on a different base. The power of Dionysus rested on the soldiers of a citizens' army which sustained a pure military monarchy. It is untypical and offers no specific interest for us. The Attic confederation was the creation of democracy, also, a burgher association. It was inevitably pressed into a course of developing a politics of civic rights which subordinated the confederated city to the organization of the dominating city. The size of the tribute of subject cities was not fixed by agreement but, at times, pre-fixed in Athens if not by the demos itself by a contradictorily handled commission chosen by the demos. All legal affairs of the confederates were transferred to Athens leaving no small burgher guild in the locality to restrict the lords of the wider empire. Thereafter with few exceptions the outfitting of ships and contingents was imposed by way of money payments upon the subjects while the dominant citizenry (of Athens) was assigned to sailor service. A single decisive destruction of the fleet of the demos could then bring the domination of the demos to an end.[29]

The power positions in the city of Carthage were occupied by large plutocratic patricians fusing gains from trade and piracy in typical ancient manner with large landed holdings. These holdings were operated capitalistically with slave labor as plantations and defended by an army of mercenaries. (In connection with its expansion politics the city shifted over for the first time to a system of coinage.) The relation of the army leader, whose army was bound personally to him and its fate correlated with chances for booty, to the patrician families of the city could not be without tension. Until Wallenstein it was true that any privately recruited war fol-

---

29. As in the disastrous Sicilian venture under Nicias.

lowing may turn against its commissioner. The never stilled mistrust between the mercenary army and patricians weakened military operations so that the superiority of the professional army as against the Italian burgher militia could not be lastingly maintained. As soon as the army consolidated behind the person of a permanent field commander the corporals and soldiers of the mercenary army became a match for the patricians. The suspicion of the Carthaginian plutocracy and the Spartan ephors of the victories of the field commander corresponded to the development in the Attic demos of the institution of ostracism.[30]

A number of factors reveal the intrinsic self-limitations of the classical world-power formations. In the military monarchies of the time, the disinclination of the ruling strata to share power with subject people weakened their expansion possibilities. Furthermore all ancient hoplite systems were restrained by the power of economically profitable political monopolies which the cities represented. The decisive groups within the cities were disinclined to relax the restrictions on citizenship, thus opening access to the privileges of the political association. This made it practically impossible for a number of individual city communities to develop a single system of rights under a common civic law. All tendencies toward inter-local community formation on the basis of city law could only shrivel in this barren soil. The individual city community represented everything that the burgher conceived as right and fundamental to his prestige and ideal burgher pride as well as to the enjoyment of economic opportunities dependent on his membership in the militaristic burgher-association and the rigid exclusiveness of the cult community. It was a powerful limitation upon unified state formation.

That inter-local forms were not completely impossible is illus-

---

30. In Athens in Cleisthenes' time a new institution was originated which weakened the position of the Areopagus by depriving it of the political function of guarding the constitution and protecting the state against tyranny. *Ostrakismos* was the ordinance that, in the sixth prytany of each civil year, the question should be laid before the Assembly whether they willed that an ostracism be held or not. If the vote was affirmative, an extraordinary assembly was summoned in the market place. The citizens were grouped in tribes and each placed in an urn a piece of potsherd (*ostrakon*) inscribed with the name of the person he desired to be "ostracized." Whoever had the most *ostraka* against him was condemned to leave Attica within ten days and not set foot in it again for ten years. He could, however, retain his property and he remained a citizen.

trated by the Boetian Confederation which developed a common
Boetian civil right, common officials, representation by individual
city delegations, assemblies, a common coinage and a common army
alongside the autonomy of individual cities. However this was an
isolated case in the Ancient world. The Peloponnesian confederation
signified nothing similar and all other confederations were formed
along other dimensions. Only the special social conditions of the
Roman community permitted the development of a quite divergent
type of international politics.

Special Character of Roman Democracy
in Contrast to the Greek

More than in any other ancient polis, in Rome dominion was
in the hands of nobles of strongly feudal stamp. Despite temporary
interruptions their hold on the community was ever and again
renewed. Their effect on the institutions is evident even today.
The victory of the plebs did not bring about a redistribution of
power in the Hellenic sense, for while presenting the form of a
domination by tribal peasants, the city was in fact dominated by
resident landlords who controlled the political life of the city. It,
alone, was economical "dispensable"[31] and qualified for the senate.
The same stratum was more or less exclusively qualified for the
important administrative offices of the polis, constituting an office
nobility. Under these circumstances feudal and semi-feudal relations
of dependence assumed unusual strength and significance. Though
its old military character declined, in Rome the institution of
clientage played a role to latest times. Furthermore, as we have
seen, the enfranchised, in the nature of the case, appear in the relation of almost slave-like legal bondage. Caesar had one of his enfranchised persons executed without objection to this being pos-

31. The economic position of the nobility in Rome was such that its members were free to devote full time to politics. In other contexts Weber drew the
distinction between men who live "off" and those who live "for" politics. The
first category are persons who make a living from their political service; the
second, of which the Roman office nobility represents a relatively pure type,
are economically independent and can devote themselves to politics without
compensation directly. It goes without saying that such a stratum of persons
living "for" politics will run political affairs in a manner enhancing their private
economic situation. One recalls modern American dollar-a-year men of World
War II who did yeoman service for their companies.

sible. Increasingly over time, the Roman office nobility represented a stratum which in terms of its landed possessions found a weak analogy in early Hellenism only in the figures decried as tyrants of an interlocal nobility of the type of the Miltiades. In the time of Cato the Elder persons reckoned as estate owners had considerably larger landed possessions than persons in Greece assumed to be estate owners by Alcibiades or Xenophon.

Individual noble families undoubtedly already accumulated numbers of such possessions which, in accordance with their status, they controlled directly while, through their slaves and enfranchised persons, they were indirectly partners in all sorts of business throughout the world, though such businesses were not in accord with their status. No Hellenic noble stratum compares to the economic and social level of the Roman patrician of the later republic. With the increasing land possessions of the Roman nobles the numbers of sub-farmers (coloni) grew as well. They were outfitted with equipment by the lords. Their economic conduct was controlled and with each crisis they were plunged more deeply into debt. In fact their position of complete dependence upon the lord was hereditary. In the civil wars of the party leaders (even as by the field commanders in Numa's wars of clients) they were summoned to war service.

It was not merely individual persons who appeared in a client relation. The victorious field commander took subject cities and areas under his personal protection and this patronage remained in his family. The Claudian family had Sparta and Pergamon as clients. Other families had other cities in clientage, receiving their envoys and representing their wishes in the senate. Nowhere in the world has such a political patronage been consolidated in the hands of single and formally quite private families. Long before the monarchs, privileged lordly powers were held by them such as ordinarily are only possessed by monarchs.

Democracy was not able to break through the power of this office nobility resting on clientage. A communalization of the sibs into *demes* and the elevation of the organization of the *demes* into constituents of a political organization for the purpose of destroying the power of patrician organization in Attic manner was not possible in Rome. Even as little was it possible as in Attic Democracy after the destruction of the Areopagus, by free decision of the

demos as an administrative assembly to constitute the entire citizenry
into a sworn body of legal associates. In Rome the institution representative of the office nobility and most closely corresponding to
the Areopagus was the Senate. As the standing body counterposed
to the growing structure of appointed officials administratively controlled by victorious military monarchs, these patricians were not
at first thrust aside but only disarmed and restricted to the administration of pacified provinces.[32]

The patrimonial constitution of the ruling strata also revealed
itself in the manner of conduct of official business. Initially the staffs
of the bureaus were composed of the officials themselves. Within
peaceful administrations the appointment of subaltern personnel was
extensively carried through. Field marshals supported themselves
by use of their clients and enfranchised adherents along with a personal following of free political friends or obligated families in the
conduct of their offices. Also the prince who in the first stages of
the military monarchy conducted his administration without restriction, came to depend so completely upon enfranchised persons, that
this stratum rose to the height of its power and threatened to place
a Claudian emperor over the senate. Also, under the circumstances,
even formally the conduct of the administration lay in the hands
of the personal subjects of the prince. And like late republican
patricians the prince found the point of gravity of economic power,
as for example under Nero, in a powerful extended landlordism in
such areas as Egypt. If such areas were not, as has been maintained,
legally so employed, they were, nevertheless, actually administered
in the form of a personal patrimonial domination.

This patrimonial-feudal trend so apparent in the late days of the
Roman republic and its administration of honoraries is peculiar to
Rome as an unbroken tradition of old. To be sure it was originally
confined to small circles. It was the fundamental source of important
contrasts to developments in the Hellenic world. This appears even
in characteristics of external life conduct.

In Hellas in the time of chariot warfare the nobleman began
to wrestle in the ring. The *agones*,[33] the product of individual

32. Caesar made the mistake of opposing the Senate directly; the patricians
executed him. Augustus played a more skillful game, apparently favoring it but
in fact maneuvering it into position where it was in charge of pacified provinces
without armies. See footnote above.
33. Struggle for victory, gymnastic exercise, wrestling.

knightly combat and the ecstasy of knightly war heroism were the source of the decisive course of Greek development. In contrast to the tournaments of the Middle Ages where wagons and horses make up so much of the foreground an important difference appears from the beginning. All forms of the official festival were established by the form of the *agones* alone. With the emergence and dominance of hoplite technology the sphere of the *agones* was widened. All events of the gymnasium assumed this form and were thereby made "socially acceptable": spear fighting, wrestling, fist fighting, above all prize races. The ritualistic song of honor to the gods was supplied by the musical *agones*. To be sure, eminent men displayed the quality of their possessions through the horses and wagons they permitted to run for them. However, in the nature of the form, the plebeian *agones* had to be recognized as equal. The *agones* were organized with prizes, umpires, contest rules and interpenetrated the whole of life. Alongside the Epics it became the single most important bond of Hellenic world in contrast to all barbarians.

Even in the oldest forms of Hellenic sculpture the qualities special to them appear: nakedness, lack of all clothing, showing nothing but weapons. From Sparta, the place of the highest military training, an influence diffused over the Hellenic world and even the loincloth fell away. No community on earth has ever brought an institution such as this to the center of all interest such that all artistic practice and conversation were dominated by it, even the Platonic dialogues. Until the late times of Byzantine domination the circus parties were the form in which schisms of the masses clothed themselves and the bearers of revolution in Constantinople and Alexandria appear.

In Italy the institution, at least in the form of its development in classical Greece, remained alien. In Etruria the city nobility demonstrated its dominance over the scorned plebeians in the contest of the Lucumones[34] but it was represented by a chosen athlete. Also in Rome the nobility declined to make common cause with or before the mob.

Never have prestige feelings suffered such a loss of distance and value as in these naked tournaments of the Greeks. They could remain as little as in the cultic dance song of Dionysian orgiasticism

---

34. A Lucumo was a priest or ruling noble with priestly functions among the ancient Etruscans.

or the *abalienatio mentis* of ecstasy. In Roman political life the significance of the speech and exchange of the Agora and Ecclesia receded as completely as the foot races of the gymnasium. Speech-making arose later, but in the senate where it assumed a completely different character from the rhetorical art of the Attic demagogues. Tradition and experience of old former officials set the tone of politics. The old rather than the young provided the standard for the order of exchange and form-feeling of value. Rational considerations, not lust for booty of the rhetorically inflamed *demos*, and the emotional excitement of young manhood, gave politics its tone. Rome remained under the guidance of experience, consideration, and the feudal power of a stratum of notables.

Selective Bibliography

(The following bibliography is not intended to be in any sense complete. It is highly selective with respect to Max Weber's own sources and the problems he brought particularly into focus.)

Nels Anderson and Eduard C. Lindeman, *Urban Sociology* (New York: 1928).

W. A. Ashley, "The Beginnings of Town Life in the Middle Ages" *Quarterly Journal of Economics*, Vol. X. (1896).

A. Ballard, *Domesday Boroughs* (Oxford: 1904).

A. Ballard and James Tait, *Borough Charters* (Cambridge: 1923).

George von Below, *Territorium und Stadt* (Munich: 1923).

_____ "Die Entstehung des modern Kapitalismus und die Hauptstädte, *Schmoller's Jahrbuch* XLIII (1919).

_____ "Das ältere deutsche Städtewesen und Bürgertum", *Monographien zur Weltgeschichte* (Leipzig: 1898).

Donald J. Bogue, *Population Growth in Standard Metropolitan Areas: 1900-1950* (Washington: 1953).

E. W. Burgess, *The Urban Community* (Chicago: 1926).

Fustel de Coulanges, *La cité antique*. Trans. by Willard Small (28th Ed. Paris: 1924).

Maurice R. Davie, *Problems of City Life* (New York: 1932).

Robert E. Dickenson, *The West European City* (London: 1951).

W. W. Fowler, *The City-State of the Greeks and Romans* (London: 1895).

Patrick Geddes, *Cities in Evolution* (London: 1915).

W. Gerlach, *Die Enstehungszeit der Stadtbefestigungen in Deutschland* (Leipzig: 1913).

Gustav Glotz, *La cité greque* (Paris: 1928) Eng. trans. N. Mallison (London: 1929).

Amos Hawley, *Human Ecology* (New York: 1950).

Karl Hegel, *Geschichte der Städteverfassung von Italien seit der Zeit der römischen Herrschaft bis zum Ausgang des zwölften Jahrhunderts* 2 vols. (Leipzig: 1847).

_____ *Städte und Gilden in den germanischen Völkern im Mittelalter*, 2 vols. (Leipzig: 1891).

Richard M. Hurd, *Principles of City Land Values* (New York: 1924).

F. Keutgen, *Untersuchungen über den Ursprung der deutschen Stadtverfassung* (Leipzig: 1895).

_____ *Urkunden zur städtischen Verfassungsgeschichte* (Leipzig: 1901).

[231]

Grace Kneedler, "Functional Types of Cities", *Public Management* (1945).
_____ "Economic Classification of Cities", *Municipal Yearbook* (1945).
René Maunier, *L'Origin et la function économique des villes* (Paris: 1910).
Henry Sumner Maine, *Village Communities in the East and West* 7th ed. (London: 1913).
F. W. Maitland, *Township and Borough* (Cambridge: 1898).
Louis Mumford, *The Culture of Cities* (New York: 1938).
William B. Munro, *Municipal Government and Administration* (New York: 1926).
_____ "The City", *Encyclopedia of the Social Sciences.*
William F. Ogburn, *Social Characteristic of Cities* (Chicago: 1937).
Robert E. Park and others, *The City* (Chicago: 1925).
Theodor Petermann, "Die geistige Bedeutung der Grosstädte, *Die Grossstadt* (Dresden: 1903).
Elmer Peterson (Ed.) *Cities are Abnormal* (Norman, Okla.: 1946).
H. Pirenne, *Medieval Cities* (Princeton: 1925).
Hugo Preuss, *Die Entwicklung des Deutschen Städtewesens* (Leipzig, 1906).
James A. Quinn, *Human Ecology* (New York: 1950).
S. Ritschel, *Markt und Stadt in ihrem rechtlichen Verhältniss* (Leipzig: 1898).
_____ *Das Burggrafenamt* (Leipzig: 1905).
_____ *Die civitas auf deutschen Boden* (Leipzig: 1894).
Michael Rostovtzeff, "Cities in the Ancient World" in *Urban Land Economics* Richard T. Ely (Ed.) (Ann Arbor: 1922).
Arthur Meier Schlesinger, *The Rise of the City* (New York: 1933).
Georg Simmel, *Die Grosstädte und das Geistesleben* (Dresden: 1903).
R. Sohm, *Die Entstehung des deutschen Städtewesens* (Leipzig: 1890).
Oswald Spengler, *The Decline of the West* (New York: 1926-1928).
Josiah Strong, *The Twentieth Century City* (New York: 1898).
Graham Romeyn Taylor, *Satellite Cities: A Study of Industrial Suburbs* (New York: 1915).
J. G. Thompson, *Urbanization: Its Effects on Government and Society,* (New York: 1927).
H. A. Toulmin, *The City Manager* (New York: 1915).
Adna F. Weber, *Growth of Cities in the Nineteenth Century* (New York: 1899).
H. Waentig, "Die Wirtschaftliche Bedeutung der Grosstädte" in *Die Grosstadt.* Ed. by Th. Petermann (Dresden: 1903).
Leonard D. White, *The City Manager* (Chicago: 1927).
Delos F. Wilcox, *The American City* (New York: 1906).
Louis Wirth, "Urbanism as a Way of Life," *American Journal of Sociology* (1938)
_____ "The Urban Society and Civilization," *A. J. S.* (1940).
Robert A. Woods, *The City Wilderness: A Settlement Study of South End, Boston* (Boston: 1898).

Index